The Symbiotic
Character

A NORTON PROFESSIONAL BOOK

The Symbiotic Character

STEPHEN M. JOHNSON, Ph.D.

W. W. NORTON & COMPANY • *New York* • *London*

Printed in the United States of America

First Edition.

Library of Congress Cataloging-in-Publication Data

Johnson, Stephen M.
   The symbiotic character / Stephen M. Johnson.
      p. cm.
   "A Norton professional book."
   Includes bibliographical references and index.
   ISBN 0-393-70115-8 : 27.95
   1. Object relations (Psychoanalysis)   2. Separation-individuation.
3. Personality disorders.
   [DNLM: 1. Personality Disorder—therapy.   2. Psychotherapy.   WM
190   J69s]
RC455.45.023J64   1991   616.89—dc20   91-1964
DNLM/DLC

W. W. Norton & Company, Inc., 500 Fifth Avenue, New York, N.Y. 10110
W. W. Norton & Company, Ltd., 10 Coptic Street, London WC1A 1PU

1 2 3 4 5 6 7 8 9 0

To Ellen with love

Leaving home is a kind of forgiveness, and when you get among strangers, you're amazed at how decent they seem. Nobody smirks at you or gossips about you, nobody resents your successes or relishes your defeats. You get to start over, a sort of redemption.

— Garrison Keillor
Leaving Home

ACKNOWLEDGMENTS

THIS BOOK WAS WRITTEN while I was a Professor at Pacific Graduate School of Psychology in Palo Alto, California. I am grateful to the school's administration for providing the necessary time and resources and particularly to Robert Morgan for his support of this form of academic research. Sue Hully and Louise Woffington served as research assistants on this project, and Sue, with my collaboration, created the two appendixes.

My former mentor, Ed Muller, was largely responsible for starting me on the path reflected in this series of books, and my personal guides, G. Timothy Scott, Gypsy Frankl-Podolsky, and Bruce Johnston, have contributed greatly to this journey. Susan Barrows served as editor for these volumes and provided just the right mix of freedom, support, and skillful editing.

My closest personal friends, Peter Alevezos, Larry King, and Ron Wagner, have consistently given me the faith that has enabled me to increasingly trust my own judgment.

My clients are the co-authors of these books. Their courage, vulnerability, honesty, and trust have inspired me and this work. And my wife, Ellen, to whom this book is dedicated, has done more than words can say. But, then, she knows.

CONTENTS

Acknowledgments   vii

Introduction: Psychotherapy as a Post-Modern Art Form   1

I. A THEORY OF CHARACTER FORMATION

1. A Characterological-Developmental Theory for
   Psychotherapy   13
2. Characterological Issues of Attachment and Bonding   28
3. Characterological Issues of Self-Development   42
4. Characterological Issues of the Self in System   61

II. THE SYMBIOTIC CHARACTER

5. The Owned Child   77
6. Insights from Psychoanalysis and Family Therapy   105

III. TREATMENT OF THE SYMBIOTIC CHARACTER

7. Therapeutic Themes   133
8. Symptoms as Internal Object Relations   153
9. Internal Object Relations and the Negative Therapeutic
   Reaction   175

APPENDICES

A. Psychoanalytic Developmental Concepts: A Selected
   Glossary   197
B. A Research-Based Chronology of Development   208

References   219
Index   231

The Symbiotic
Character

Psychotherapy as a Post-Modern Art Form

THE POST-MODERN ERA IS characterized by diversity and integration. Art forms, in particular, self-consciously reflect an appreciation of both classic and modern forms while, at the same time, flaunting an irreverent detachment from them. Post-modern art involves the integration or combination of two or more classic or modern forms, often with an experimental, even humorous, spirit concerning what may go with what. Not all of it works, of course, but the fusions, the crossovers, and the juxtaposed forms often make for interesting artistic expressions, connecting us with forms of the past unmistakably expressed in the post-modern present. From architecture to painting, to fashion and haircuts, this interest in the possible combinations and permutations of human expression surrounds us.

It is not coincidental, then, that in psychotherapy, we are in the midst of an overdue period of openness and integration. Many therapists are finally learning what competing schools of thought have to say about the task of understanding and helping people. Even in the two most conservative camps of behaviorism and psychoanalysis, there are many who are willing to learn new perspectives and loosen former rigidity (e.g., see Messer, 1986). Stephen Mitchell, addressing psychoanalytic techniques, writes "One of the great, generally unacknowledged truths about analytic technique is that it is developed on a trial and error basis, personally designed in the interaction with each individual analysand" (Mitchell, 1988, p. 212).

Psychotherapy is truly an improvisational, theatrical art form. Whatever theories are used in its execution, they must be well in the background for this moment-to-moment interpersonal interplay. As

in any interactional theater, the stimulus and demanded response
are too immediate to permit one to check in with all the relevant
theories or prescriptions that might influence that response. Anyone
who attempts to do even a fraction of that will be hamstrung in the
process and neglect her own intuitive, human resources, which are
certainly more essential than the theories. As with any art form,
psychotherapy relies on the particular disposition, temperament, and
talents of the artist. Therapists, of course, gravitate towards those
grounds of being and therapeutic techniques that suit their personal
style and that prove to be most effective for them. In the post-modern
period, it is probably useful to become more flexible in this regard,
yet there will be personal and artistic choices in that flexibility.

In this book, I will once again present a general unifying theory of
character and development which I believe can productively "hold,"
explain, or justify this integrative and flexible approach to psychotherapy. This "post-modern art psychotherapy," which I dub PMAP,
is conducted using one cardinal rule. It is this: *The PMAP is not
the territory* (a slight misquote of Korzybski). The truly interactive,
intersubjective, interpersonal, spontaneous exchange of psychotherapy is the territory. And it is never a solo act. Here, I hope only to
provide an integrative theory that will inform and direct it and I
intend to take a stand here for this integrative approach as a legitimate, state-of-the-art expression of where the mental health profes-
sions and their supporting basic sciences have brought us in the
post-modern era. In other words, this is not a "whatever works"
eclecticism. Rather, the theory is a product of generations of basic
research in psychology, psychiatry, and the social sciences. In this
approach, there is a reverent respect for all those who have labored
to bring us data, observations, theories, and techniques. But there is
also the irreverence of a child of the post-modern era, particularly
for the rigidity of most of our founding mothers and fathers.

At the level of therapeutic technique, for example, I believe it
is very important for educated therapists to know why the classic
psychoanalysts have insisted on neutrality and abstinence in the analytic process. Similarly, it is critical to know why humanists like
Carl Rogers and Heinz Kohut have so emphasized accurate empathy,
attunement, prizing, and even indulgence. These two positions, which
frequently prescribe very different therapeutic responses, are each
based on a separate rationale, which may or may not apply in any given

case or at any given therapeutic choice point. To be a truly effective post-modern art psychotherapist, one needs to know the underlying rationales and to know to what extent each applies at the moment. Then, the therapist makes the best therapeutic response she can, realizing that it may represent one pole or the other or an integration of the two. Finally, one must keep one's eye on the interactive partner—not on the theorists and their rationales—to determine the appropriateness of the response. To follow Korzybski's metaphor, *we must keep our eyes on the road, not on the map* (or PMAP).

I have made a list of analogous polarities which may need to be evaluated or integrated at various therapeutic choice points. I offer it here (Table 1) as representing only a few possibilities and as a preview of this volume's treatment of the dimension of technique. One's moment-to-moment choices in the midst of the interactive art form will, of course, not always be perfect. But they are far more broadly determined than therapeutic expressions that are constrained by a rigid adherence to one classic or modern form.

In making this point I am always reminded of an old story. It is about a man in a small European town who had achieved considerable success and, wishing to celebrate and announce it, went to the best tailor available, a man by the name of Zumbach. He ordered the tailor to make for him his finest suit. After several fittings, the

Table 1
POLARITIES AT PSYCHOTHERAPY CHOICE POINTS

Authenticity	Neutrality
Intersubjectivity	Abstinence
Supportive	Expressive-uncovering
Directive	Nondirective
Behavioral focus	Hermeneutic focus
Containment learning	Expressive learning
Focus on cognition	Focus on affect
Prohibition of transference	Provocation/allowance of transference
Empathy	Intervention
Current determinants	Historical determinants
Interpersonal focus	Intrapsychic focus
Systemic focus	Dyadic focus
Strengthening defenses	Weakening defenses

man came for his suit and, trying it on, noticed that one sleeve was longer than the other. He said, "Zumbach, I don't want to give offense, but this sleeve is half an inch longer than the other. You must fix it." Zumbach took afront. "It is not the suit, it's the way you are standing. Stand like this," he said, as he pushed the man's shoulder down so that the sleeves matched perfectly. Then, standing sideways to the mirror, the customer noticed the improper fit of his jacket and said, "Zumbach, there is this big pucker here in the back of the neck. My wife hates it when my jackets have that pucker in them. You must fix it." But again Zumbach said, offended, "It's not the suit, it's the way you are standing. Stand like this," and he pushed the man's head down firmly. Well, this went on for two or three more tailoring problems until the man, completely cowed by Zumbach and fearing even to breathe, left the store. Riding home on the bus, the man was approached by a stranger who, noticing the suit, said, "What a beautiful suit. Zumbach the tailor must have made that suit for you." Surprised, the man turned and said, "That's right. How did you know?" "Well," said the man, "Only someone as talented as Zumbach could fit someone as crippled as you."

The point? Only someone as talented as Freud, as brilliant as Skinner, or as creative as Perls could fit someone as crippled as you if you try to do this improvisational art, while restricting yourself to their theories and techniques. To do it their way requires a kind of twisting of yourself, a restraint of your spontaneity, a bridling of your intuition and good sense. As Frank (e.g., 1982) has repeatedly documented, it is psychotherapy's nonspecific effects that account for most of the variance in outcome, and those effects are related to these human factors. Other researchers, largely from the psychoanalytic side, are consistent in showing therapeutic alliance as the best predictor of success among several variables investigated (e.g., see Horowitz, 1984, p. 32).

It is time that therapists who practice this improvisational art form, which is based on sound psychological principles but unconfined by any particular dogma, declare themselves and stop feeling guilty about what is really state-of-the-art work. This is a book about individuation. That very process is required of any psychotherapist, who must finally individuate from his mentors and masters. It is not necessary to disrespect or lose them, but only to transmute their gifts so that they fit us and the multitude of situations in which we find ourselves. It means that we grow up, leave home, and learn about the rest of the world.

The theory that I will be developing in this volume relies a great deal on the classical observations and theories about character which are pervasive in psychiatry generally, but which owe the greatest debt to the analytical tradition beginning with Sigmund Freud and Wilhelm Reich (e.g., 1949) and continuing through Alexander Lowen (e.g., 1958), David Shapiro (e.g., 1965), and Mardi Horowitz (e.g., 1984). The early figures in that historical chain emphasized more the conflict properties of character and the energetic expressions of defense. The later members of the chain have emphasized more the cognitive style and, influenced by object-relations theory, the self-representation and object representations associated with each characterological expression.

The other major intellectual line represented here is that of psychoanalytic developmental psychology summarizing the strains of ego psychology, object relations, and self psychology. This integration provides a characterological-developmental view of personality and psychopathology. I think of the therapy that derives directly from this intellectual tradition as *developmental psychotherapy*. But, like many others, I have been frustrated by the lack of any concrete information concerning how developmental psychotherapy is done. Masterson (1976, 1981, 1985) and Kernberg (1975, 1976, 1984) have been the most concretely helpful. But even by their work I have usually been more informed than assisted in knowing exactly what to do. In my earlier books (Johnson, 1985, 1987), I have tried to be as precise and concrete as possible about how I have created an art form that suits my particular experience, temperament, and style. I will continue to do that in this book: not to document *the way to do it* but simply to demonstrate *a way of doing it*.

I would like to emphasize that, for me, the integrated characterological-developmental theory not only informs my therapy at all levels but, not infrequently, *is* the therapy. There is very little in this volume that is of purely theoretical and unapplied nature, even if it is only potentially applicable. For example, I frequently tell clients of the basic existential life issues underlying the basic characterological adaptations with which I see them dealing. Further, I share with them what I know and ask for their collaboration in understanding how these issues became problematic for them. In my contributions to that understanding, I include not only the evolving understanding of the precise nature of the environment in which they grew up, but also what their *child's mind* would have made of that environment. Among other things, this knowledge of a child's perceptions of and assumptions about the world and self often helps the client understand why some events, which his adult mind now sees as relatively inconsequential, could have been so devastating to him as a child.

Characterological development is a function of not only the evolving demands of the child and the environment's ability to meet them but also the child's evolving *consciousness* and what meaning the failures will have concerning self, others, and the world. Script decisions (Berne, 1964) or pathogenic beliefs (Weiss & Sampson, 1986) are typically arrived at by a child who not only has a very limited view of the world but also has predictable distortions about how the world works (i.e., about cause and effect, about his own exaggerated or diminished responsibility, about the boundaries of the self, etc.).

THE PROCESS OF PSYCHOTHERAPY

I think of the psychotherapy process, as I execute it, in these three basic steps: (1) *"getting the story straight,"* (2) *corrective emotional experience* both in and outside psychotherapy, and (3) *repertoire expansion* through interaction and special technique.

"Getting the Story Straight"

The comedian Jerry Lewis has referred to himself as "the keeper of the idiot"—i.e., the Jerry Lewis idiot. I think we are all keepers of our own idiot—our personality, our complexes, our areas of sensitivity, and those other places where we are not really up-to-date with ourselves and our circumstances. The better we know and understand the "idiot," the more able we are to keep her or help him become less idiotic, more mature, more contemporary with our other development, etc. This is what "getting the story straight" does. It is a largely hermeneutic or meaning-oriented intervention, and, in that, it is in most debt to the classic form of psychanalysis. But, both for the therapist and the client, there is in that hermeneutic dimension one additional and very important element—that is, the understanding it provides about the way out, the way to maturation and resolution of the complex, point of sensitivity, or arrested development.

An additional element of the hermeneutic intervention is the contemporary adult understanding it can help achieve of one's own parents, siblings, childhood friends, etc. The adult's reconstruction of his childhood is just that—a reconstruction. But in that reconstruction is the opportunity for a conscious re-sorting of what it all really meant and an understanding and correction of what it meant to the child's mind. The hermeneutic intervention, as such, is valuable, as are all such interventions in helping the person understand and thereby have an increased sense of control or mastery not only of the historical situation but of current situations.

Like most therapists, I have seen accurate interpretations, reconstructions, and explanations followed not only by a sense of relief and completion, but also by a diminution or even a disappearance of symptoms. On occasion, I have seen symptoms recur and then disappear again with the self-administration of the accurate interpretation. Behaviorists and cognitive therapists have erred in diminishing the potentially pervasive importance of this kind of understanding. Kohut (1977, p. 184) has written "The purpose of remembering . . . is not to 'make conscious' the unconscious . . . but to strengthen the coherence of the self." Such coherence through knowing is, I believe, the best content beginning for psychotherapy.

Corrective Emotional Experience

As Gustafson (1986) has noted, Alexander and French's concept of the corrective emotional experience has been widely misunderstood. They presented a truly sophisticated concept which was oversimplified by the classic psychoanalysts who attacked it and the legion of overly supportive therapists who used it to justify almost anything (Gustafson, pp. 38–39). Extending the work of Ferenczi and Rank, Alexander and French's central point was this: It is pointless for the patient to experience again and again the trauma of his childhood. What is therapeutic, maturing—indeed healing—is facing that trauma and mastering it in a "strengthened context." That strengthened context can, among other things, exist in the therapeutic alliance of psychotherapy. For Alexander and French, a semi nal part of that alliance is the belief on the part of the client that the therapist will not reinjure her in the way she was originally injured.

Weiss and Sampson are probably the most articulate representatives of this intellectual lineage, with their emphasis on the client's therapeutic tests of this proposition. Their hypothesis is that clients try to provoke the therapist into delivering the very psychic injury from which they are trying to recover. The client's unconscious hope is that the therapist will not fall for that gambit but will truly assist and help the client understand and master it. As the therapist passes the test by not rising to the bait or by correcting her error if she does, the client becomes more and more confident that this is indeed a "strengthened context." The therapeutic alliance that is so rein-forced strengthens the therapist's interpretations, explanations, and reconstructions and helps the client to gain the understanding—and thereby the hermeneutic control—and, eventually, the environmen-tal mastery of the injury and its related existential issue. Psychothera-peutic process, in this view, involves the continuous here-and-now reexperiencing and relearning surrounding this issue, resulting in its maturation, resolution, and completion. We have to thank the intellectual lineage of that buddy system represented by Ferenczi and Rank, Alexander and French, and finally Weiss and Sampson for explicating this process. In the acknowledgments for explicating this essential process, we shouldn't fail to credit Winnicott, Kohut, and Rogers for, each in his own way, strengthening the position that advo-cates both *holding* and *interpretation* (e.g., see Winnicott, 1987).

What I would like to add to this intellectual lineage is that we as psychotherapists can help our clients structure their lives in such a way that their whole life becomes a "strengthened context" or an opportunity for corrective emotional experiences. One or even five hours a week of psychotherapy is not that much in a client's total life experience, particularly insofar as that small amount of time has as its objective the correction of complexes and patterns based on an entire life's experience. The therapist's and the patient's evolving understanding of what is a strengthened context, of what a corrective emotional experience for her would be, of the normal human learn-ing processes involved in the existential issue in question, creates the possibility of engineering a life of altered context. Here the contribu-tions of the sociological, social work, and behavioral schools can be appreciated and integrated into a psychotherapy that directly im-pacts the patient's day-to-day life.

Additionally, psychotherapy can help provide the strengthened extratherapy context by assisting the client in understanding not only his projected contents but also others, their history, motivation, etc. Here the characterological-developmental theory can also be quite useful. To the extent that the client understands his significant others, their character, and where they are coming from, he is more able to understand their actions and thereby less prone to react with his own overdetermined responses. Sometimes the client needs to learn that certain of his wife's reactions have to do with her own phenomenology, and this understanding can assist him in both responding to her and controlling his own overdetermined reactions to her. This kind of understanding can insulate the narcissist from a reinjury to self-esteem, it can keep the oral character from being drawn into a co-dependent role, or it can prevent the symbiotic character's typical overreaction to another's distress. In other words, knowledge that will help the client discriminate the present from the past includes the phenomenology and motivation of significant others in the present. This provides, in a very special way, a strengthened context for one's day-to-day life experience.

Repertoire Expansion

Here is where I place many of the special techniques from psychoanalysis, gestalt, bioenergetics, hypnosis, neurolinguistic programming, cognitive-behavioral psychotherapy, etc. These techniques and their more subtle talk-therapy derivatives are certainly used by many therapists to facilitate the first two processes—getting the story straight and the corrective emotional experience. But in addition to this, these more active procedures provide the opportunity for a kind of direct learning that might not otherwise be available.

We have learned, for example, that people who are phobic or who have panic reactions, particularly those who are agoraphobic with panic attacks, require more than insight and intratherapy experience to reliably face the feared circumstances. The insight may be useful, but repeated direct learning with the phobic stimuli in strengthened contexts is usually necessary. The strengthened context may involve a relaxed state achieved in systematic desensitization, a new way of looking at oneself and the situation as provided by a cognitive reframe, or most commonly, the presence of a soothing other who accompanies the agoraphobic in the in vivo desensitization to the feared stimuli. Although agoraphobia provides the clear-

est and best documented example of the need for direct learning of
new behaviors, I believe that there are any number of problematic
affects, behaviors, and ideas which similarly require direct experience of some kind. In general, the special techniques of this third
category may be used to provide these experiences that increase the
flexibility of the patient's repertoire.

The desensitization metaphor from behavior therapy is a good
one for understanding one aspect of the necessary intervention in
any number of characterological problems. The schizoid needs to be
desensitized to people, the obsessive-compulsive to his own warded-
off feelings, the oral to his own needs, the symbiotic to his expression
of aggression, to separation, and often even to success in the world.
Getting the story straight about how one was sensitized and learning
precisely to what one was sensitized can be extremely useful. But
the actual desensitization *experience* is usually required for any real
transmutation of character. Such new learning can occur spontaneously, but the therapist's prompting and arranging for this learning,
both within and without the therapy contact, is often necessary and
usually facilitative. While it can often be arranged in a less formal
manner than that typically emphasized by traditional behavior mod-
ifiers, cognitive therapists, hypnotherapists, or neurolinguistic pro-
grammers, more deliberate strategies are often valuable adjuncts to
the therapist's repertoire of skills for engineering new learning.

Psychopathology can accurately be seen as universally restrictive
of the repertoire of human responses. Indeed, it is this rigidity that
hampers the organism's otherwise rich array of possibilities for han-
dling situations. Often, the arrest of development and learning surrounding a certain existential issue has cut off the natural learning
and adaptation process, and it is that process that must be reacti-
vated. Special techniques for doing this are the legacy of those more
modern, usually active, forms first initiated by Wilhelm Reich and
furthered by such pioneers as Alexander Lowen, Fritz Perls, Joseph
Wolpe, B. F. Skinner, Milton H. Erickson, and many others. It is
time that we integrate these unique contributions within the main-
stream of psychotherapy. Of course, not every therapist will learn
or feel comfortable with all of these techniques, but one who has
not exposed himself to at least a few of them or who is unable to
identify with any of them is not really operating with the fully available therapeutic repertoire. Such a therapist will be particularly ham-

pered wherever the engineering of new learning is a critical part of the therapeutic program.

In integrating a number of approaches to understanding psychopathology and doing psychotherapy, I have done what any practicing therapist must do—employ these various perspectives in developing my own unique view of things and my own unique style of working. In so doing, we interpret the work of others. Interpretation is not necessarily a literal translation. Wherever I am aware that my interpretation is substantively different from the original, I will acknowledge that. However, it should be clear that it is not my intention to present an exact replication of the original author's work. Rather, I intend to acknowledge the sources behind the development of my own integration and offer my interpretation of that work as it has been useful in my clinical thinking and practice. In short, this work represents an integrative interpretation of a number of schools of thought and practice rather than a literal translation. This approach is consistent with the theme of this particular volume on the development of autonomy, individuation, and self-expression.

The section that follows this introduction presents a thorough introduction to the characterological-developmental model which is the bedrock of this approach. Although I have done this in each of the other books in this series (see Johnson, 1985, 1987), this section represents the most comprehensive and integrated presentation of the model. Each of the basic existential issues that underlie character development are presented, together with a greater emphasis on the current developmental research that applies to the model.

In this book, I also attempt to provide the reader with a number of tools to assist in learning this way of looking at human behavior and change. This includes the summary tables outlining each character structure in Chapters 1 through 4, one appendix that summarizes the most useful concepts from object relations (Appendix A), and another (Appendix B) that summarizes chronologically the results of relevant developmental research.

For one to fully utilize the conceptual and change approaches to the symbiotic character suggested here, one must understand the entire model underlying them and be prepared to deal with those themes that are representative of other characterological issues. I have never seen a client who could be understood solely through the insights provided by understanding one character structure. The issues underlying the structures are common to the human condition, and we all share more or less the human dilemmas that they represent. I believe that it is the integrative model presented in Chapters 1 through 4 that is perhaps my most useful contribution to the practicing therapist—this is reflected in the length of this section and the auxiliary tools provided for understanding it.

Chapter 5 is an expanded, detailed presentation of the etiology and defining characteristics of the symbiotic character. My objective here is to assist the reader in not only recognizing the character structure, but also developing a resonant empathy with the phenomenology of a person with these issues. Understanding the phenomenology is helpful in getting inside the often neurotically complex expressions of the disorder and making change safe.

Chapter 6 presents a selected review and integration of theoretical approaches that particularly apply to the symbiotic issue. Most central to this chapter, as well as the subsequent ones on treatment, are Fairbairn's ideas about the internalization of bad objects. Fairbairn's work leads to the very useful modeling of the psychopathology as internal self-object relationships. This view is potentially very powerful in explicating and exorcising the problem. This chapter also reviews the similar and very helpful work of Masterson on the essential etiology of the symbiotic issue, the contributions of the family therapists, and the insights of Weiss and Sampson on control mastery and test theory.

The final three chapters explicate the treatment of the symbiotic character using these theoretical structures and incorporating a potentially broad range of techniques. These chapters are particularly influenced by Fairbairn's theoretical propositions, which are made quite concrete by the ways in which these patients symptomatically express their internal object relations. The therapeutic process derived from this model is essentially aimed at releasing patients from the internal, closed, and autopoetic system that blinds them to the freedom of experiencing a social system that is external, open, and potentially corrective.

In writing this book, I have attempted to make all this as easy to understand as I could without losing the necessary complexity of the human being. I hope that this complexity has been retained and that truly grasping this material will be difficult enough to represent new and meaningful learning.

PART I

A THEORY
OF CHARACTER
FORMATION

A Characterological-Developmental Theory for Psychotherapy

THIS CHAPTER IS AN ATTEMPT to integrate what we now know about human development with what we know about the common constellations of character. Though our knowledge of both character and development is evolving and determined by our cultural perspective, I believe this integrated view gives us the most useful map of the territory of personality and psychopathology for the purpose of conducting psychotherapy. An approach to understanding and helping people, which is grounded in the significant issues of their development, provides a generalized map which calibrates the most essential territory—it is a map that is sufficiently general yet appropriately targeted so that it fits the task at hand. Particularly when a characterological-developmental perspective can remain open to the evolution of knowledge and culture, it provides a view that integrates the effects of the developing human potential with the effects of environmental conditions, and it documents how potentials affect learning and how either can be derailed from an optimal course.

Psychoanalytic developmental psychology, which is an umbrella label for object relations, ego, and self psychology, has been of great clinical use to many of us because it has consistently asked some of the most useful questions: What are the child's most basic needs and drives? What does the child need to achieve optimal human development? How does the person formulate a cohesive, robust sense of self? How does cognitive development unfold, and how does it relate to character and psychopathology? How does indulgence, trauma, or chronic frustration affect the development of the human being? Are there critical periods for the development of certain human qualities? If so, what are they? Does the human being internalize aspects of the environment; if so, how?

A cognitive map, which is to serve as the underpinning for the endeavor of psychotherapy, also does well to include the most prevalent constellations of personality and psychopathology. The current *Diagnostic and Statistical Manual* of the American Psychiatric Association (1987) certainly provides a running start for this, albeit atheoretical and democratically derived. In my earlier work (Johnson, 1985, 1987), I have argued that a contemporary character-analytic point of view provides a very similar yet more theoretically derived view of the constellations of personality and psychopathology. Further, when this approach is informed by more developmental and interpersonal perspectives, one can derive a clinically useful model which can hold a wide variety of therapeutic techniques and suggests their appropriate application.

In this characterological-developmental view, each character structure is the outgrowth of one basic existential human issue. Each issue is fundamental to the human experience and requires a constant resolution over the life span. Yet, there are predictable periods in life during which each issue is of particular importance. And the first time the issue is dealt with can be particularly important, especially when the individual's experience is severely traumatic. In that case, early forms of resolving the issue tend to become fixed. In other words, the current model is not one of lockstep development asserting that crucial life issues are resolved in one life phase so that the child may move on to resolve others in subsequent phases. These issues are too important for that. Rather, what is proposed is that these extremely fundamental human issues are faced early on in life, and that some early attempts at resolving them are based both on limited equipment and limited experience of the world. Furthermore, when the issues are faced in trauma, their early resolutions tend to become rigid and resistant to change. In this view, these early solutions were often quite adaptive given the limitations of the environment and the limitations of the individual's capacities, but they often achieved an imperfect escape from trauma.

The work of Solomon and Wynne (1954) has documented the extreme resistance to extinction of a response learned in an analogous escape conditioning paradigm. In these experiments, dogs learned to avoid electric shock when signaled. Once established, the avoidance response never extinguished unless the dogs were confined in the original box and only then with a great deal of "resistance" and emotionality. The rigidity of similarly established solutions may explain the character and psychopathology of humans who come for psychotherapy. People often need to learn that the shock has been turned off—that their original escape solutions are no longer necessary.

The characterological-developmental model is further appealing as a cognitive map for all this because it suggests a resolution to one of the central conflicts of psychoanalytic theorizing. This conflict has been elucidated best by Greenberg and Mitchell (1983), who argue for the essential irreconcilability of the classical drive theory of psychoanalysis, which conceptualizes unconscious conflict resulting from instinctual impulses and societal inhibitions, and the interpersonal model, which conceptualizes the contents of the psyche as all interpersonally derived. In the interpersonal view, the dynamic conflict between two or more internalized aspects of the person derives from others in the interpersonal matrix.

The contemporary character-analytic model includes recognition of primary instinctual impulses such as sexuality and aggression but places equal importance on the environmental response to the individual's impulses and needs. Most importantly, the theory asserts that what is also definitional of character and resulting psychopathology comes from the person's pattern of dealing with the natural organismic response to the environment's frustration of the instinctual needs. Thus, much of what is character and much of what makes up psychopathology are understood in terms of the individual's complex reaction to environmental frustration. Conflict is interpersonally derived, but based on what is inherent in the human being.

More and more, contemporary theorists are willing to acknowledge the humanly inherent need for relationship (e.g., Fairbairn, 1952, 1958; Mitchell, 1988; Stern, 1985), as well as the sometimes competing need for individuation (e.g., Mahler, Pine, & Bergman, 1975; Masterson, 1976, 1981). With these latter "instincts" firmly in place, constellations of personality and psychopathology can productively be conceptualized as deriving from those existential lifetime issues: the extent to which they are allowed, frustrated, or resolved, and the individual's reactions to their continued frustration. Developmental knowledge, not only about babies but about people over the life span, informs us of the various expressions of each issue, as well as the developing nature of the human equipment at various ages and the nature of the kinds of cognitive and other errors and distortions made over the life span (e.g., see Kegan, 1982).

There are additional practical advantages to this characterological-developmental approach for psychotherapy. First among these is the beneficial effect that this essentially "therapeutic reframe" can have on both the client and the therapist. With respect to the client, this is a reframe which often finds easy acceptance because one's problematic behavior, attitudes, and feelings often seem so immature. Presented correctly, this reframe can have a beneficial effect on the self-labeling process, prompting compassion and understanding for oneself in place of self-denigration. As with any other hermeneutic intervention that "takes," one achieves the satisfaction of understanding and thereby achieving some control over the problem. But the developmental therapeutic reframe can do much more. For purposes of prescribing new learning and the intervention required to achieve it, the reframe can specify what has not been learned or resolved and can elucidate the required context and learning processes necessary for growth or resolution.

These same advantages of compassion, understanding, and control accrue to the therapist as well. Of particular importance here is the reframe's effect in helping the therapist distance from her own negative personal reactions. For example, the narcissistic client, who can relate only through idealization and ultimately devaluation or, alternatively, through using one as an audience for his grandiosity, will easily stimulate some not-very-therapeutic reactions in most people. But a therapist who can see the child in the adult and understand that this form of relationship is all that he is up to at that moment can attenuate her reactions and more easily respond with what is useful. It will often be important for the therapist to remember that this developmental model is merely that—a model or analogue of reality that can both generate and justify a plethora of therapeutic responses. Finally, the characterological-developmental model not only directs the therapist's attention to some of the more important issues, but also offers a model of how these issues may be resolved.

To the extent that we are correct about the basic processes of resolution in the infant or child or adolescent, we can assist the client in going through that very process. Developmental research on such things as perception-taking and object constancy, for example, has shown that the ability to take another's perception or to simultaneously hold conflicting feelings about an object develop through a number of iterations as one develops cognitively and emotionally. The young adult can take another's perception at a much higher level of sophistication than can a latency-aged child, who, in turn, can have empathy for another at a much more sophisticated level than can the 18-month-old who has demonstrated such abilities. Similarly, when an adult client needs to learn such an ability, that learning will not be the same as in an infant or a latency-aged child or an adolescent, but some of the essential processes will be the same. The therapeutic encounter, the learning procedures, and the level of conceptualization will be age- and situation-appropriate in good developmental psychotherapy, but knowledge of the process at each documented iteration cannot help but be useful.

Kohut's (1971) formulation of the archaic transferences of merger, twinship, mirroring, and idealization offer another useful example of this iterative maturing process. While, on the one hand, these transference behaviors are definitional of narcissistic personality disorder for Kohut, they are also the basic building blocks for his conceptualization of the development of self. Kohut asserts that a need for these selfobject relationships continues throughout the life span, but that, as the individual matures psychologically, the selfobject needs also mature, so that the individual needs others and ideals to respect, relations with others who are similar to him and who admire him, etc. Seen in these ways, the therapeutic derivatives from this developmental perspective are reparative but not regressive, in that they acknowledge the analogue nature of the model and recognize the contemporary strengths of the client.

According to the theory I will present here, personality and psychopathology develop in particular constellations as a consequence of the interaction of a broad but finite range of instinctual needs of the person and the environment's ability or inability to respond appropriately to them. These instinctual needs go well beyond those oral, anal, and phallic internal pressures posited by Freud and include the infant's well-documented need to attach or bond to a primary caregiver (e.g., Bowlby, 1969); the child's need to individuate through exploration, self-determined activity, and the building of psychic boundaries (e.g., Mahler, 1968); the need for self-determined expression (e.g., Kohut, 1971, 1977; Lowen, 1958, 1983);

and the need for an attuned self-other relationship (e.g., Kohut, 1971; Stern, 1985). In this theoretical construction, the nature of personality and psychopathology is, then, largely determined by the kinds of interpersonal frustrations that are encountered by the developing person as she attempts to meet these many needs. Personality and psychopathology are further defined by both her natural instinctive response to the frustration in question and the methods she chooses to use in dealing with, adjusting to, or suppressing those natural responses. Her choice of adjustment maneuvers is further determined by the structural capacities at her level of development at the time of frustration as well as by the possible maneuvers that are modeled or accepted by the interpersonal environment. It is this interplay of instinctual needs with the impact of the interpersonal environment that makes this a truly integrative theory.

Character-analytic theorists (e.g., Levy & Bleecker, 1975) have delineated the development of character in five stages: (1) *Self-affirmation* is the initial expression of the instinctual need. (2) The *negative environmental response* is the social environment's blocking or frustration of that need. (3) The *organismic reaction* is the natural, "wired in" response to frustration by the environment—usually the experience and expression of intense negative affect, particularly rage, terror, and grief at loss.

These first three stages are relatively straightforward. It is in the final stages that character is formed. (4) The fourth stage is labeled *self-negation*. This more elaborate form of turning against the self involves the individual's imitating the social environment in blocking the expression of the original instinctual impulse *and* blocking the instinctual response to that block as well. It is this identification with the environment that sets the person against himself, makes the block to self-expression internal, and creates psychopathology. This is the beginning of an internal conflict, which can persist throughout a lifetime, between the irrepressible instinctual need and reaction, on the one hand, and the internalized blocking of those needs and reactions, on the other.

Wilhelm Reich, Alexander Lowen, and other energetically oriented therapists have emphasized how the blocks to self-expression are literally present in the body, represented by chronic muscular tension which can result in postural distortion. This blocking or self-negation originally served the purpose of avoiding the pain and frustration of experiencing the environment's block. It continues to serve that purpose, and thus it is very resistant to change. The blocking on a body level is simply the organism's way of not experiencing the original need and the uncomfortable reaction to its frustration. Furthermore, the body blocks avoid the inevitable anxieties of being vulnerable again and risking the anticipated reinjury.

Fairbairn's (1958) position appears completely consistent with this and adds to it. Fairbairn's view was that these original organismic self-expressions (i.e., instincts, libidinal impulses, etc.) were object-seeking. When the objects (others) were frustrating or blocking, the individual internalized them and then rendered them unconscious. The original impulses, as well as what Fairbairn characterized as the individual's "aggressive" responses to frustration, became unconscious. What Fairbairn's view adds, which will be reviewed in much more detail in Chapter 6, is the emphasis on the resulting unconscious and fixed internal object relations, which account for the resulting static psychopathology and the resistance to new relationships, learning, and change. Change is resisted not only because it may cause the resurrection of internalized "bad objects" and repressed impulses toward them—an intolerable psychic state that motivated repression in the first place—but also because of the individual's attachment to these objects as internalized. "It is above all the need of the child for the parents, however bad they may appear to him, that compels him to internalize bad objects; and it is because this need remains attached to them in the unconscious that he cannot bring himself to part with them" (Fairbairn, 1974, p. 68).

In other words, the self-negation process is relational and uniquely personified in each case. The constructs emphasizing splits in the self and explaining pathology and resistance in terms, for example, of an internalized object suppressing "libidinal" expression, are very useful clinically. Much of gestalt therapy is based on processes that bring to consciousness and actualize these splits of the self and play out their interrelationships.

(5) The fifth and final step in the sequence, labeled the *adjustment process*, essentially consists of making the best of it. This involves the construction of any number of compromises in an attempt to resolve the unresolvable conflict. This is analogous to Sullivan's concept of the "security operation" or Winnicott's "false self." In this conceptualization, the budding narcissist, for example, who cannot

get well-attuned prizing from caretaking figures by his natural self-expression, will identify with the image of himself that these caretakers require for their own purposes, and he will do everything in his power to live up to it. By so doing, he can achieve some semblance of the mirrored attunement that he requires. Simultaneously, he can avoid the recurrence of painful narcissistic injuries, which come as a result of his true self-expression. To the extent that he can live up or down to the environment's expectations, the compromise appears to work, and this, in part, explains why the successful narcissist is notoriously difficult to change.

The self-negation process defines what the individual must deny or suppress. The adjustment process defines what he must exaggerate. What parts of the real self the individual suppresses and what parts he exaggerates succinctly define his character as discussed here. Psychopathology is seen in the suppression, in the exaggeration, or most often, in the individual's natural reaction to this kind of habitual, unnatural accommodation to avoid pain while maintaining contact.

The infusion of psychoanalytic developmental theory and developmental research (both observational,`a la Mahler, and experimental,`a la Stern) enriches and continually updates this model of character development. These sources provide data on the exact nature of the original organismic self-expressions (instincts) and document when they first seem to appear as naturalistically observed or as experimentally demanded. Further, these sources directly catalog environmental-social frustrations and the infant's or child's responses to them. Finally, these sources suggest the kinds of structural abilities and inabilities that occur throughout the life span and provide the basic equipment for the self-negation and adjustment processes. Though these sources all contain a mixture of empirically derived fact and inductive and deductive theory, there is a remarkable degree of convergence concerning the essential processes, despite all the apparent disagreement concerning their timing or the debates concerning what is inherent vs. what is learned. Further, there are empirically derived facts from the data that, without much interpretation, provide solid building blocks for a characterological-developmental theory.

The perspective of ego psychology can be useful here, if only at the level of description, by helping us make sense of a continuum of psychopathology. Along with others in this field (e.g., Masterson, 1976, 1981; Meissner, 1988), I have suggested that we see various basic forms of psychopathology along a spectrum. I believe the most central underlying dimension of such a spectrum involves the structural (often termed ego) functioning of the individual. This model posits that the same basic underlying characterological issue may be expressed all along this spectrum.

Just as other authors have discussed high-, medium-, or low-functioning borderlines or narcissists, I have been suggesting a similar demarcation along other characterological dimensions. Since I see these characterological dimensions as reflecting existential issues, the categorization will reflect the extent of psychic and behavioral disruption in relation to the issue in question. I am asserting that people are best understood *in relation to* these existential issues, recognizing that people can operate at different levels of structural integration depending on which issue they are dealing with. For example, an individual who typically operates with a high level of integration may more or less disintegrate or regress when faced with perceived threats to safety, threats to self-esteem, threats of another's abandonment, etc. This model is similar to that of Gedo and Goldberg (1973), who asserted that differing psychoanalytic *Models of the Mind* were appropriate to understand the differing types of psychopathological functioning.

Table 2 provides as comprehensive a map of all this as I could get into one table. Each characterological issue is subsumed under one of three developmental periods suggested by the developmental research and theories—attachment/bonding, self and other development, and self in system development. The six basic characterological issues and their respective expressions in behavior and attitudes are briefly presented. On the right side of the table the continuum of structural development is presented with three marker points along that continuum: personality disorder, character neurosis, and character style. The continuum reflects a descending disruption in structural or ego functioning, particularly as it relates to that particular characterological issue.

Considering the schizoid (safety) issue, for example, full-blown schizoid personality disorder would be characterized by a very low level of structural development and high disruption in functioning, particularly around issues of social involvement, safety, and smooth

Table 2

CHARACTEROLOGICAL ISSUES AND STRUCTURAL DEVELOPMENT

Developmental Period	Character	Issue	Characterological Expression	Structural Development Continuum and *DSM-III-R* Diagnosis		
				Personality Disorder	Character Neurosis	Character Style
Attachment/ Bonding	Schizoid (safety)	Others the source of pain not comfort	Dissociation, withdrawal. Polarity: Presence-absence	Schizoid ——————— Schizotypal Functional Psychoses	Avoidant ———————	>
	Oral (need)	Needs are denied or too great to be met	Dependency on or gratification of others at the expense of the self. Polarity: Seeking dependency gratification – providing dependency gratification	Dependent ———————	Compensated Dependent* ———————	>
Self and Other Development	Symbiotic (self boundaries)	Identity found in others, not in the self	Fusion defines an alien self-expression. True self elicits guilt. Polarity: Autonomy-enmeshment	Borderline ——————————————— Dependent ———————————————		> >
	Narcissistic (self-esteem)	Identity found in the "false self," not in the impoverished real self	Attempts to maintain the grandiose self. Polarity: Worthlessness-grandiosity	Narcissistic ———————————————		>
	Masochistic (freedom)	Control of self-initiative surrendered to overpowering other	Subservient, guilt inducing, passive-aggressive, spiteful. Polarity: Controlled-controlling	Self-defeating* ———————————————		>
Self in System Development	Oedipal (love-sex)	Disruption and often splitting of the sexual and love impulses	Denial or exaggeration of sexuality, competition, and love. Polarity: Sexual-asexual	Obsessive-Compulsive ——————————————— Histrionic ——————————————— mixed ———————————————		> > >

Note: Psychoanalytic developmental psychology = ego psychology (Hartmann, A. Freud), object relations (Mahler, Masterson, Kernberg, Stern, Winnicott, Fairbairn), self psychology (Kohut, Gedo, Goldberg), and character analysis (Reich, Lowen, Horowitz, Shapiro).

*Diagnoses not recognized by *DSM-III-R*.

affective regulation, with a tendency toward extreme use of dissociation and withdrawal in defense of threatening involvement. Schizotypal personality disorder and functional psychoses would also be listed under the character disorder column, evidencing high disruption in ego functioning, particularly around these kinds of issues.

At middle levels of structural development with the schizoid issue, one is more likely to find the behavior more characteristic of the avoidant personality disorder in *DSM-III-R* terms. Here there is an overuse of social withdrawal as a defense, with some cognitive and affective dissociation, especially under social stress, but serious structural disruption is absent, particularly outside this area of concern. What defines this midpoint character neurosis, is a long-standing and life-disrupting internal conflict which yields behavior that is "neurotic." In Shapiro's words, "The neurotic personality or character . . . is one that reacts against itself; it reacts, reflexively, against certain of its own tendencies. It is a personality in conflict" (Shapiro, 1989, p. x). Thus, in *DSM-III-R*, what distinguishes a schizoid from an avoidant personality disorder is that the avoidant wants to be with others but is anxious about doing so. The tendency to approach reflexively brings on anxiety, but the tendency to avoid yields dissatisfaction. This "house divided against itself" personality can then produce elaborate compromise solutions to simultaneously accommodate the competing tendencies that carry that unmistakable neurotic quality.

At still higher levels of structural development, one would see more of what I would characterize as schizoid personality style. Here, the problems of schizoid adjustment are less obvious on the surface, the individual is far better defended and more able to present a social facade which covers underlying fear and anxiety. The individual often uses more mature defenses, such as intellectualization, to handle his anxiety, but there is an underlying fear of others and an inability to fully experience social contact with a concomitant restriction in the affective range.

In the structural-development continuum of the table, I have attempted to do a loose, generalized translation to *DSM-III-R* personality-disorder terminology. With the exception of the avoidant personality classified under the schizoid issue, there are really no middle and high-end positions, because, in general, the manual is devoted to a description of severe personality disorders. The arrows within the structural development section are meant to communicate that the basic issues represented in these personality disorders may be extended to understand the character neuroses and the character styles that could just as well carry the same names. The table, which plots a characterological issue by level of structural development, can also be used in a general way to evaluate a client on more than one dimension, much like an MMPI profile. Thus, any given individual may show structural development in the low to middle range on the issue of narcissism, with a higher, yet disrupted, level of functioning on the schizoid and oedipal issues, etc. I have found that an orientation to all of this, which emphasizes the existential life issue as opposed to character typology, deepens and broadens understanding of ourselves and others and humanizes our approach to psychological problems.

The model of character and psychopathology presented here is a "functional" one, meaning that it covers that which can be attributed to environmental as opposed to organic or genetic causes. Thus, those severe disorders that are documented to be organically or genetically related are not listed. Here I would include psychoses, bipolar disorders, antisocial (sociopathic or psychopathic) disorders, and autism. Some object-relations theorists would argue that sociopathic functioning is arrested development in the earliest (i.e., schizoid) period, but I have come to feel that much of it may be organically related.

Table 3, a companion to Table 2, further elucidates the structural development continuum. Here I've simply listed the characteristics of higher structural development, which can be evaluated for an individual overall or, even more interestingly, for each characterological issue. An individual may have very good reality perception in general, but, because of his narcissistic issue, may misperceive social cues which are seen to affect his self-esteem in any way. Or, one's modulation of affect might be quite good except when one's fear of abandonment is triggered, etc. It is my experience that understanding this intersection of characterological issues and structural development for an individual provides the most useful diagnostic information and accurately predicts the themes of psychotherapy, its likely pace, and, to some extent, the interventions that will be useful, ineffective, or harmful.

Now, I will turn to an exposition of the six basic characterological issues and the developmental factors that influence their course.

Table 3
THE STRUCTURAL DEVELOPMENT CONTINUUM

HIGH	MEDIUM	LOW

Affective
Affective stability
High anxiety tolerance
Anxiety serves as signal
Good self-soothing abilities
Good differentiation of feelings
Smooth modulation of feelings
High frustration tolerance
Experience of self-cohesion
Insusceptible to regressive states

Cognitive
Objective self-perception (good "observing ego")
Constancy of self-perception
Predominance of mature defenses
Mature development of moral sense
High-quality reality perception
High quality of judgment
High quality of synthetic abilities
Formulation and execution of clear intentions
Regressions creative and ego mediated
Projections or regressions "owned"

Interpersonal
Object constancy
Good self-other differentiation
Distance and closeness well modulated

Intimate others usually assumed to show object constancy

Perception of others is reality based

Affective
Affects highly labile
Low anxiety tolerance
Anxiety traumatic and disorganizing
Poor self-soothing abilities
Poor differentiation of feelings
Feelings undermodulated
Low frustration tolerance
Self-fragmentation
Susceptible to regressive states

Cognitive
Self-perception not reality based
Self-splitting
Predominance of immature defenses
Morality founded on immature bases
Poor reality perception
Impaired judgment
Impaired synthetic abilities
Intentions and planning impaired
Regressions not ego mediated
Projections and regressions not "owned"

Interpersonal
Object splitting
Blurring of boundaries
Relationships characterized by clinging, detachment, or ambivalence
Relationships characterized by fears of other's abandonment, rejection, or destructiveness
Relationships characterized by merger, twinship, mirroring, or idealization transference behavior

CHAPTER 2

Characterological Issues of Attachment and Bonding

HAVING NOW REVIEWED the basic theory, in the remaining chapters of this section I will follow the central dimensions of Table 2 in presenting a summary of characterological issues. In this chapter, I will present the characterological issues that derive from the earliest period—attachment and bonding. These *schizoid* and *oral* issues will be discussed with illustrations of their expressions along the structural continuum—personality disorder, character neurosis, and character style. Similarly, in Chapter 3, I will present those issues of self development—symbiotic, narcissistic and masochistic— along the same continuum. Finally, Chapter 4 will be devoted to the issues of the "oedipal" period, where the negotiation of self beyond the dyad becomes more crucial.

THE SCHIZOID ISSUE

The bulk of recent developmental research indicates that the human infant is seemingly "hardwired" at birth for social interaction (see Appendix B for a chronological listing of social and cognitive developmental markers as established by observation and experimental research). The data indicate, for example, that the neonate can discriminate its own mother's voice from another woman's voice reading the same material (DeCasper & Fifer, 1980). These same authors have shown that at one week, infants can recognize the difference between a passage read aloud to them in utero and a control passage which had never been read before. This shows a kind of social interaction even across the birth gap. Stern (1977, p.

36) notes that, even in the first few weeks of life, infants' eyes converge at approximately eight inches from the face, which is the typical distance between the mother's and the infant's face during nursing. Indeed, by the end of the first week, the behavioral evidence strongly suggests that the infant is sufficiently familiar with the mother's face to become visibly disturbed if it is obscured by a mask or matched with a voice other than the mother's (Tronick & Adamson, 1980, p. 141).

By one month, infants begin to show appreciation of more global (nonfeatured) aspects of the human face, such as animation, complexity, and even configuration (Sherrod, 1981). Even in the first two days of life, infants can discriminate between and even imitate happy, sad, and surprised expressions (Field et al., 1982). By three weeks of age, babies are able to perform the fairly complex activity of audiovisual crossmodal matching of the absolute level of stimulus intensity (Lewcowicz & Turkewitz, 1980), indicating that they are, even at this point, up to the kind of mutual attunement with another that Stern (1985) characterizes as the essence of early human relations. Young infants are so predetermined to be social that they react emotionally to signals of distress from another individual (Sagi & Hoffman, 1976; Simner, 1971). Other studies have shown that infants will work to receive human contact or the opportunity to watch others. Lichtenberg (1983, p. 6) concludes that, "study after study documents the neonate's preadapted potential for direct interaction."

All this indicates that the infant is preprogrammed and attuned to the kinds of social responses he receives. So, very early on, a baby will track not only whether he is being handled roughly or subjected to painful stimulation, but he will be able to track the affective tone with which he is handled and the attunement, or lack of it, to his needs, emotional states, etc. Tronick et al. (1978) have documented that three-month-old infants will react with mild upset and social withdrawal if parents simply go "still-faced" in the middle of an interaction with them. Stern's (1985) work also shows that, from birth, the child can do things to tune out overstimulation. While challenging Mahler's earlier view of a "stimulus barrier," these findings further demonstrate the child's ability to discern and respond to aversive stimulation of a more social nature.

The schizoid issue (see Table 4) is one of safety in the social world. It is clear that the infant has more than the necessary equipment to discriminate the nurturing or depriving nature of the social environment. Babies can very quickly discriminate if caretakers are cold, distant, unattuned, even indirectly hostile. Essentially, the schizoid and oral issues come first developmentally because they involve the frustration of instinctual needs that are present at birth and that can be discriminated at birth or very shortly thereafter.

Yet, while the infant's ability in the discriminative realm is impressive, there are obvious limitations to its repertoire of adaptations to serious frustration. Turning away from and tuning out aversive stimulation are essential aspects of the infant's limited repertoire of responses to aversive stimulation. While these mechanisms may certainly be used extensively to deal with later traumas, they can be used as early as the beginning of life. The characterological-developmental theory merely states that to the extent that these mechanisms are used in the earliest period of life to avoid and escape nonoptimal frustrations in that period, they will tend to persist throughout life in response to situations that are perceived as similar (i.e., harsh, threatening, cold, etc.). Furthermore, to the extent that the early environment is indeed harsh, the theory simply asserts that the individual will be inclined to generalize his early experience and anticipate harshness in subsequent social situations. That harshness, both early and contemporary, may involve anything from abuse to inattention to poor attunement. The theory predicts that individuals with the schizoid issue will be particularly vigilant to harsh social environments, especially to harshness that resembles the early forms in which it was experienced. Further, the theory predicts a tendency toward social isolation, withdrawal, and forms of mental migration that will help avoid or escape any stress, particularly of a social nature.

Up to now, this process is all very simple and straightforward. However, what many clinicians have noted about schizoid individuals is that (a) they tend to be harsh with themselves, and (b) they often tend to gravitate towards relationships and environments that are themselves harsh. These phenomena are explained by the self-negation hypothesis of the characterological theory, which is consistent with the hypotheses of a number of relational-interpersonal theorists (e.g., Fairbairn, 1952; Mitchell, 1988; Weiss & Sampson, 1986; Winnicott, 1958, 1965). The individual is thought to imitate the caretakers and eventually internalize their attitudes toward the self. Fairbairn (1958) suggests that this internalization is particularly important when the child's objects are traumatically frustrating or "bad," because the child will render the internalized object and his own identification with it unconscious in order to escape pain. Thus, an internalized self and self-other relational model are rendered unconscious and thereby permeate his experience of self and his relationships with others. Also, the individual's relational needs are met in the context of this kind of negative self-other relationship, and the modes of self-negation and compromise solutions arrived at earlier are designed for just that kind of interpersonal entanglement. So, the patterns persist, both intrapersonally and interpersonally.

Because a common experience of each character expression is very valuable in communicating about them, I use illustrations from films in teaching about them whenever possible. In the schizoid's case, Timothy Hutton's portrayal of Conrad in *Ordinary People* is illustrative of one in the character neurosis range. William Hurt's portrayal of Macon Leary in *The Accidental Tourist* illustrates the extreme social withdrawal of a well-adapted schizoid personality disorder, if one discounts his quick recovery in falling in love with Muriel, portrayed by Geena Davis. The multiple personality portrayed by Sally Field in *Sybil* illustrates the extremes of dissociation that can be used to escape pain.

Psychotherapy of a person with a schizoid issue revolves around the projection as well as the reality of harshness in the social environment and harshness toward the self. People with this issue tend to see harshness where it's not, to be persistently harsh with themselves, and also to gravitate unnecessarily to harsh environments where their relational needs have been met, albeit very imperfectly, and their coping defenses are appropriate. At lower levels of structural development, there is typically a history of more severe and prolonged trauma. One finds the extreme inability to bond with another and the capacity for dissociation and withdrawal developed to a high degree. At higher levels of development, there tends to be more social skill and involvement, with concomitant tendencies toward intellectualization and spiritualization of life. Anxiety in social situations, while better compensated, is nevertheless present.

In this clinically derived correlation between personality, symptom constellation, and reconstructed history, therapists have often emphasized the role of terror in explaining and maintaining the often extreme levels of dissociation and withdrawal of these individuals. This is exemplified most dramatically with those who have experienced the kind of physical violence, sexual abuse, and sadistic torture that leads to the extreme dissociative cases of multiple personality. But we often find such intense terror present where we are able to uncover far more benign, if troubled, histories. It is unclear in many of these cases what exactly has happened to the individual, though it is quite conceivable that one very traumatic incident which has been repressed, and/or a chronically cold and barren social environment could be the cause.

In any case, schizoid individuals at all levels of structural development will show an almost automatic tendency to dissociate—to be unaware of their feelings and out of touch with thoughts or even visual memories that might disturb them. To some significant degree, these individuals are really out of touch with themselves and significant aspects of their experience. They tend, in particular, to isolate their feelings from thoughts. It is believed that this tendency to separate themselves from their own experience keeps them safe from the intense levels of terror that may emerge as this defensive strategy is relinquished. As this occurs, these individuals also typically access a good deal of retaliatory rage, which has also been kept in check by this ability to separate oneself from one's own experience. Typically, the treatment of the schizoid individual will involve not only the uncovering and expression of these difficult feelings but also some learning of better ways to control them. As all this occurs, the individual becomes more and more able to be vulnerable with respect to others and to access and connect to truly affectionate and nurturing feelings about others.

Successful therapy with a schizoid person really involves a desensitization to people, to intimacy, even to the experience of dependency on another for understanding, attunement, compassion, and love. It also involves attenuating the hostile "evoked companion" (Stern, 1985) or internalization of the harsh other and the hostile, retaliatory self. Finally, a good therapeutic outcome with a schizoid person involves the development of relational needs met in a more highly relational context, not in the context of a harsh, unwelcoming other.

Therapeutic errors with these individuals typically revolve around the timing of the process of desensitization to dissociated feelings and thoughts as well as to other people. At one extreme, a very

Table 4
SCHIZOID CHARACTER

---

1. *Etiological constellation*: Parenting is abusive to harsh to unattuned, cold, distant, and unconnected. The child experiences itself as hated, unwanted, or insignificant. With the limited resources of an infant the individual can only withdraw, dissociate, or internally migrate. The blocking of the most basic expressions of existence and the withdrawal of energy from external reality, others, and life itself produce deadness and disconnectedness.

2. *Symptom constellation*: Chronic anxiety, avoidant behaviors, conflict over social contact, trust, and commitment are definitional. There is usually evidence of self-destructive or self-damaging behavior, self-hatred or disapproval of self, poor self-care and self-soothing. The individual often shows an inability to know her own feelings and to make sustained social or intimate contact. To a great extent, this individual can be defined as one who is out of contact with self and others.

3. *Cognitive style*: Isolation of thinking from feelings with abstract thinking often well developed. Concrete operations in relation to the physical world often poorly developed. "Social" intelligence is often impaired.

4. *Defenses*: Projection, denial, intellectualization, "spiritualization," withdrawal, isolation of affect, dissociation, and fugue states. The individual may have poor memory, especially for interpersonal events, conflict, and childhood.

5. *Script decisions or pathogenic beliefs*: "I have no right to exist. The world is dangerous. There is something wrong with me. If I really let go, I could kill someone. I will figure it all out. The true answers in life are spiritual and other-worldly."

6. *Self-representation*: The self is experienced as damaged, perhaps defective or evil. The individual questions his own right to exist and invests in intellectual or spiritual pursuits identifying with his intellect and spirit.

7. *Object representations and relations*: Others are seen as nonaccepting, threatening, and more powerful than the self. The individual is particularly sensitive to harshness in the social environment. She often projects hostility onto others and elicits hostility through projective identification.

8. *Affective characteristics*: The person experiences chronic fearfulness and often terror. Affect is isolated and/or suppressed. The individual doesn't know how he feels and can appear cold, dead, and out of touch with himself. Primitive, suppressed rage underlies the fear and terror.

---

distant therapist might collude with the schizoid in very intellectualized reconstruction or mechanical, behavioral therapy for some aspect of this problem. At the other end of the spectrum, a very
feeling-oriented therapist might rush such a client to premature affective and social experiences which would retraumatize him and
thereby deepen the dissociative defense. Very often, these clients
elicit impatience in therapists who fail to appreciate the profound
level of terror that motivates their stubborn, out-of-touch demeanor.
Retaliation for the very slow and uneven progress of these individuals, if not quickly repaired, can provide the death knell for their
therapy. It is perhaps more with the schizoid issue than with any
other that the therapist needs to provide at least a potentially holding
environment while, at the same time, being careful not to push the
client with more closeness, intimacy, or understanding than his
shaky structure can handle. It is the "corrective emotional experience" offered in therapy and engineered outside it that is the essence
of the required psychotherapy.

For each character issue or structure, I have composed a table
summarizing some of the central features. In each summary, I have
used the following categories: (1) etiological constellation, (2) symptom constellation, (3) cognitive style, (4) defenses, (5) script decisions or pathogenic beliefs, (6) self representation, (7) object representations and relations, and (8) affective characteristics. Though
these summary statements are oversimplified and, in general, do not
discriminate along the dimension of structural development, I have
found them to be very useful heuristically. They are repetitive in
places, but that repetitiveness is deliberate; in part, because I have
found it often necessary for the real learning of this material, and
also, because the slightly different slants or particular choice of
words may be quite useful clinically in more accurately matching a
specific client.

THE "ORAL" ISSUE

In clinical practice, problems that revolve around the themes of
need, dependency, and dependency gratification are fairly common,
giving rise to the labels of "oral" character, dependent personality
disorder, and co-dependent (see Table 5). As with all other characterological patterns outlined here, this one derives from clinical expe-

rience with adults. The developmental theorizing has been derived from a combination of clinical experience with these individuals involving a reconstruction of their history and the developmental data (both naturalistic and experimental) that is available. In formulating this theory, it has always been obvious that infants ask to be fed almost immediately after birth and that their relationship to "feeding" may very well become isomorphic for their relationship to need gratification in general. In recent psychoanalytic theorizing, we emphasize more the interpersonal needs for relationship and mother-infant attunement. All the developmental research is consistent in emphasizing these themes, making the "oral" label a bit out-of-date as far as the regional specificity it implies, but it is still an appropriate label if it is understood metaphorically.

In any case, what clinicians have repeatedly found with those patients who present with problems in the "need constellation" is a history marked by either deprivation or unreliability in the need-fulfilling capacity of their parents. <u>The severely "oral" patient gives one the impression that he has never really been thoroughly filled with those nutritional and emotional supplies that all human beings require.</u> The body language as well as the presenting complaints and historical data all tend to confirm this impression of deprivation (see Johnson, 1985, or Lowen, 1958, for a description of this body language). In trying to reconstruct the etiological picture for these individuals, we notice that their defenses, from a psychodynamic point of view, are rather primitive in nature, and that their relationships have a distinctly one-up/one-down character revolving around need gratification.

In looking for developmental origins of these patterns, we have always known that young children need a great deal of attention and attunement quite early on; now, observational research documents these facts as never before (e.g., Mahler, Pine, & Bergman, 1975; Stern, 1985). Clinically, we also notice that people with these issues often have parents who, even in the first months of life, were unable to hold up their end of the relationship. We may see a history of depression, alcoholism, or extreme circumstances which made normal parenting difficult (e.g., single-parent families, stresses of war, or dire economic circumstances). This environmental block or frustration of natural dependency is, almost without exception, replicated by the individual, who harbors unresolved dependency issues.

Even in those individuals with this etiology who appear the most dependent, one typically sees self-disapproval of the neediness, as distinct from the more self-syntonic dependency of the symbiotic character.

In those individuals who have achieved a higher level of adjustment, the self-negation process is usually seen most clearly. The individual's needs are typically denied and/or expressed very minimally. Indeed, these individuals often experience their needs as alien or wrong and require themselves to be extraordinarily deprived before their own needs can be seen as legitimate. The adjustment process in these higher functioning individuals often involves a great deal of caretaking of others, as has often been observed in adult children of alcoholics. Often, these same individuals tend to take on much more caregiving than they can really sustain, ultimately breaking down and failing to deliver the level of gratification that they promised. It is at these times of breakdown that their needs become so great that they must be acknowledged and, at least to some extent, met. But, once this painfully won indulgence is allowed (and often guiltily), the individual will quickly return to the pattern of denying his own needs and attempting to gratify those of others. In this adjustment process, I believe there is the attempt: (1) to maintain contact with the environment which is essentially ungratifying, (2) to experience need gratification vicariously, and (3) to "fix" others so that they may at last gratify the self.

Developmental data, both observational and experimental, as well as psychoanalytic theory, can allow for this self-blocking of need and the attempts to nurture the insufficient caretaker from very early on. The developmental research shows that young infants respond empathically to others' distress (Sagi & Hoffman, 1976; Simner, 1971), that infants condition early and rapidly to frustrated feeding experiences (Gunther, 1961), and that by 10 weeks infants show differential responses to joy, anger, and sadness when these are displayed by the mother (Haviland & Lelwica, 1987). By three months of age children respond differentially to another's depression as expressed by facial expression and voice cues (Tronick et al., 1982), by nine months children can notice congruences between their own affective state and the affective expression observed on another's face (MacKain et al., 1985) and demonstrate attunement through crossmodal matching to the mood state of the mother (Stern, 1985), and by 10 months, they have the ability to match joyful and angry responses (Haviland & Lelwica, 1987). Further, Stern (1985) reports data that document that the quality of the attachment at one year is an "excellent predictor of relating in various other ways up through five years." Lewis et al. (in press) have found that anxious attachment at 12 months is predictive of psychopathology at age six in boys.

Psychoanalytic theory posits a number of instinctual vicissitudes and early developed defensive strategies that allow for the kind of self-denial and other-directed need gratification that orals exhibit. These strategies are: identification, displacement, reversal, and turning against the self. Blanck and Blanck (1974), in summarizing psychoanalytic ego psychology theory, indicate that all of these cognitive operations develop early and just after the most primitive defenses of denial and projection. Further, children begin to show primitive caretaking responses early (see Appendix B for additional developmental research summaries).

The characterological-developmental position is that, once there is a blocking of the need "impulse" and the ensuing compromises and internalizations are in place, these solutions will be quite fixed and resistant to change in spite of experiences that could potentially change them. This is due to the fact that, among other things, one's relational needs have been met with these blocks and adjustments and that these maneuvers were forged in the crucible of painful deprivation. The "pathogenic belief" (Weiss & Sampson, 1986) or "script decision" (Berne, 1964) underlying all this typically involves the idea that releasing the block and experiencing the need will lead to a repetition of the painful disappointment and deprivation. Further, it is often believed, albeit unconsciously, that failing to meet the needs of others will also lead to abandonment. Other common underlying beliefs are: "I don't need. I can do it all myself. I find myself in giving and loving. My need is too great and will overwhelm others."

As a result of living her life in this untenable, undernourished, and inhuman way, the oral character is prone to drop into very collapsed states. This often involves physical illness and depression. The physical illness is common because the individual is chronically undernourished in many respects and, therefore, more susceptible to all kinds of illness. Furthermore, getting sick is a culturally sanctioned way to procure nurturance, both from others and the self, and may well have been the only circumstance in which the compensated oral person was able to get caretaking from her parents. Serious illness, in particular, is a sort of honorable discharge from the often overwhelming and unconsciously resented responsibilities of adult life.

The "emotional illness" of depression can occur for the same reasons and be sustained by the same secondary gains or payoffs. Of course, depression also serves the function of defensively suppressing the oral's aggression, hostility, and much more intense but real grief at deprivation and the consequent loss of self which she feels. In any oral character with even marginally effective compensation, there is a compensatory state juxtaposed with this state of collapse, which is often more positive but can often veer off into elation, euphoria, and, in extreme cases, to manic episodes. In such states, the compensated oral character tends to exhibit the overnurturing of others, to take on more responsibility and independent action than she can sustain, and to make plans that are optimistic to grandiose.

The oral character is typically quite grandiose in her underlying omnipotent belief that she can meet the needs of others, and this oral grandiosity serves a defensive function. It is during these times of compensation that the individual takes especially poor care of herself, effectively setting up the collapse which inevitably follows. All character structures may show a juxtaposition of what I have alternatively termed the symptomatic or *collapsed self* and the compensated or *false self*. Both characterological expressions are defensive of the underlying real-self structure, which includes the archaic, real, and vulnerable demands of the child. This alternating pattern is perhaps just more obvious in many oral personalities, who tend to show this cyclothymic-like pattern.

The oral character is also typically out of touch with his natural aggression and his considerable hostility. Even where he can identify his needs, he is not able to mobilize aggression in such a way that he can get what he wants or organize his life so that it really works. As a function of his character development, his nature is passive, and he usually becomes more passive when anxious. In other words, anxiety does not serve as a signal to mobilize aggression, but is more traumatic in nature, increasing passivity. After all, the arrested dependent child believes that it is really someone else's job to take care of her. While she may defensively take care of others or collapse, she cannot take care of herself. The aggression and hostility often show up residually in a kind of chronic irritability, which is typically self-dystonic but which she is, nevertheless, unable to fully control. That irritability is the leaking through of the rage at chronic disappointment and the deep resentment at having to rise to self-sufficiency and the care of others prematurely.

The oral self-representation also follows this compensated-collapsed polarity. The person alternately sees himself as all-giving, all-nurturing, and even all-powerful in his abilities to heal the world in the compensated state, and as defective, powerless, damaged, and depleted in the collapsed state. This same polarity is useful in observing and understanding the relationships of the oral character, which tend to be characterized by dependency. The description of the compensated oral character and the co-dependent are virtually indistinguishable, although the co-dependent behavior can derive from other characterological solutions. Yet, in all but the most well-compensated oral personalities, others often get the message that this individual is really after his own dependency gratification. This message can come through in the longing look in the eyes, the manipulative feeling of the oral collapse, or in the transparency of the oral's nurturance, which demands even more nurturance in return.

One way or another, sooner or later, with the oral personality, we often feel that nothing will ever be enough, and that this person is truly a bottomless pit. And there is truth in that. The very real, legitimate needs of the infant, the child, and the adolescent were not really met. In a very real sense, he can never go back. What was missed then will be missed forever. To resolve this is as much a part of the oral's recovery as is his realization that human needs are legitimate and *can* be met within the real limits of adult relationships.

The characterological-developmental theory posits that releasing the block and relinquishing the adjustment will also remove the block to the natural organismic reaction of rage at the depriving other. It is true that one gripped by overwhelming need and rage may well alienate others and elicit abandonment and retaliation.

Successful therapy with the oral character addresses all of this and essentially repairs the individual's relationship to his own need; reclaiming the *right* to need; learning to discriminate one's own needs and express them; desensitizing the fear of disappointment, abandonment, or rejection at such expression; and legitimizing the very

Table 5
ORAL CHARACTER

---

1. *Etiological constellation*: Parents are unreliable or insufficient in response to the child's needs and are frequently excessively needy themselves. The child relinquishes the dependent position before being satisfied, thereby remaining chronically needy and dependent. He attempts to consistently deny the dependency that may be apparent or compensated but that is always disapproved of by the self.
2. *Symptom constellation*: The individual cannot get his needs met. Failures include the inability to identify needs, the inability to express them, disapproval of one's own neediness, inability to reach out to others, ask for help, or indulge the self. Self-soothing and self-nurturing abilities are impaired. The individual tends to meet the needs of others at the expense of the self, to overextend, and to identify with other dependent people while denying the similarity. Frequent illness, depression, or other forms of collapse, which coerce and justify support while permitting self-indulgence, are common. Compensations for dependency continue to be attempted irrespective of how well they work.
3. *Cognitive style*: Prone to swings of overactive, euphoric, and sometimes creative thought to underactivated, depressed, and uninspired cognition. May show poor judgment and reality testing in elated periods.
4. *Defenses*: Denial, projection, identification, reversal, displacement, and turning against the self. The compensation of caring for others and elation as well as the collapse of illness and depression are defensive and involve splitting of self and object representations. Grandiosity is shown in the oral's exaggerated responsibility for and attempts to meet others' needs.
5. *Script decisions and pathogenic beliefs*: "I don't need; I can do it all myself. I find myself in giving and loving. My need is too great and will overwhelm others. If I express my needs, I will be disappointed, abandoned, or rejected."
6. *Self-representation*: Split, emphasizing the giving, loving, healing, nurturing, and empowered self in the compensated state and the damaged, depleted, weak, defective, and powerless self in the collapsed state.
7. *Object representations and relations*: Split, with others seen as figures with more resources who may give the needed supplies or as weak and unable to take care of themselves and in need of gratification. These individuals tend to relate as dependent or co-dependent. When the individual's dependency is apparent, others feel they can never do enough — that the person is never really able to be satisfied.
8. *Affective characteristics*: These individuals are prone to a cyclothymic-like pattern of euphoria, elation, and mania alternating with physical collapse and depression. They are out of touch with aggressive impulses and hostility but tend to be irritable. They often show fear of aloneness, fear of abandonment, and jealousy.

---

natural rage at being frustrated for being a normal human being who needs. Where the needs are, indeed, infantile and in some sense meaningfully arrested, they cannot be met currently and a realization and mourning of that fact is necessary. However, at the same time, the individual typically can have more of his needs met than ever before. I have often said to clients with this issue, "You can't get all that you really want, but you can get much more than you have ever had." Even those of us who are very needy can get a lot of those needs met if we go about it properly. Denying one's needs, meeting them vicariously or only when collapsed, or, alternatively, express-ing them in a demanding and entitled way are not among the strate-gies that work very well.

The oral character, whether compensated or not, needs to learn that his needs are alright. If his needs are exaggerated, he comes by that honestly, and he must realize that his needs cannot be met vicariously, that intimate relationships can exist outside his historical experience of them, that needs can be reciprocally met, etc. Further-more, he needs to experience, understand, and work through his own natural reactions to deprivation and unreliable caretaking. He comes by his "oral rage" honestly, and the same is true for the grief he experiences around that insufficiency and the fear that is a natural consequence of caretakers who could not be counted on when, liter-ally, his life depended on it. The extended treatment of the schizoid and oral characters was the subject of my first book in this series, *Characterological Transformation: The Hard Work Miracle* (John-son, 1985).

CHAPTER 3

Characterological Issues
of Self-Development

THIS CHAPTER IS DEVOTED to those characterological issues that underlie difficulties in the development of a firm sense of a separate self. Though vastly different in expression, these "self disorders" have in common the individual's alienation from his or her real self. For such a real self to develop there must be an environment that encourages a full range of self-expression, accurately and sympathetically mirrors that expression and provides optimal frustration to such expression when necessary. All of the characterological issues reviewed in this chapter show the common etiology of environmental failure of the preceding prescription.

The symbiotic, narcissistic, and masochistic character structures essentially derive from a history in which children were used to fulfill the agendas of caretakers. There is, then, a resulting confusion in identity wherein the externally imposed identity agenda is consciously accepted while remaining somehow ill-fitting, inauthentic, or incomplete. Simultaneously, the more natural forms of self-expression that are discouraged remain undeveloped and the source of internal conflict. Finally, the traumatic constriction of real self-expression yields developmental arrests which require recognition and maturation.

THE SYMBIOTIC ISSUE

This characterological issue revolves around separation from the matrix of interpersonal life which surrounds the human child from the earliest days. Stern (1985), whose work is perhaps best known for challenging Mahler's concept of early symbiosis as a universal illusion in the early months of life, writes of the child of one year that "most of the things the infant does, feels, and perceives occur in different kinds of relationships. . . . The infant engages with real, external partners some of the time and with evoked companions almost all of the time. Development requires a constant, usually silent, dialogue between the two. . . . This subjective sense of being with (intrapsychically and extrapsychically) is always an active mental act of construction, however, not a passive fear of differentiation" (Stern, 1985, pp. 118–119).

All of the developmental research already reviewed attests to the young child's exquisite social sense, attunement, and responsivity to social contingencies (e.g., see Appendix B). It is at about the one-year point that the child begins to develop the ability to stand upright and walk. The latter ability gives him the capacity to initiate separation and engage in autonomous activity at a far higher level than ever before. The development of speech, which also occurs at about this time, introduces another very powerful individual function, allowing differentiation at a symbolic level.

Mahler has called the period between 10 and 15 months the practicing subphase of individuation and characterizes it as a period during which the child has a love affair with the world and with his own emerging abilities. It is during this period that the child is observed to wander further away from the parent with far less apprehension than before and is relatively impervious to falls and other frustrations. It is called *practicing* because the child is practicing these new, exciting abilities which open new opportunities for experiencing the world. The characterological-developmental theory that I espouse and develop here contends that this is an especially important period for the development of autonomy, particularly as it relates to autonomous adventure, initiative, and the development of a sense of agency and self-efficacy.

The experimental, developmental research indicates that, as early as 12 months, a child will look to his parent to signal whether adventurous moves are dangerous or safe (Emde & Sorce, 1983). Early and, I believe, critical incidents that discourage separation, initiative, and adventure, occur when these parental signals err in the direction of danger, where the caretaker is threatened by this "practicing" of autonomous functions and this early exercise of self, or where these moves are actively punished because they are experienced as contentious or inconvenient. Such incidents may be even more powerful during the subsequent "rapprochement" period of 15 to 24 months when the observational research shows that the child particularly appreciates the implications of his separateness, vulnerability, and dependency on parents. It is at this same time that other researchers have witnessed an increase in the imitation of conventional social behaviors (Kuczynski, Zahn-Waxler, & Radke-Yarrow, 1987).

Whether or not a child in these circumstances has the illusion of symbiosis or fusion either through a natural tendency to make that error, à la Mahler, or on the basis of his ability to construct reality, à la Stern, the child's experience is one of intense involvement, indeed enmeshment, with another. But, at about 12 months there is enhanced ability and impulse to move out of that symbiotic orbit at times and to become one's own person by walking, talking, exploring, etc. When that impulse is blocked, the child learns that he must restrain himself in these respects and develops a compromised false self, which maintains contact with the parents through continued dependency and enmeshment. This leads to a kind of false self where, as in all other such adjustments, identity is found in the relationship with the other at the expense of the identity established through the exercise of autonomous functions.

Levy and Bleeker (1975) outlined the five steps of character development for each of the five classic characters described by Alexander Lowen. I reproduced these in *Characterological Transformation* (1985) with slight modifications and added a similar outline which I derived for the symbiotic character. I reproduce this latter outline here to enhance understanding of the process in general and this structure in particular. This outline (see Table 6) presents a quick summary of what will be presented in greater detail in this particular volume.

This description and etiological schema of character apply to structures from the extreme borderline patient, who experiences extreme fusion states, panic, or acting-out at abandonment or engulfment, to symbiotic character neurotics, who are extraordinarily conflicted and tormented about their exaggerated responsibility and obligation to others, to those whose character style is less subject to neurotic conflict, but who have some difficulty finding or owning their autonomous identity and who overly define themselves by who they are with instead of by who they really are. Even in those of the

Table 6
THE SYMBIOTIC ETIOLOGY

Self-affirmation: I have the right to separate and be myself.

Negative environmental response: Withdrawal, panic.

Organismic reaction: Panic.
Chronic environmental frustration impels a squelching of the organismic reaction.

Self-negation process:
— Retroflective attitude: I don't want to separate.
— Muscular holding pattern: Holding still, holding breath, maintaining an undeveloped, undercharged body.

Adjustment process:
— Ego compromise: I will live through another.
— Characteristic behavior: Dependent, clinging, complaining, afraid of separation.
— Ego ideal: I will be loyal.
— Illusion of contraction: I am safe as long as I hold on to you.
— Illusion of release: I will be abandoned and helpless.

---

latter character type who function rather well in the world, there is often a limited sense of self and self-agency, which can express itself in the lack of truly self-initiated preferences, tastes, and abilities. Even though there may be a very high level of competence and apparent self-expression, it is often not fully owned and integrated into a unified self-concept. In more technical language, the self is more likely to be formed through the incorporation of others or through the idealization of or identification with others rather than through a more fully developed process of internalization. Separation guilt and survivor guilt (Modell, 1965, 1971; Niederland, 1961; Weiss & Sampson, 1986) are often very useful concepts in the process of liberating the symbiotic character.

Among the more common themes in the psychotherapy of the symbiotic character is permission for the expression of natural aggression, which is a central part of the separation process as well as for the natural hostility that these individuals harbor as a result of being blocked in many forms of self-expression. Concomitantly, the

Table 7
SYMBIOTIC CHARACTER

1. *Etiological constellation*: Parents block self-agency, adventure, and self-control by anxious, withdrawn, threatened, or punitive responses to these behaviors that serve to produce distance, establish difference, demonstrate aggression, or establish a self-determined identity. Concomitantly, merger, empathy, and identification with and dependency on parents are overvalued. This yields an adopted, accommodated, other-determined self based to the overuse of incorporative introjection and uncritical identification. Identity formation relying on the more mature transmutative processes of assimilation and accommodation are underutilized.

2. *Symptom constellation*: Deficient in a solid sense of identity, self-concept, and behaviors that define a unique self. Identity found in relationship to intimate others with whom the individual merges. This lack of firm boundaries can lead to confusion about responsibility, susceptibility to invasion by the affects or thoughts of significant others, and, in borderline functioning, to actual fusion states. This propensity to be taken over by others can lead to fears of loss of autonomy and to fears of total engulfment which prompt rigid distancing. These maneuvers, in turn, lead to fears of abandonment and identityless isolation. Many other symptoms serve to preserve the original merged relationship, rebel against it, or, more commonly, both. The actual preservation of family pain going back generations is not uncommon. Separation guilt, survivor guilt, and weakened aggression are common.

3. *Cognitive style*: Boundary confusion results in poor reality testing with regard to who is responsible for what. In lower functioning individuals (i.e., borderlines), this leads to overexternalization of responsibility and blame. In higher functioning individuals, this results in excessive responsibility for others leading to the cognitive errors of separation and survivor guilt. These individuals often have difficulty discriminating their own likes and dislikes, beliefs, opinions, etc. Except at the lowest levels of structural development, aggression is denied and projected and is thereby unavailable for use.

4. *Defenses*: Merger, denial, projection, identification, coercion, manipulation, externalization, omnipotent responsibility (an expression of grandiosity), turning against the self, projective identification, splitting.

(continued)

Table 7
(continued)

5. *Script decision and pathogenic beliefs*: "I am nothing without you. You are taking me over or swallowing me up. I owe you myself. I am responsible for you, and/or you are responsible for me. I can't be happy if you aren't happy. I can't tolerate difference between us. I can't tolerate being too close. My happiness, success, survival will hurt you or is at your expense. Your separateness, success, or happiness that does not include me, hurts me and is gained at my expense. I can't survive without you."

6. *Self-representation*: Depends on connection with the other but is otherwise unclear with varying degrees of boundaryless features. Based excessively on incorporative introjection and identification. An independent, assertive self is denied or split off.

7. *Object representations and relations*: Others experienced as exceedingly important with blurring of self-other differentiation. Others often experienced as engulfing or abandoning (i.e., split). Particularly at lower levels of structural development, these individuals are experienced by others as manipulative and coercive.

8. *Affective characteristics*: At lower structural levels, the affective instability is characterized by panic and rage at abandonment and/or engulfment. At higher levels, guilt is common and associated with excessive responsibility for others. Anxiety may be stimulated by anything that leads to separation (e.g., differences of opinion, success, freedom from symptoms, etc.)

---

therapy usually has to deal with the natural fear that will be aroused as the individual begins to separate from the fused relationship and identity. A common interpretive theme with this structure involves the many, and other intricate, ways in which the person preserves the underlying, original relationship with all its limitations. The affects, behaviors, cognitions, and symptoms of these individuals may often be best understood for their preserving function. Neurotic compromises, which allow some expression of autonomy but simultaneously negate or deny it, are common.

Successful therapy with the symbiotic character involves breaking the bonds of restraint that fuse the individual and his identity to others. It may very well involve withstanding aggression and hostility in the transference, and in the higher functioning cases it will typically involve pulling for just that aggression and hostility and working through its disavowal. Successful therapy will also involve eroding the disavowal of whatever real, autonomous sense of self has been developed. Finally, to the extent that a real self must still find true expression and receive attuned support, this self-building must occur, and, to the extent that real internalization of relevant abilities such as self-soothing, responsible limit setting, etc., have not been acquired, this internalization process must also be initiated and supported. In general, at lower levels of ego development, there will be a longer process of therapy devoted to this self-development. At higher levels of development, there will be more real self available for the person to own, and a greater proportion of the therapeutic task will center on achieving that ownership, dispelling unconscious, pathogenic beliefs having to do with excessive obligation and responsibility, and eroding neurotic compromises which express but deny the true self.

THE NARCISSISTIC ISSUE

Narcissism is the issue of self-esteem (see Table 8). The characterological-developmental theory espoused here asserts that this character structure comes out of the nonoptimal frustration of self-expression, just as does the symbiotic's. Here, however, the frustration is somewhat more complex and variable. It is not the separation per se that yields the unattuned or negative response from the caretaker. Rather, it is some form of the child's self-expression that is "not enough" or "too much" for the other. The reconstruction of narcissistic cases often yields the fact that the individual was repeatedly put down or "narcissistically injured" in the expression of his ambitious self-expression, or he was idealized, and therefore expected to provide far more gratification, excitement, or meaning for his parents than was possible, or both. It is not uncommon in the reconstruction of these cases that one parent was more idealizing, and that the narcissistic injury initiated by that parent came from the child's inability to live up to the inflated expectations. Simultaneously, the other parent can be threatened by the child's real magnificence and the spouse's extravagant attention to the child. Unable to deal with all that, the other parent may humiliate and shame the child, narcissistically injuring him more directly.

All narcissistic individuals live with the unresolved polarity of grandiosity and worthlessness. The true expression of their real magnificence and limitation did not bring accurately attuned recognition and praise as well as optimal frustration. Rather, it brought disappointment, humiliation, or, at best, it was ignored. The environmental block was then reinforced, as always, by the individual who blocked those parts of himself that were not reinforced and inflated those parts that were so highly valued. This latter adjustment process constitutes Winnicott's "false self," which, in the narcissist, is experienced as more false or inauthentic, both by the self and others, than in any other character structure. But the false self is the individual's only source of self-esteem and is therefore typically guarded with intense vigilance. He doubts himself, because his real self has been undervalued, if not humiliated, and he easily projects or finds disapproval in the environment and is exquisitely sensitive to slight disapproval or failure. When well-defended, the narcissistic person aggrandizes and adorns himself, plays to the audience for superlative approval, manipulates, objectifies and devalues others in service of his grandiose, false self, and seems to believe in his own grandiosity. However, everyone becomes part of the audience that is manipulated for the desired effect, but the inevitable frustrations of life will elicit the opposite pole of worthlessness, self-depreciation, and self-inhibition of activity. This will elicit again the defense of the grandiose false self, which is typically an even more desperate and sometimes unrealistic version of that compensation than existed before the threat.

Again, there has been controversy among developmental theorists as to when this issue initially arises and, therefore, at which point it can be earliest arrested. In many ways, this question is of little importance clinically. It is more the process than the point at which it happens that is important. Still, much evidence suggests that this process could happen fairly early. It is around the activities of Mahler's practicing period (10 to 15 months) that a great deal of self-expression is first seen, and the child obviously has the powers to discriminate and participate in attuned interaction at this point. Children have been consistently observed to be quite taken with themselves and their new abilities at this time. More recent research on children indicates that they become self-reflective at about 18 months of age, indicating that at this point they can at least begin to have some capacity for a self-concept (Stern, 1985). It is also between one and two years of age that children demonstrate that they react to activities in terms of standards of performance that could affect self-esteem (Gopnik & Meltzoff, 1984; Kagan, 1981). Even at this "late date," children would presumably base that construction on prior, as well as continuing, experiences, and, to the extent that these events were narcissistically injuring, the issues of self-esteem would likely arise.

Perhaps more than any other theorist, Kohut (1971, 1977, 1978) has been the most definitive in suggesting both ambition and idealization as inborn vicissitudes—ambition requiring accurate mirroring and idealization requiring idealizable others for optimal development. According to Kohut, it is the mishandling of these needs that prevents the optimal frustration and results in the narcissistic character formation.

At the low end of the ego development continuum, one sees those blatantly narcissistic individuals whom most laymen could diagnose after a couple of minutes of casual conversation. These people show the gross levels of entitlement, grandiosity, manipulation, devaluation, and objectification of others which are definitional to all as narcissistic. Some of these people can be relatively effective in life in spite of all this, because they are able to mobilize a good deal of their aggressive self-expression and, particularly when they are bright and talented, may be quite successful in some areas. Interpersonally, they are a disaster, and if the "false self" fails, they break down into serious forms of void and fragmentation, often becoming truly dangerous to themselves and others.

In narcissistic character neurosis, these traits and issues are far less obvious, but this personality is at war with itself around the issue of self-esteem. There is typically more rapid vacillation between the poles of what I have termed the symptomatic self and the false self in the second book in this series, *Humanizing the Narcissistic Style*. The individual at this level of structural development is typically far less obvious in his expression of the grandiose false-self features such as entitlement, omnipotence, and the narcissistic use and devaluation of others. But self-esteem is fragile and is typically propped up by perfectionism and an extreme reliance on achievement. There is some awareness of a real self and a desire to express it, enjoy it, and have it well received. The narcissistic neurotic will say, "Why can't I relax, why can't I accept myself, why can't I let myself enjoy things, why do I always have to be number one, why do I procrastinate important projects until the last minute and then pull them off in an anxious frenzy, etc., etc., etc.?" The war with self produces the neurotic symptoms, which usually have strong components, of course, of anxiety, depression, and the self-involvement of rumination about self-worth, physical symptoms, procrastination, and feelings of worthlessness.

At the level of narcissistic style, there is typically less torment, a less severe history of narcissistic injury, and more effective defenses, particularly if the person is capable. Still, there are threads of narcissistic issues of all the types mentioned earlier, including an exaggerated commitment to the persona or public self, which, often very gracefully, hides any aspect of the real self that would lead one to be seen in less than the most positive light. One feels, perhaps consciously, perhaps not, that if "they" know all there is to know about me, they wouldn't like and admire me as much as they do now. In short, there is *something* about me which is bad or not enough or too much and which must be hidden. Though there is less symptomatology at this level, there still is often a measurable amount of it, and, more often, one's loved ones or family have a sense of missing something in the relationship, which is not quite real or authentic. The person at this level is often a bit "too good to be true" and, in that, is not.

As with the symbiotic character, the treatment of the narcissist involves the resurrection and development of the true self, including the injuries, the arrested development, the pathogenic beliefs, and the disavowed aspects of the "self." Those disavowed elements usually involve the less agreeable, narcissistic features such as entitlement, grandiosity, and objectification of others. It is the injured and undeveloped real self of the narcissist that needs an advocate in the psychotherapy, and this is why Kohut was so correct in his emphasis on the greater need for empathy in the treatment of this structure. The empathy is also required here, of course, for the tender fragility covered by the false-self mobilization. When the narcissistic person is really *understood* (seen, heard, recognized) for who he really is, he experiences the safety to discover who he is and to reexperience the injury to that real and often young and vulnerable person. Then, he can experience the necessary therapeutic shift where he begins to

Table 8
NARCISSISTIC CHARACTER

1. *Etiological constellation*: Parents narcissistically cathect the child and disallow the child's legitimate narcissistic cathexis of the parents. The child is used to mirror, aggrandize, or fulfill the ambitions and ideals of the parent. The child's real magnificence and vulnerability are not simultaneously supported. Rather, the parents need the child to be more than he is for self-fulfillment and idealize him or need him to be less than he is and humiliate him, or both. This results in a deep injury to the experience of the real self and a consequent deficit in self-esteem regulation. The natural system of feedback and correction affecting the balance of ambitions, ideals, and abilities fails to mature such that ambitions and ideals remain grandiose, while corrective negative feedback about abilities must remain rigidly disavowed.

2. *Symptom constellation*: The individual harbors a grandiose false self characterized by omnipotence, pride, self-involvement, entitlement, perfectionism, and excessive reliance on achievement for the maintenance of self-esteem with manipulation, objectification, and devaluation of others. When this compensatory false self breaks down, the individual shows great vulnerability to shame or humiliation, feelings of worthlessness, difficulty in self-activation, and work inhibition. This low self-esteem dominated depression may be accompanied by hypochondriacal preoccupations, psychosomatic illness, anxiety, and loneliness. An even deeper real-self crisis includes the deeply felt enfeeblement and fragmentation of the self; emptiness, void, and panic at the realities of an arrested development; and long-suppressed real affects relating to the original narcissistic injuries.

3-4. *Cognitive style and defenses*: In the grandiose, false-self state, the narcissist demonstrates cognitive errors that will maintain the grandiosity, e.g., externalization of responsibility (i.e., blaming others), denial of negative input, disavowal of his own negative attributes, devaluation of positive contributions from others, unrealistic identification with idealized others, etc. In the symptomatic or collapsed state, there is a preoccupation with symptoms, defensive rumination on self-worth, physical symptoms, procrastination, or other preoccupations that keep the demands and affects of the underlying real self at bay. Splitting keeps these two states separate and unintegrated. Feeling his real self, the narcissist always experiences at least some disorganization, vulnerability, and unfamiliar but vital affects. Here the individual may feel he is losing his mind, but, if managed correctly, it is here that he begins to find himself.

(continued)

Table 8
(continued)

5. *Script decisions and pathogenic beliefs*: "I must be omnipotent, perfect, special. I must know without learning, achieve without working, be all powerful and universally admired. I must not make a mistake or I am worthless, nothing, and disgusting. I must be a god or I am nothing. If I am vulnerable, I will be used, humiliated, or shamed. I can't let anyone really matter to me. All that I own, including my friends and family, must reflect and confirm my perfection and superiority. I will never be humiliated again. Others are superior to me. Others are inferior to me."

6. *Self-representation*: Split — grandiose or worthless as outlined above.

7. *Object representations and relations*: Object representations are best understood using the four basic narcissistic transferences suggested by Kohut: (1) *Merger* — where the individual achieves a sense of security and worth through fusion. Here the individual will freely use the other without recognizing the actual self-other boundary; (2) *twinship* — where the individual achieves a sense of enhanced identity and self-worth by assuming exaggerated similarity between the self and other; (3) *mirroring* — where the individual relates to the other solely as one who enhances self-esteem by serving as a prizing, understanding, acknowledging "part-object;" and (4) *idealization* — where the other enhances self-cohesion and esteem by being perfect in one or more respects and serving as a source for emulation. Idealization may also serve to create the perception of the perfect merger, twinship, or mirroring object. Others typically feel used by the narcissist, but if he is effective in his false self, others are attracted to him for his charisma and talent. The use of others to discover the real self, rather than aggrandize the false self, is pivotal in the desired maturation of the narcissist's relationships.

8. *Affective characteristics*: Narcissists are frequently noted for the "as if" or artificial quality of feelings, the inability to feel for others, and their extremely easily wounded pride. At lower levels of ego development, acting-out and impulse control disorders are common. At higher levels, there is great intolerance for most feelings, although a high level of affective responsiveness is held in check. Silently born shame and humiliation are common.

use others for the discovery and development of his real self rather than to bolster and aggrandize his false self.

With what I have termed the "borderline" narcissist, this treatment process is longer, more repetitive, more supportive, more "reluctantly indulgent" (Kohut) of both the grandiosity of self and the idealization of the therapist or others. And this therapy must be more devoted to the real development of a true self rather than working on its simple uncovering and ownership.

At higher levels of ego development, where many false-self abilities have been finely honed but not really experienced as one's own, as the source of pleasure for oneself, or as an authentic gift to others, the therapeutic problem is easier because it represents more of a shift in orientation and experience than a "redo" of the essential developmental processes.

At the middle or neurotic level of this issue, there is relatively more emphasis on helping the person to enjoy the exercise of his autonomous functions, which are indeed grand at times and which can be experienced and enjoyed without the neurotic entanglements that give achievement its typical pain for these people. In a sense, successful treatment of the narcissist involves reclaiming the healthy or normal narcissism that is the birthright of every human being— exercising it, enjoying it, and liberating it. Yet, to be human is to be in some ways vulnerable, limited, needy, dependent, weak, and even stupid at times. We all need to accept that part of humanness in ourselves and others. We need to be loved and to love ourselves when we are vulnerable in these ways. When there is a taming of normal narcissism, there is a self-directed object constancy in which the self is loved in all its magnificence and in all its humility.

MASOCHISTIC ISSUE

Masochism involves the issue of control (see Table 9). As Lowen (1958) has suggested, an understanding of this structure can be gained by simply imagining what an animal such as a dog or cat would do if it were forced in the natural processes of intake of food and elimination. However docile the animal might be, intrusion in these natural organismic responses would undoubtedly elicit strong aggressive responses, and, if this highly intrusive intervention continued and aggressive responses were eventually eliminated, one can imagine highly pathological consequences for the animal. Such is often the case with the masochistic human, whose history is often replete with intrusion, control, and humiliating subjugation of the will.

Lowen (1958) reports these historical memories from one of his masochistic clients: "To my mind, as I look back, it's not that I didn't eat as much as it was that I didn't eat enough. My mother forced enormous quantities of food into me. . . . I remember at the age of three to four, running around the kitchen table, my mother running after me with a spoonful of something I didn't want in one hand and a belt in another hand, threatening to strike me, which she often did. . . . One of the worst things my mother did was to threaten to leave me or to go up on the roof and jump off and kill herself if I didn't finish my food. She actually used to step out of the apartment into the hall, and I used to collapse on the floor in hysterical crying."

In relation to "toilet troubles," the same client recalled, "My mother forced me under pain of hitting me to sit on the toilet for one or two hours and try to 'do something,' but I couldn't." This same client recalls that after the age of two, he was constipated, and his mother inserted her finger into his anus, stimulating it. He received frequent enemas through age seven and was plagued with horrible-tasting laxatives (Lowen, 1958, pp. 196–197).

The individual's innate need or disposition to exert some control over these bodily functions appears obvious, as does the nature of the innate response to their excessive frustration. According to Reich, Lowen, and the contemporary analysts, the masochistic character is the result of this kind of relentless intrusion and control, which very naturally expresses itself most profoundly in the parents' attempts to socialize the child, often, but not exclusively nor always, in the very basic processes of food intake and elimination. In cases as serious as the one I've just reviewed, we can assume that these intrusive parental tendencies expressed themselves very early on and continued throughout childhood and beyond. What is often critical in the understanding of masochism is the point at which the child capitulated—the point at which the will was broken. It is at this point, when the self-negation expressed as a self-imposed block, particularly against the organismic reactions to frustration, is most fully imposed. It is due, I think, to the fact that many character analyses have uncovered these memories of intense parent-child battles prior to such capitulation that the formation of this structure is often seen as occurring at or beyond the second-year.

The clinical picture that this character label is invoked to summarize and explain is represented by those seen as long-suffering, self-depreciating, self-defeating, and often self-torturing individuals who seem to have a need to suffer and, in their suffering, torture others. There is, in these unfortunate people, a strong tendency to complain, a chronic absence of joy, and the kind of chronic stasis in behavior and attitude that was labeled by Reich the "masochistic bog or morass." This hopeless immobility is highly frustrating to anyone who tries to help. Others typically experience being defeated by this hopeless, helpless person who can't be helped, and they sense her underlying passive aggression.

It is as if the intense rage at intrusion was turned against the self, leading to a bind in self-expression. In these individuals, there is a noteworthy absence of trust in others, and that absence of trust is expressed in hopelessness for the self and, for that matter, the world. Related to this dynamic is the oft-noted "negative therapeutic reaction" with these individuals, such that any improvement is often quickly followed by a relapse. Such return to suffering may be seen both as an expression of the underlying distrust, a justification for it, and a spiteful retaliation against the helper, who, because he is in the more powerful role, is associated with the injuring parent.

The bound negativity of the masochistic person is extremely virulent. To release these bonds, to really ask for help from another, to accept that help and even enjoy it, severely threatens a structure held together by a great deal of conflicting energy. To open oneself to trust and hope opens one to the possibility of being tricked, humiliated, and overpowered again. The resistance to all of that is legion and is reinforced by the individual's attachment to the self and "bad object" forged in the crucible of all this pain. Hence, the masochistic client frequently returns to the maddening position of burdened suffering in which complaints and self-depreciation are directed at whomever would help or offer real support in his exit from the hell of this particular "closed system of internal reality" (Fairbairn, 1958, p. 381).

It is in this that others usually feel the masochist's held resentment or spite, which is not very far below the surface of his self-effacing and pleasing nature. Indeed, it is thought that this pattern, which in therapy is represented in the negative therapeutic reaction, serves to provoke the retaliation and hostility of the other which justifies the distrust and, when that retaliation is sufficient, serves to release the expression of the held-back aggression and hostility of the masochistic person. Like a beating in a sexual context, it is not the beating itself that is desirable but the intensification of the physical charge, which provokes a sexual release that is, in fact, satisfying. And it is the release that the masochistic person desires most profoundly—a release not only of the pent-up hostility, but also of the overcontrolled impulses of love and tender expression. Yet, it is the release that opens the masochistic structure and the discouragement and hopelessness of the original position. The recycling and progressive understanding of this pattern comprise the primary theme in the masochist's treatment. Pleasure is a sin, trust is to be distrusted, hope leads to disappointment. If you expect the worst, you won't be disappointed or, worse yet, tricked.

It appears that this structure may be relatively less prevalent now than it was at one time, certainly in the western United States. This kind of very intrusive, dominant, and punitive parenting may well have been more typical of earlier generations where cleanliness training was more valued, where women had fewer forms of self-expression, etc. Those who work with battered women and incest survivors report seeing many of these features currently, but there is reason to believe that this structure, in its predominant and severe form, may be waning in the general population.

Whatever the validity of this speculation, however, I certainly have seen relatively few cases of clearcut, severe masochistic pathology. Rather, and of particular interest for this volume, I have seen a number of cases where the central issue seems to be symbiotic, but where the adopted identity replicates the more masochistic adjustment of the parent—particularly the mother. I think the understanding of the masochistic issue is important not only for itself but also for the treatment of many symbiotic individuals, because it is with this kind of parent that the phenomena of separation guilt and survivor guilt can be quite paramount. It is very difficult to enjoy life when one comes out of the matrix of the masochistic parent. Even though that parent may have the sense not to deliver the same kind of abuse to her offspring as was visited on her, the masochist's self-torture is torturing to others—particularly to the offspring, who are

Table 9
MASOCHISTIC CHARACTER

1. *Etiological constellation*: Control-oriented, dominating parents are intrusive and invasive of appropriate boundaries. These experiences of being overpowered, which often occur around the child's food intake and elimination, are finally recapitulated by the individual's overpowering her own aggressive, hostile, and retaliatory impulses. To maintain contact and receive the necessary support, the individual typically develops a compliant and servile personality, which may often contain passive-aggressive features that are out of awareness.

2. *Symptom constellation*: Long-suffering, self-torturing, self-depreciating, and self-defeating behavior often suggests a "need to suffer." A chronic immobile depression that has been termed the masochistic bog or morass is common. Bound self-expression is accompanied by hopelessness, distrust, and passive-aggressive behavior. In therapy, resistance of a passive nature and "negative therapeutic reaction" are more common and obvious than in many other structures. The residuals of the masochist's considerable life energy often appear to exist only in her spite, which is tightly bound. Interpersonal difficulties of the kind outlined in other sections of this outline are common.

3. *Cognitive style*: Plodding, unimaginative, burdened cognition. Chronic, low-grade depression dulls cognitive functioning. There is an expectation of the worst and a distrust of the positive in life.

4. *Defenses*: Denial, projection, and disavowal, particularly of aggression and hostility, identification with the aggressor, reaction formation, and chronic holding back, often in the musculature, of unacceptable or distrusted impulses.

5. *Script decisions and pathogenic beliefs*: "I give up. I will be good. I'll never give in. I'll show you. I can punish you by withholding from both of us. Deprivation will hurt you more than it hurts me."

6. *Self-representation*: The individual experiences himself as being obligated to serve and as trying to live up to that obligation. The masochistic patient is usually aware of her lack of spontaneity, difficulty in aggressive movement, and her comparatively stuck and uninspiring life-style. Often she wishes for more adventure, release, etc., but she can't seem to marshall the energy to achieve this, or she will plead that she simply doesn't know how. However, she often sees her ability to endure pain and deprivation as an admirable quality.

(continued)

Table 9
(continued)

7. *Object representation and relations*: The masochist seeks to make contact with others through being of service and complaining. But the service is tainted by its suffering, joyless, guilt-inducing quality and the complaining, which brings attention and suggestions, never ceases. "Why don't you, yes but" is a typical masochistic game. Through these actions and other passive-aggressive maneuvers, the masochist provokes retaliation and can then occasionally get some release of the pent-up spite in response. In particular, the masochist can be seen as one who deprives himself of satisfaction in order to punish another by depriving them of satisfaction. Since the masochist is used to this form of deprivation (i.e., of satisfaction) she is better than most at tolerating it, and it doesn't *appear* to punish her as much as it punishes the other.

   Intrapsychically, others are seen as those who should be served at one's own expense. Unconsciously, others are the object of a great deal of pent-up hostility which can only be passively expressed, except with extreme justification.

8. *Affective characteristics*: Restrained, muted, depressively tinged affect. Guilt at obligation failures is common. The individual is out of touch with aggressive or hostile feelings, but others may be well aware of them. The masochist often feels she is the victim of others or of life itself and feels victimized.

prone to take responsibility for their parent's suffering. In view of this, it is important in the process of diagnosis to distinguish between the process of characterological adjustment, which is essentially symbiotic in nature (more prevalent, I believe, in our time), and the truly masochistic disorders, which typically come from a more severely invasive etiology.

A successful therapy with a masochistic client must involve a therapist who does not get too irrevocably trapped in the web of repeated failure and discouragement which typically motivates any helper's retaliation. A therapist who has a comprehensive understanding of the masochistic issue and who expects this course of events will be far less likely to take it personally and to react in the usual ways.

This same analytic understanding will, of course, help the client as well. Both parties can be greatly assisted by reviewing the many similar circumstances involving defeated helpers of the past. These historical and contemporary analyses will be most useful where they elicit the masochist's underlying hostility and distrust of the helper. As Fairbairn (1952) pointed out, it is with these clients, who most exemplify the "negative therapeutic reaction" and who led Freud to hypothesize the "death instinct," that the theory of internalized, unconscious, bad objects can be most easily seen to fit.

In these cases, the therapist is needed to assist in releasing those internal negative forces from repression, while interpreting them as natural consequences of intrusion, invasion, and suppression of the individual's healthy inclinations. At the same time, the therapist must offer a real and good relationship in the outer world to replace the closed inner reality of the client, which contaminates all of his interactions with others. To quote Fairbairn (1952, p. 74), "the appeal of a good object is an indispensable factor in promoting a dissolution of the cathexis of internalized bad objects, and . . . the significance of the transference situation is partly derived from this fact."

The therapeutic tests (Weiss & Sampson, 1986) of the masochist can be tough because they pull eloquently for seeing him as bad, hopeless, inferior, and deserving of retaliation. The therapist will find that passing the tests, and there may be many, is greatly facilitated by understanding the internal self and object structures of the masochist and consistently and supportively refusing to become a participating part of them.

CHAPTER 4

Characterological Issues of the Self in System

CLASSICAL PSYCHOANALYTIC THEORY traces all neurotic symptoms to the oedipal conflict, and, where personality disorders have been considered, these have typically been seen as pre-oedipal in origin. The position taken here, which is consistent with many contemporary psychoanalytic theorists, is that this dichotomous view is not only oversimplified but is incorrect. It seems clear now that "neurotic" psychopathology can revolve around a number of basic existential life issues, which exist throughout the life span, though they may be differentially important in the early years. Furthermore, the constellation of symptoms or problematic situations for people struggling with the oedipal etiology may, in general, be defined with far greater specificity. Finally, the characterological-developmental theory would place importance both on the child's sexual and rivalrous impulses, including the internal struggles that these impulses provoke, *and* on the environment's ability to optimally frustrate and indulge around the child's expression of early sexual interest and rivalry.

In this way, oedipal impulses are not essentially different from any other basic, inborn form of self-expression that require appropriate environmental responses. The symptom constellations that derive from the oedipal issue can be complex because both sexuality and rivalry are involved and because the issue is triadic, involving a system rather than a dyad. Such complex interactions can occur with other issues as well, but they always occur with oedipal ones.

The oedipal issue is that classic complex involving love, sexuality, and competition, originally delineated by Freud. Understanding of this complex of issues is immeasurably enhanced by simply viewing it as similar, in most essential respects, to all other developmental challenges shared by the individual and his environment. The oedipal complex, like the schizoid, narcissistic, or masochistic complexes, comes out of the environment's inability to optimally indulge and frustrate these existential demands of the individual. Specifically, I believe that psychopathology of an oedipal nature is related to either the exploitation of or the anxious, threatened, and often punitive response to sexually related love and competition that children receive. This was certainly Freud's original position, and both social history (e.g., see Miller, 1984) and a century of clinical case reports give us every reason to return to it.

Of course, it is true that the oedipal issues are, in many ways, more difficult to handle optimally than some of the simpler issues presented. Oedipal issues typically involve three or more people, and they can interact easily with other issues that precede them developmentally, thus yielding more permutations and combinations of etiological factors. But, what essentially happens in the oedipal case is that the child's sexuality is not lovingly permitted and supported by the optimal frustration of clear boundaries. Rather, it is exploited or punished or, in most cases, both. For example, you may find one parent exploiting sexuality and the competitive urges that go with it, both for sexual satisfaction and for the indirect expression of hostility toward the other parent. Simultaneously, the other parent may be threatened by such behavior and, both directly and indirectly, act threatened and retaliate toward the child. A parent may also encourage and exploit the sexuality and competition, but when it becomes too much or when it threatens the relationship with the spouse, may withdraw from the child, or humiliate or punish him for these previously encouraged behaviors. Where there is only exploitation, children may fear punishment and, in any case, will find such exploitation of their sexuality overwhelming.

Learning that it is unsafe to love sexually with an open heart and to experience natural human rivalry, these children will pull back, block off, and restrain these thoughts and feelings by whatever defenses are available. By the time these oedipal issues are salient, children have access to a very broad range of defensive maneuvers to ward off these troublesome thoughts and feelings. This is another reason why the oedipal constellations can be quite complex. Individuals can, for example, marshall affect as a defense and develop an ability to blot out their troublesome internal experience by the histrionic overdramatization of any feeling. Or individuals may keep themselves preoccupied by compulsive behaviors and/or obsessional thoughts. Children, too, have a large repertoire of abilities to enhance the process of adjusting to this particular type of narcissistic injury. It is not uncommon for these individuals to seek acceptance and avoid reinjury by trying to develop a perfect persona and achieve perfection in every area of endeavor.

Lowen (1958) has associated the oedipal etiology with a number of characterological expressions, including hysteric or histrionic, obsessive-compulsive, passive-feminine, and phallic-narcissistic. Some of these constellations involve the interaction of the oedipal issue with other pre-oedipal issues (i.e., the phallic-narcissistic character is an interaction of the narcissistic and oedipal issues, and the passive-feminine is the interaction of the oedipal and masochistic issues). It seems to me that there are two basic oedipal characterological adaptations which provide the essential underpinnings for the other permutations and combinations: the *histrionic* (formerly hysteric) and the *obsessive-compulsive*. The histrionic represents the etiological pole characterized more by inappropriate encouragement and exploitation of sexuality and competition, and the obsessive-compulsive represents a preponderance of punishment for these same expressions. While the clinical literature classifies women as histrionic with far greater frequency, males can also receive this diagnosis. Males are the sole bearers of Lowen's phallic-narcissistic diagnosis, and, while the behaviors of this character differ from the histrionic, the etiological dynamics are often quite similar.

It is crucial to note here that obsessive-compulsive behavior, in particular, can derive from other etiological constellations. It is becoming increasingly apparent that obsessive-compulsive disorder per se may be a neurological problem. It is a strategy that can keep many unacceptable feelings at bay and can provide a kind of artificial structure in the absence of authentic structure. But it is also a common neurotic compensation for unacceptable oedipal impulses and can derive from this etiologic constellation. Similarly, certain kinds of dissociation, denial, and affect defenses typical of the histrionic character can also be seen as a result of other etiological circumstances, but these defenses are commonly seen as sequelae of these etiological circumstances.

The Oedipal Issue in the Histrionic Character

Most histories of histrionic people (mostly women) in the literature are replete with rigid, cold, and rejecting mothers and seductive, emotionally infantile fathers. The following case (Horowitz, 1989) is archetypal:

Miss Smith's mother was rigid and moralistic. Her family found her joyless and often depressed. Devoted to the Catholic church, she served on its committee on pornography and was concerned throughout life with social propriety. . . . Mr. Smith was unusual . . . one of his greatest eccentricities was nudism. He insisted on practicing his nudism around the house, including taking his breakfast while naked. He assumed the function of waking each daughter and would lie undressed on their beds above the covers until they arose. During early adolescence, this so embarrassed and upset the patient that she begged her mother to make him stop. Her mother would cry and claim that she was helpless. . . . While the father overtly chided his oldest daughter for her sexual behavior, covertly he was interested and teased for details. Later when Miss Smith was in college, he wanted to visit her to flirt with her roommate. (Horowitz, 1989, pp. 202–204)

Paul Chowdoff (1978) reports another typical case of histrionic personality:

The product of a family background of wealth and social position on both sides, O. had lived with her mother, whom she saw as cold, distant and ungiving, after her parent's divorce when she was age five. Her handsome, "perfect" father became the focus of her longings and fantasies, the summers spent with him the high point of her life. During these visits, she reported episodes when she'd wake up to find her father standing beside her bed rubbing her back under her nightgown. Twice in her life, she was in the course of achieving some autonomy—as a nineteen-year-old college student and later when caring for herself and her children after the failure of her initial marriage. The first period was terminated by a summons from her father to return and finish college while living with him, and the second by the promise of her present husband to rescue and take total care of her.

Very often in these cases, the isolation from the mother and the special, sexually charged relationship with the father persists well into adult life with continuing dependency of the daughter on the father and inappropriate sexual advances or sexually tinged interaction occurring between them. These fathers do such things as sharing their intimate lives with their daughters, telling seductive off-color jokes, or maintaining romantic symbols of the special relationship which are more appropriate to lovers than to a father-daughter relationship.

Just as in families where the incestuous child abuse goes much further, the family of the histrionic is characterized by denial and rationalization. The child, of course, models these strategies, which protect everyone in the family from facing the uncomfortable realities of their existence together. The child, caught in the middle of this incestuous drama, must often go further to distance herself from all the overwhelming emotions and thoughts. This, then, can lead to what Shapiro (1965) has labeled the impressionistic cognitive style of the histrionic, wherein there is "an incapacity for persistent or intense intellectual concentration," a "distractibility or impressionability that follows from it," and a "nonfactual world in which the hysterical person lives" (Shapiro, 1965, p. 113). This more global cognitive orientation is accompanied by an emotional overreactivity which can serve as an affect defense and often serves to coerce the environment into taking responsibility for her and perpetuating the dependency.

Histrionic people frequently see themselves as childlike and get into relationships where they play "baby doll" to "big daddy." Histrionic women often gravitate toward older men who can take care of them, thereby replicating the father-daughter relationship where caretaking is exchanged for a kind of sexual favor. Histrionics were first identified by Breuer and Freud for their conversion reactions, which they typically relate to with "la belle indifference," exemplifying their cognitive style and belying the defensive underlying purpose of the symptom. Dissociative episodes can also occur when stress is too high to manage with more adaptive defense mechanisms.

The relationships of histrionics, like their thinking, are often superficial and have an "as if" quality in which it seems that the person is playing a role. There is also a strong underlying unconscious hostility to the opposite sex, which, on the surface, is so overvalued. Their relationships are also marked by a repetitive, gamelike quality where sexual seductiveness is often followed by sexual submissiveness to a greater force at times, or by rage, outrage, or forceful rejection at other times. Another common symptom in relationships is a split between those who stimulate sexual arousal and those who stimulate more heartfelt affection. This split, in which sexual and affectional needs may be met but only in isolation from one another, protects the individual from entering the original vulnerable situation in which she was injured.

Successful treatment of the histrionic personality demands a genuine human connection where all of the affective, behavioral, and cognitive maneuvers used to avoid forbidden thoughts and feelings and feared intimacy are slowly melted away. The histrionic needs to learn of her sexual and competitive impulses, her history of being exploited and deprived of love, and her hostility that results from this exploitation and deprivation. She needs to relearn how to open her heart, to be real and vulnerable, and to mature sexually and relationally. Further, she needs to relinquish the false-self histrionic phoniness and the investment in her particular brand of perfectionism, and to reinvest that energy in reclaiming her birthright to deeply felt and sexual love. Finally, she needs to mature in her relationships with other women so that rivalry is neither dominant nor denied in her experience but becomes merely an evolved human proclivity.

As in every other structure, the histrionic will provide "tests" which encourage the therapist to become a participating figure in the "closed system of inner reality." When this gambit succeeds, therapists are seduced, either sexually or into inappropriate and counter-therapeutic caretaking and authority roles which perpetuate the existing adaptation. The oedipally derived histrionic character is summarized in Table 10.

Table 10
OEDIPAL CHARACTER

General etiological constellation: Caretakers exploit or react negatively to the child's natural sexuality and competition. These bipolar responses often occur together with one parent being seductive and exploitive, while the other is threatened, cold, or directly punitive. Or this ambitendency toward sexuality and/or competition can be promulgated by the same parent. This conditioning results in any number of affective, behavioral, and cognitive strategies for suppressing or keeping from awareness these instinctual responses. This suppression or disavowal results in the removal of these drives from optimal frustration and indulgence so that they fail to mature and become appropriately integrated into the adult personality. While the permutations of these triadic constellations are legion, two basic themes are apparent: (1) The symptomatic and personality constellations resulting from relatively more exploitation of sexuality and competition (e.g., histrionic and phallic-narcissistic characters) and (2) symptom and personality constellations resulting from relatively more restraint or punishment of these behav-

(continued)

Table 10
(continued)

iors (e.g., obsessive-compulsive character). These will be outlined separately — histrionic below and obsessive-compulsive in Table 11.

Histrionic

1. *Etiological constellation*: At least one parent exploits natural sexuality and uses the child as a sex object. The other parent is often cold, distant, or directly punitive, particularly concerning sexuality and/or competition, or is seen as being so out of the child's guilt and associated projections.
2. *Symptom constellation*: Overly emotional reactivity, exhibitionistic and dramatic behavior, sexualized relationships with a denial of the sexuality, shallow emotional experience, global and imprecise thought processes, excessive attention to and toward the opposite sex, conversion reactions, dissociative episodes, high propensity to act-out, highly distractable with difficulty in sustaining concentration, sexual difficulties including difficulty with arousal, pre-orgasmic syndrome, dismeneuria, retarded or premature ejaculation, unsatisfying (superficial) orgasms, etc.
3. *Cognitive style*: Global, nonlinear, imprecise, and emotionally dominated thought processes that serve to keep "dangerous" affects and thoughts out of awareness. Thinking is often visually dominated and impressionistic resulting in fast and shallow judgments about the meaning of events, ideas, and feelings, and an absence of factual detail and reality based discrimination.
4. *Script decisions and pathogenic beliefs*: "Sex is bad. Competition and rivalry are bad. My worth depends on my sexuality and attractiveness. All gratification comes from the opposite sex. I can't love, be sexual, be competitive. I need to be more attractive. If I love fully I will (1) be exploited or rejected, (2) hurt my parents, or (3) be shamed."
5. *Defenses*: Denial, repression, acting-out, conversion, dissociation, externalization, impressionistic and global thinking.
6. *Self-representation*: Imprecise and fluid with self-concept tending to rely more on appearance, social acceptance, and immediate experiences than on accomplishments or other more stable grounds.
7. *Object representations and relations*: Relationships frequently sexualized, impulsive, and characterized by superficial "role playing" behavior. Individuals of the opposite sex are extraordinarily important consciously, but unconsciously they are the target of considerable hostility,

(continued)

Table 10
(continued)

which is frequently expressed after some stereotyped excuse has been created. There is typically unconscious competition toward members of the same sex. Themes of victimization and nurturing-parent to helpless-child role relations are common in often repetitive, "gamelike" relationships.

8. *Affective characteristics*: Shallow, "as if" affects that are overly dramatic. A high level of sexual titillation with an absence of deep and mature sexual feelings. The individual may be easily overwhelmed by affective states with thoughts blocked or largely controlled by impressionistic and affective experiences. There is a tendency to act-out in response to feelings. Hostile and competitive feelings are not conscious but are expressed in repetitive "gamelike" interactions.

The Obsessive-Compulsive

The obsessive-compulsive was the first such personality constellation described by Freud, and, until recently, it was clearly the most well-described syndrome. It is also the most frequently diagnosed personality disorder and is more often attributed to men (Frances, 1986). Indeed, it is so commonly discussed and demonstrated in so many people, at least to some minimal extent, that we tend to give its study short shrift, because we think we know what it means. It really warrants more serious attention than this, particularly for professionals, because understanding the nuances of the typical history, phenomenology, and psychological processes involved can significantly impact our empathy for and effectiveness with people who suffer from this disorder.

David Shapiro (1965) has helped me to understand this disorder by emphasizing the role of distorted volition or will directed at controlling and prescribing what cannot be prescribed or controlled — namely, drives, spontaneous interests, and affects. In Shapiro's words, "willful directedness has been distorted from its most subjective significance as an extension, and, so to speak, representative of one's wants, to a position of precedence over wants, aimed even at directing them. Impulse in this order of things is not the initiator of the full stage of willful directedness and effort, but its enemy" (p. 37).

Shapiro also points out the extent to which the obsessive-compulsive experiences "his own overseer issuing commands, directives, reminders, warnings, and admonitions" (p. 34) as external to himself. The overseer's values and directives are accepted but are not the result of free choice. And, particularly as the obsessions or compulsions appear more neurotic or absurd, the individual is puzzled, annoyed, or troubled by them, and experiences them as truly alien to himself. This external or alien quality of the "overseer sitting behind and issuing commands" has all the earmarks of an unassimilated, introjected other. Further, it leads to the projection outside the self of this introject, as Meissner (1988) has so cogently pointed out, which explains why the obsessive-compulsive often claims that he behaves in the way he does in order to satisfy an objective necessity or a social imperative which the rest of us do not experience as so absolute.

This demanding overseer phenomenology is consistent with the repeated experience of clinicians, who find that these patients remember and often currently perceive their parents as stern, exacting, rigid, and rule-bound. Parents of these individuals are often found to have been particularly threatened or disgusted by the child's alive, animal nature and were interested in producing the perfect little lady or gentleman. Not infrequently, the reconstruction or even current experience of parents is that they are threatened by competition or success that would diminish them by comparison.

As with all other general etiological constellations, not all of these descriptors apply to all cases. Here and in the summary tables, including Table 11 for this character, I deliberately use a number of related but different words to describe etiological factors for their clinical utility. In one case, the words "stern" and "exacting" may be precisely descriptive for the client and, therefore, quite helpful to her. In another, the phrases "threatened by success' and "disgusted by one's animal nature" may be more precisely descriptive and helpful.

So, the characterological-developmental theory for the obsessive-compulsive is simply this: The child introjects and identifies with the parent and the parent's standards or values and, over the course of structural development, tries to use his willpower to meet these introjected standards and live up to these unusually rigid, life-denying, and body-alien values. The will is used to block the original

organismic expressions as well as to promulgate a false self consisting
of the correct attitude and behavior that is necessary for some semblance of positive contact with the very contingent and often not very
positive parent. This is a clear-cut example of a characterological
reproduction—i.e., obsessive-compulsive parenting producing an
obsessive-compulsive child.

It is critical to point out that the obsessive-compulsive person is
not always best understood through this more "anal" and "oedipal"
etiology as expressed in traditional psychoanalytic language. Even
Lowen (1958), who gives the clearest argument for the oedipal etiology of this syndrome, acknowledges that these traits will often be
seen in primarily oral and masochistic characters (p. 157). I would
add that one can often see extreme rigidity exhibited in low-functioning individuals who have a poor sense of self. In these cases, the
obsessive-compulsive behavior is not defensive in the classic sense
but literally protects the person from the void and fragmentation of
an enfeebled self. In other words, the individual actually finds himself in his orderliness or in his rigid moral, political, or religious
beliefs, and organizes his life around living up to them. The rigidity,
then, does not serve to defend against unacceptable impulses as much
as it serves to organize a disorganized structure. What I am offering
in this section is the development of an understanding of obsessive-
compulsive behavior when it is based on a more oedipally related
etiology and when it serves a more classically defensive function.

When that is the case, the behavioral compulsions, cognitive obsessions, and less symptomatic activities consistent with this personality can be best understood as the organism's attempts to ward off
or keep in check these unacceptable impulses, which tend to be sexual, aggressive, competitive, and affectively spontaneous. These "activities" include the obsessive-compulsive's tendency to live "under
the gun" of constant, pervasive tension and pressure to do, feel,
and think the right thing. This constant pressure keeps him busy
cognitively and behaviorally and keeps him in check so that any
spontaneous expression, which may be potentially wrong or dangerous, is inhibited. Similarly, his intense and narrowly focused attention, particularly to detail, and his characteristic isolation of thinking
from feeling keeps him busy and away from truly self-initiated behavior, thought, and feeling that might threaten, anger, or displease

the other. Similarly, his well-noted doubt, indecision, and procrastination keep him from committing to a course of action that, in the final analysis, must reflect a personal commitment and choice.

Furthermore, the obsessive-compulsive's social behavior, which is often noted as being stilted, emphasizing the correct social role behavior, and his pedantic, self-possessed, and affectless way of presenting himself, keeps him distant from his own distrusted impulses and from any dangerous feelings toward and for others. Finally, the obsessive-compulsive's tendency to be very aware of and responsive to others along the dimension of submission-subjugation also can be seen to derive from this overall personality organization. Others are seen as the personification of the external imperatives, social rules, and objective necessities to which the individual must live up or as subordinates who must be set straight by these rules. Others may also be seen to be threatened or injured by the individual's competitive nature or successes as was the parent in the oedipal struggle. Again, the preoccupation with correct rules, the proper behavior, the proper attitudes, and the possible adverse effects of one's interpersonal actions keeps the individual busy and keeps the dangerous impulses out of awareness.

Symptomatically, the suppression, self-regulation, and life-denying holding back create depression. When the individual is really pressed by stressful events and/or the increased pressure of unresolved, unexpressed impulses, the obsessions and/or compulsions can take possession of the individual to such an extent that he is driven to absurd lengths in his obsessive preoccupations and compulsively driven behaviors. Not infrequently, the failure of the defenses to manage all of this leads to intrusive thoughts which are frequently of a sexually sadistic or otherwise hostile nature. These thoughts are, of course, extraordinarily ego-dystonic, because they are so far away from the good person that this individual is trying to be.

Frequently, the obsessive-compulsive is also perfectionistic. While there can be some similarity to the perfectionism of the narcissist, this is a good example of how characterological theory can be useful in yielding the most accurate and empathic understanding of people. The obsessive-compulsive's perfectionism is driven more by a determination to willfully do the right thing and avoid the wrong thing. It is as if he is trying to please or appease that external authority and avoid its punishment. The perfectionism is motivated to avoid censure, control what is bad in the self, and hold in check what will threaten or displease the other.

In the case of the narcissistic etiology and orientation, the perfectionism is better conceptualized as a developmental arrest in grandiosity. Trying to be perfect maintains the grandiose false-self illusion and protects one from dipping into a state of worthlessness or void. Here, a perfect performance, achievement, or self-presentation enhances self-esteem. On the other hand, with the obsessive-compulsive, the perfectionism is directed more to the individual's attempts to control his own feelings and motivations so that he is the right kind of person and does not offend. The latter is a far more passive and interpersonally defensive position than that of the narcissist, who is better known for being able to mobilize his aggression and impress others with behavior that he himself often experiences as shallow, hollow, or phony.

So, the characterological-developmental theory is important for clinical work because, among other things, it assists the clinician by suggesting what to look for in the history, belief structure, attitude, self-presentation, and symptomatology that will aid her in understanding what lies beneath the observed expression and in helping the client understand this himself. Once this is done, the developmental theory has some prescriptions about how issues may be resolved. In the case of perfectionism, does the individual need to learn that his sexual, aggressive, and competitive impulses are normal and human and all right and that they cannot be subjugated to his will, or does he need to learn that his perfectionism is an expression of an unresolved grandiosity in early development which requires him to learn a more realistic, well-modulated, "constant" self-esteem based on the integration of what is marvellous and what is limited in himself?

Returning now to the problem of the obsessive-compulsive, we may ask, when does all this develop? It is not possible to answer that question as completely as we would like. Nevertheless, we do know that children begin to operate on the basis of standards at about two years of age (Gopnick & Meltzoff, 1984). The experimental, developmental research indicates that a number of the factors operative in this particular adaptation do not develop until quite a bit later than we have seen in the characterological issues heretofore reviewed.

For example, children cannot distinguish between mental and physical events (Wellman & Estes, 1986) until about three years of age. It is also about this time that they begin to be able to distinguish between intended and accidental outcomes in their judgements of stories and what happens to characters in them (Yuill & Perner, 1988). This research is relevant because it documents the long period of childhood existence during which there is confusion about the realistic relationships between causes and effects. Furthermore, it is not until six years of age that children begin to use purely mental strategies to regulate their feelings (Bengtsson & Johnson, 1987) and to take moral and conventional rules seriously (Tisak & Turiel, 1988). These findings would indicate that the strategy for living by such rules and the purely mental strategy of trying to regulate drives by will develops relatively late. Further, naturalistic observation tends to confirm Freud's original position that the sexual interest, seductiveness, and rivalrous behavior that children can display also does not come until about three years of age. So, when obsessive-compulsive behavior is the result of these oedipal events, all the available information would indicate that this one adaptation develops relatively late to begin with and that it continues to develop over some period of time.

Parenthetically, it is probably also true that these strategies in service of other functions (e.g., to bolster an enfeebled self) are also mastered at a relatively late period, even though they may be motivated by a developmental lesion occurring considerably earlier. This phenomenon of the later overlay of more sophisticated strategies to deal with a more primitive complex is quite consistent with the kind of characterological-developmental theory I am trying to integrate for clinical practice.

The final piece of the theory, which needs to be emphasized here, is the extent to which the obsessive-compulsive solution binds the individual to the parent, who is, particularly in this case, supremely contingent in his or her response to the child. When the child is very good, he may get praise or at least the absence of criticism. When the parent is very exacting, however, the child will receive qualified praise, with notation of how she might have done a bit better. This latter response, of course, promotes the perfectionism of the child, who can nurture the illusion that if she could only be a little better, she could have a more unqualified positive contact with the parent.

Be that as it may, the most critical point to understand here is that the child's adoption of and attempts to live up to the parent's standards provides the social connection and the self-identity within that connection that all of us require. This living up to the family standard and being the kind of child you're expected to be defines the self and maintains the needed contact. The rigidity of the pattern can be explained by the combination, in this case made so obvious, of the avoidance of the punishment and the maintenance of contact and, through contact and emulation, identity. Thus, it is the fear of a repetition of the punishment, as well as the fear of isolation both from the self as defined and from the family, that maintains the pathological pattern which may otherwise seem so absurd even to the individual himself.

The therapeutic themes in these cases are, of course, the gradual challenging of these tight defenses and the gradual acceptance and expression of the disavowed drives, affects, and thoughts. Insight concerning the basis for these rigid defenses which require so much safety is usually very helpful. "Getting the story straight" about the history which motivates this extreme need for control and proper functioning in all realms can yield the kind of sympathetic understanding for the self that these individuals absolutely require. The individual needs to learn slowly that these extreme guarantees of safety are not necessary any longer, and that novel patterns of thinking and behaving, while anxiety provoking, do not lead to anywhere near the danger that is affectively anticipated. Through all this, the individual needs to learn to tolerate the anxiety that the relinquishing of defenses and the release of underlying contents will provoke, and a good therapeutic alliance which is not exclusively abstinent will often facilitate that.

In a sense, the obsessive-compulsive needs to be desensitized to his own feelings, and a gradual process of uncovering and optimal frustration is necessary for that to occur. Almost all experts on this syndrome agree that it is important to keep the client in the here and now in this process and encourage greater attention to feelings than to thoughts. In this regard, the therapeutic relationship—transferential, countertransferential, and real—is a particularly good choice for therapeutic focus because of its immediacy and potential realness. The most common therapeutic error in these cases is a collusion with the intellectualized, distant, affectless relation to events and others by a therapist who is himself obsessive-compulsive or whose method may easily err in that direction (i.e., cognitive and behavior therapies and pedagogic psychoanalysis).

Table 11
OEDIPAL CHARACTER: OBSESSIVE-COMPULSIVE

1. *Etiological constellation*: Exacting, rigid, persistent, rule-bound parenting occurs, especially around socialization training, impulse control, and the "taming" of sexual, competitive, and aggressive expression. There is not, in this control, the invasion and intrusion into the organism's natural processes nor the crushing of the will that occurs in masochism. Rather, the child is encouraged through punishment, reinforcement, and example to use his will to tame all aspects of his animal impulses, spontaneous behavior, competitive nature, tender feelings, etc. As the individual achieves this exaggerated self-possession and reserve, he acquires the kinds of rigid, judgmental, and driven behavior that characterize this personality. The obsessions and compulsions serve to maintain this emotionally restrained stance by warding off affects and drives.

2. *Symptom constellation*: Possessed by a driven, pressured tension to do the correct, necessary, or imperative thing. This imposition of objective necessity or higher authority is constant and pervasive resulting in a life of continuous effort related to sanctioned purposes. Spontaneous expressions, personal choices, or any genuine feelings are difficult to access. Rigidity in bodily posture, moral and other judgments, or routine activities is definitional. This rule-bound personality is uncomfortable with freedom, and release from one concern will lead to anxiety and quick replacement with another pressing concern as the subject for stewing rumination. Perfectionism and procrastination are often present and related to the fear of doing the wrong thing. Similarly, difficulty in decision making reflects fears of self-initiated expression which may be wrong. Social behavior can be pedantic, affectless, and stilted with an emphasis on correct social role behavior. Depression and intrusive thoughts, especially of a hostile or sexually sadistic nature, are often problematic along with troublesome obsessive thoughts and compulsive behaviors that, at this symptomatic level, are experienced as alien and as taking over the individual.

3. *Cognitive style*: Intense, sharp, focused attention to detail is associated with a tendency to miss the essential features of things. A related char-

(continued)

Table 11
(continued)

acteristic is the isolation of cognitive understanding from the emotional meaning of events, ideas, or behavior. Cognitive activity can persist in a rigid pattern in spite of repeated failure or observed absurdity of the process. Doubt, uncertainty, and indecision often plague even the simplest activities.

4. *Defenses*: Rumination, rituals, rule-bound living serve to eliminate the need for accessing impulses or desires. Doubt, indecision, procrastination, shifting attention, and rigid posture all serve to overwhelm the cognitive and affective accessing of warded-off contents.

5. *Script decisions and pathogenic beliefs*: "I must have done something wrong, I must do the right thing. I'll never make another mistake. I have to control myself or I will totally lose control."

6. *Self-representation*: Consciously, the individual sees himself as conscientious, responsible, hardworking, morally and otherwise correct, and trying hard to be the right kind of person. He experiences himself as duty bound to follow an externally determined set of rules or principles and not as a free agent with respect for his own wishes and judgment. Unconsciously, as the script decisions and pathogenic beliefs illustrate, he harbors the feeling that he has done something terribly wrong and must hold himself under tight reign so that he will not transgress again.

7. *Object representations and relations*: The individual tends to see others as the personification of authority, to which he is subject, or as subjects of his authority. This lends a one-up/one-down flavor to his relationships, which are often formal with much attention to the proper role behavior as parent, spouse, superior, subordinate, etc. Power struggles often characterize relations, particularly where role-relationship rules are at all unclear or where there may be disagreement concerning such rules. Others often find these individuals frustrating due to the lack of meaningful connection or real communication experienced, the rigidity of values and behavior, the deadened affect, and the seemingly unnecessary pressure and tension that they create in themselves and others.

8. *Affective characteristics*: Overmodulated affect leading to a restrained and constricted manner with little access to feeling. The person will experience anxiety, particularly if defenses fail to bind it effectively. Underlying hostility is expressed indirectly or through intrusive thoughts which may be sexually sadistic or violent. The individual separates ideas and feelings such that disturbing or highly positive thoughts do not produce the usual affective impact. Tender feelings are also blocked and expressed indirectly, if at all.

PART II

THE SYMBIOTIC
CHARACTER

CHAPTER 5

The Owned Child

LIKE ALL OTHER CHARACTEROLOGICAL ISSUES, the symbiotic one is existential and lifelong. From walking and weaning to leaving home and retirement, there are recurring opportunities to master individuation and form a new identity. To the extent that any of us suffer from functional psychopathology, we must separate from the role we adopted in our family of origin to become ourselves and to know freedom. There are very important lessons to be learned from those whose problems in living are most clearly defined by their difficulties in separation and identity formation. The strategies found successful in liberating the "symbiotic character" can be of nearly universal significance. Becoming optimally integrated with others, yet remaining autonomous, is an accomplishment of only the wisest and most fortunate.

ETIOLOGY

The essence of the symbiotic's etiology is this: Natural attempts at separation are blocked, cause parental anxiety, or are actively punished. At the same time, the child's natural abilities for empathic mirroring are overvalued and reinforced by parents who require merger with the child in order to feel secure or worthwhile.

All developmental research, whether naturalistic or experimental, confirms the need of the child for the parent in the earliest months of life—for sustenance, relationship, and regulation. The developmental research reviewed by Stern (1985) documents the remarkable degree of mother-infant attunement typical of the normal child's first year. While Stern questions the psychoanalytic notion of the child's *illusion* of fusion with the mother, his work documents that the child's actual *experience* is indeed one of unique behavioral union

79

with the mother and that the infant's sensitivity to others in general, and the mothering figure in particular, from a very early age, is truly remarkable.

Concomitant with the need for relationship and all that it brings, there is also a natural human need for individuation. When does the need for autonomy first emerge in the human infant? It seems to me that it depends on what kind of autonomy one is talking about. Even in the first days of life, a child initiates and separates from the caregiver through the visual gaze interaction over which he shows control. Patterns of parental neglect or intrusion can begin immediately if this channel is used as the vehicle for communicating excessive closeness or distance. The infant develops an enhanced ability to move out of the parent's orbit of influence when he begins to walk at about 10 months. Mahler has noted that in the "practicing period" initiated by this change, the child becomes more independent, more engrossed in his own activities, more impervious to difficulties, and generally more adventurous. Clearly, the child will develop differently if these early adventures are supported, delighted in, and freely allowed than if these initial trials at independence are met with fearfulness, punishment, or excessive restraint. Developmental research documents that a child as young as 10 months will look to the mother for signals about the safety of venturing forth (Emde & Sorce, 1983). An anxious, overprotective mother will consistently signal that such initiations are unsafe, and the child will inevitably introject that overly fearful perspective. As a consequence, the child's orientation to this kind of self-expression will not be one resulting from the direct experience of trial and error but rather an adopted standard which is excessively conservative, constrained, and anxious.

This incorporative introjection of standard is prototypical of the symbiotic's entire identity. It is an identity swallowed whole as a function of experience with the parent, rather than an identity developed out of the entirety of experience in the interaction of self with environment. This fact lies behind a therapeutic theme that I have found useful with every symbiotic character. Stated simply, the theme is this: "That is not who you are" and "That's not you." This simple intervention repeatedly reminds the individual to reexamine his standards, beliefs, reactions, etc., on the basis of his actual experience of himself and the world and, in so doing, fosters individuation and the development of a real self.

Developmental experiments (e.g., Stern, 1985) indicate that children discover that there are other minds in the world and that others have changeable subjective states as early as seven to nine months of age. Mahler's more naturalistic observation of children shows that, at about 15 months of age, children evidence more noticeable behavior which indicates that they understand the concept that their experience is both different from that of others and shareable. The rapprochement period (15 to 24 months) refers to the returning of the infant from practicing to a more intense relationship with the parent. Rapprochement is begun when the child starts bringing objects to the parent, presumably to get the parent to share in the child's experience of that object. While the developmental research indicates that the child has awareness of separate subjectivity prior to this time, it would appear that during rapprochement children begin to appreciate more fully the implications of this knowledge and begin to act upon it in these more obvious ways.*

At this same time, Spitz has noted that children make the discovery of the wonderful "no" word. Like the adolescent's loud music and radical haircuts, the rapprochement child begins to assert an autonomous identity through opposition. How the environment responds to these various assertions of autonomy and requests for a new kind of intimacy will determine the extent to which the child feels comfortable in asserting this form of autonomy and requesting this form of attention. During these crucial initial periods of individuation, we may ask: Is the child allowed some negativity with limits? Is negativity completely indulged or severely punished? Is the intersubjective experience available and if it is, is there a mutuality in who leads it and who follows? Is the intersubjective experience contingent on compliance or restraint on the part of the child?

These experiences are among the first that affect the individual's sense of independent agency — a sense that is weakened in every symbiotic character. Typically, the symbiotic looks outside himself for the agenda in his life. He has a poor sense of his own likes and dislikes, as they have not been allowed to spontaneously develop nor been given adequate support. In mirroring others, he finds a greater sense of security — his "security operation" is an accommodating false

---

I believe this delay between awareness and full appreciation of the implications of that awareness accounts for the fact that experimental research (e.g., Stern) shows earlier acquisition of abilities than naturalistic research (e.g., Mahler).

self. He experiences aggression, assertion, and particularly, opposition as dangerous.

As Freud has pointed out, another type of autonomy issue develops in response to the need of the environment to socialize the child. At about 24 months of age, toilet training as well as other socialization demands become more salient. Obviously, the child's sense of autonomy is affected by how all this is handled. Is the timing of these socializations geared to the child's abilities and emerging inclination to be socialized? Is there rigidity or flexibility in the parents' orientation to the problems? Is the child gently corrected or severely punished or humiliated for errors? Is the child allowed some self-control or is she symbolically or literally invaded (e.g., with food, enemas, etc.)? In other words, is there an interaction between the abilities, inclinations, and talents of the child with the demands of the environment, or do these demands overpower and otherwise injure the child? Is the child's willfulness allowed but moderated or is it crushed? When the will is crushed, the life issue is more one of control, and I think the characterological formulation is more properly differentiated from the symbiotic issue and labeled masochistic. As is probably obvious, however, the symbiotic and masochistic issues commonly exist together because they reflect different forms of autonomy frustration. I separate them, not from a commitment to any particular developmental model, but for reasons of clinical utility. There is a distinct difference in the constellation of symptoms and therapeutic themes in these two types, even though they have some similarities and can coexist in the same person.

We can characterize these three forms of autonomy as reflecting the individual's orientation to agency, adventure, and self-control. The remainder of the individual's life will contain experiences that give the opportunity for additional or revised learning in these areas, and change is always possible. Yet, the experience of the young human the first few times around is usually of paramount importance, particularly when his experience is of a traumatic nature and the abilities, strategies, and defenses used to cope with trauma are more likely to become fixed. This very real "developmental arrest" will tend to persist throughout life in relation to the affected form of autonomy. It is also often true that parents who have any real difficulty with the child's expression of autonomy at 10 months of age are going to have similar difficulties with later varieties of autonomous expression. So, the first time the issue becomes an issue is generally prototypical of future confrontations of that particular issue.

The combination of developmental arrest with the consistently frustrating environmental response to adventure, agency, or self-control can often combine to negate the potential effects of new learning experiences which might be corrective. For these reasons, then, an otherwise normal adult may still be operating with the defenses, strategies, and belief systems that derive almost exclusively from the traumatic experiences of a very young child. This fact, which we all find difficult to believe, becomes more believable for the therapist who sees this model of psychopathology compatible with the facts again and again. It is also believable to tortured clients who directly experience their symptomatic behavior, attitudes, and feelings as childlike and outside the influence of their adult, direct experience and knowledge. Particularly upon analysis, patients experience that part of their reality that is symptomatic as based on a model of the world and themselves that is clearly discrepant from current reality. Sometimes without psychotherapy and very often with only a little of it, they can begin to say, "This is not me. This is not how it really is."

In considering the symbiotic's essential lack of self, it is important to understand how a "self" is formed. This involves an understanding of how internal functions and structures are built as well as how external functions are internalized and modify the existing structures. I have found psychoanalytic developmental observation and theory, as well as Piagetian concepts, to be particularly useful in this understanding. Basically, that which originates from the inside requires an "optimal indulgence" of the emerging person with an attuned mirroring of developing abilities. The "gleam in the mother's eye" (Mahler) at the child's developing abilities to walk, talk, and individuate throughout childhood and into adolescence exemplifies this requirement. At the same time, the environment must allow an optimal level of frustration in the child's acquisition of abilities, concepts, etc. Thus, the self is developed through exercise of self. Classically, this has often been termed the strengthening of self through the "exercise of function."

Internalization, that process by which what is outside the self is taken in and made one's own, may be understood in a hierarchical way. At the lowest level of development, or consciousness, if you will, there is a process which I will label "incorporative introjection." Here, the individual seems to swallow the other whole, and there is no assimilation of the other into the self. There is no digestive process by which what is outside is transformed into what is inside. The incorporative introjection is in some ways similar to the Kohutian concept of a merger transference in which the individual sees the other as literally part of himself, failing to differentiate or perceive realistic boundaries.

In describing this, I am often reminded of the picture I once saw of a snake that had just swallowed a rabbit. Prior to the snake's digestive processes going to work on the rabbit, the snake no longer looks like a snake, but rather an odd configuration of snake and rabbit. In the psychoanalytic literature, this is often referred to as an unassimilated introject, or an example of incorporation. One can often observe this phenomenon in adolescents or other immature individuals who embrace whole a religious, philosophical, or political cult without developing a very complete understanding of the underlying belief structure. Such action is taken in the absence of a well-developed self, and the incorporative introjection shores up a defective self.

At a higher level of development is the process of identification, wherein the individual copies or borrows or fuses his identity with someone else. In psychoanalytic theory, the primary identification is presumed to occur in that period of infancy when the individual has yet to distinguish between himself and the other. Secondary identification is the same phenomenon but occurs with the recognition of the separateness of the other. While the work of Stern and others would call this theoretical distinction into question, it is still useful to recognize that identification can take place with varying degrees of awareness or consciousness of the process itself. Identification that is conscious and selective is more cognitively mediated and thus developmentally more sophisticated. This process is analogous to Kohut's concept of the twinship transference, in which the self and other are seen as identical, as well as in the concept of an idealization transference, where the individual tries to emulate a superior figure.

At the highest level of development is the phenomenon that I will label internalization, in which there is some process of assimilation or accommodation, such that what is taken in becomes one's own. There is, then, some work involved in internalization. Typically, there is an effort over a period of time to fit the externally derived idea, belief, skill, or function into the existing experience and expression of the self so that it becomes congruent and integrated with other expressions. Even more effort is typically necessary when the Piagetian (1936) process of accommodation is required. Here, the individual must actively change some part of the self structure to congruently hold the new material brought in from the outside. In all of these "transmuting internalizations" (Kohut, 1984), there must be some tension or frustration to work through. This fact, I think, underlies the conventional wisdom that "hardship builds character."

So, how do these processes typically work in the formation of self for the symbiotic character? To one extent or another, the internal demands for individuation are not appropriately mirrored, echoed, and prized. In particular, ideas, abilities, ambitions, or behaviors that will make the person different from her caretakers or that will result in any kind of separation are not reinforced, but are ignored or actively punished. Furthermore, in the etiology of the symbiotic, caretakers often help the individual avoid experiencing the kind of frustration that would lead to the development of initiative in dealing with life. So there is a combination of overindulging dependency and undervaluing initiative. This, in turn, leads quite naturally to reliance on the more immature forms of identity formation; namely, incorporative introjection and identification. This results in "a self I can't call my own," with a diminished sense of agency, intentionality, initiative, and identity.

Therefore, a good deal of the symbiotic's life work involves the rediscovery and development of the self. This involves the rediscovery of innate abilities, capacities, and aptitudes that eventually can develop into interests, tastes, preferences, etc. This may involve the discovery of athletic, intellectual, or artistic propensities which have gone uncultivated and therefore still require recognition, support, and reinforcement. Along with this, of course, is the requirement for a kind of individualized reassessment in developing one's identifications, idealizations, and introjections. It is necessary for the symbiotic to face up to his or her own indulgence in failing to adequately internalize functions and structures which to some extent, must develop from the outside in.

I believe that the real difficulty in treating the symbiotic character is in overcoming the natural ease with which this person will remain

passive with respect to her own internal impulses while simultaneously borrowing an identity from others. These strategies are so
well ingrained, so effortless, and so insidiously capable of providing
temporary fulfillment and escape from uncomfortable frustration
that they are often very difficult to overcome. For this reason, it is
not surprising that the symbiotic characterological issue is so often
found in those who compulsively overeat. This kind of incorporation
soothes, fills a void, and often serves to blot out uncomfortable
affects, obviating the necessity for some kind of discipline in one's
social and intellectual life—a discipline that is all the harder due to
the history of deficient support for individuation and overindulgence
of dependence.

In sum, the essential message from the parent to the symbiotic is,
"You can have the sustenance you require from me only if you deny
the development of your self. You can have me or you, not both."
Autonomy in whatever form becomes a danger situation. Consequently, the need for it is repressed, and with it, that natural aggression necessary for separation is squelched. Compromise solutions in
the classic neurotic forms are then often developed and refined in
order to achieve some semblance of autonomy while preventing the
feared abandonment. Herein lies the conflict for the symbiotic character, which can be understood through the classic psychoanalytic
model: the wish for autonomy and the fear of having it. The deficit
for the symbiotic character exists in the developmental arrest around
this issue and the failures in new learning that result from it. These
include the symbiotic's failure to form good self-other boundaries,
to develop a sense of safety in adventure, a sense of self-agency, and
all these in aggregate—a good sense of self. Rather, there is the
development of a chameleon-like false self in which the individual
looks for his identity not in himself but in the other.

AFFECT, BEHAVIOR, COGNITION

Behavior

The symbiotic's life is exceedingly object related. There is no
sphere of her life that is not almost continually involved with others,
and indeed, activity that is independent, autonomous, or discon-
nected from others is experienced as dangerous, selfish, immoral,

and injurious to others. The symbiotic experiences her experience only in relation to others and can have great difficulty in self-activation if another is not present in that activity somewhere. The needs of the other are necessary to initiate activity, and the other's responses are necessary to sustain it.

One client reported that, just as she began to become interested in reading a book, she would begin to think of other friends and family who would be interested in or benefit from the book. With these thoughts, her own self-determined interest in the book would wane, and she would fail to attend to what she was reading. She would then put the book down, never return to it for herself, and deny herself what she experienced as a great pleasure.

As the symbiotic person gains insight, he will confess to the fact that there is very little of intrinsic interest to him; he doesn't know what activities, hobbies, or fields of interest draw him personally. Typically, he will not have a very well-developed sense of taste in things, for his preferences and activities have been adopted rather than acquired. These phenomena are a reflection of the absence of any real developed sense of self apart from relationship. He molds himself to the interests and tastes of others and, in a sense, finds his only real sense of self in losing himself in the other.

This lack of self-other boundary makes the symbiotic person exceedingly vulnerable to the affective states of others. He can easily absorb or be invaded by others' affects, and his equilibrium can be easily affected by them. He is particularly vulnerable to a significant other's upset with him and may well be prone to interpreting such upset as a threat of abandonment or rejection. Thus, a disruption of the affective tone of important relationships is upsetting or even disorganizing, and a good deal of the symbiotic's activity at such times, both cognitive and behavioral, will be directed at restoring the relationship equilibrium.

Though these propensities can be highly problematic, the higher functioning symbiotic person can be particularly well attuned to the needs and feelings of others, and his empathic abilities may be quite profound. The ability to get under another's skin, as it were, can serve him in many ways as long as the relationship is relatively conflict-free and unthreatened.

Perhaps the most interesting aspect of the symbiotic's behavior is his tendency to engage in thought patterns and behaviors that serve the purpose of preserving the original, pathogenic relationship. Behaviorally, this involves such things as selecting friends, colleagues, and mates who replicate in some significant way the binding features of the original object or, through projective identification, recreating that in others. The symbiotic's life is often filled with people who require a good deal of sensitive mirroring, whose feelings can be easily hurt, who actively or passively demand attuned holding, and who are very difficult to satisfy. In short, the symbiotic picks others for close relationships who justify her projections, or she helps them to provide such justification. By so doing, the symbiotic character now has a role to fill, and thereby she has a self. The void and fragmentation of the real self are avoided by the immersion in the other. Such immersion can, at least at times, look compulsive in the behavioral realm and obsessive in the cognitive realm. Thus, the person with a symbiotic issue may go to great lengths to placate or accommodate the other, particularly where this may reduce the other's negative affect. The symbiotic individual not only absorbs the other's negative states but also takes responsibility for them.

In psychotherapy, the *interpretation of preservation* of the pathogenic relationship is usually a ubiquitous theme in the symbiotic's treatment. However, what is important is to anticipate that accepting such an interpretation, much less acting on it, will elicit anxiety, guilt, and even emptiness of the self. For, while the symbiotic can keep herself busy, either accommodating or resisting the needs of the other, to live without that kind of relationship may seem literally impossible, not to mention morally wrong. Fairbairn's (1952) work, which will be reviewed in the next chapter, is particularly helpful in achieving an understanding of the role of this deep human need to preserve object ties in maintaining psychopathology.

The person who develops a symbiotic character often becomes the carrier of responsibility for the family pain. It is as if that pain has been absorbed by the individual not necessarily by direct experience but by a kind of assimilation or uncritical inheritance. The trap, of course, is in the assumption of responsibility for something so pervasive that it may well span generations, and the individual's power to affect it is virtually nil. The assumption of responsibility is executed by an innocently egocentric child who doesn't appreciate the magnitude of the burden assumed. The psychopathology of the symbiotic person often yields to understanding when seen as the expression of the family's pathology passed on, rather than as the direct result of trauma experienced directly by the patient. This accounts for the fact that the symbiotic's symptomatology is often experienced by him as alien in the extreme and is difficult for even an experienced analyst to understand in that it doesn't seem to derive from the patient's own history, but is a derivative of the family's history more generally.

Were there no conflict about the accommodation, enmeshment, or engulfment of the symbiotic character, there would be far less of a problem. But the individual's aggression and natural desire for self-expression cannot be so easily obliterated. Like all other characterological adaptations, this is a compromise solution to an impossible problem. There is always a deep reservoir of resentment toward the other for causing the dysphoric states of anxiety, guilt, depression, and burdening responsibility, as well as for the suppression of one's natural aggression and self-expression.

So, where do the aggression and self-expression go? They go into resisting the demands for accommodation, albeit conflictually and/ or they are turned against the self. The resistance can take many forms. The most common form is a passive resistance in which the person withdraws from the field, forgets, or in other unconscious ways refuses and frustrates the other. In these ways, the resistance is deniable, though it still may stimulate considerable guilt. Once the resistance becomes more conscious or active, it often takes on a kind of rigidity in which the person is extraordinarily sensitive to any possibility of invasion by another. This, indeed, is not an uncommon phenomenon in the psychotherapy of these individuals, because it is essentially the self-other boundaries that cannot be well modulated. The symbiotic, in the middle of such change, can be similar to the teenager who insists on defending her "rights," and the client can get stuck in such a position if the therapist cannot assist her in achieving smoother modulation. For resisting the other is just the other side of accommodating the other. In both cases, the self is found in relationship to the other, either in accommodating or resisting, but not in self-activation.

Even where a literal other is not in the picture, the symbiotic's behavior can be best understood in the accommodation or resistance of the "evoked companion" (Stern, 1985) who is demanding and often impossible to satisfy. In this activity, as well, the individual preserves the kind of role relationship to which she has become accustomed and, thereby, preserves a false sense of self. So, whether the original relationship is preserved by finding or creating others who justify the projection and living in accommodation or resistance, or is lived out purely intrapsychically (e.g., in ruminative worry), the preservation of original role relationship is at the heart of one's life. Where that relationship cannot be preserved, the symbiotic character experiences what Masterson has termed the abandonment depression, in which the individual experiences extreme difficulty in self-activation, panic, an empty terrifying loneliness, and fragmentation of the self. It is in this state that the person reexperiences the rapprochement crisis; again without the necessary connection and support, he is alone with an enfeebled self wherein individuating, separating, and autonomous activity will only serve to maintain the desolate aloneness.

The corrective emotional experience of psychotherapy with this structure involves the discovery that self-expression can now receive support. Such self-expression constitutes a "danger situation," and, both in therapy and out, the client needs to experience a kind of desensitization to it. Further, the person needs to be sustained through the separation from the enmeshed relationships that sustain a false identity, whether they are intrapsychic, transferential, or actual.

Affect

Affectively, the symbiotic character is distinguished mostly in his disturbed relationship with aggression. The aggressive impulse that is separating has been at best discouraged and at worst severely punished, so that it has not developed into a healthy, well-modulated assertiveness. Rather, the symbiotic's aggression is denied or, in borderline states, is blown off or violently directed against the self. At the lower end of the ego development continuum, hostility can appear as freely expressed rage at the perceived rejection or distancing of others or, conversely, at the perception that others are engulfing or intruding. At higher levels of ego development within this character, there is typically more defensiveness around the hostility, and its expression becomes more passive or convoluted.

The hostility exists in response to the impossible bind to which

the person has had to adjust: the threat of abandonment for individuation. Thus, it is particularly elicited by any threat of abandonment
or any experience of engulfment. The problem is that the feelings
about such hostility are, in a very meaningful way, arrested in the
experience and belief structure of the very young child. He believes
that his expression of hostility will either be exceedingly destructive
and depriving to the other or that it will be completely ineffective.
The undercontrolled, borderline symbiotic person will more often
experience his hostility as ineffectual, whereas the overcontrolled
symbiotic more often will tend to experience his hostility as destructive. But this tendency can be radically reversed, and the borderline
patient can indulge in the often more conscious magical thinking
that his hostility is destructive, and the higher functioning person
can experience that his overcontrolled responses are indeed ineffectual. At both ends of the ego development continuum, there exists
this polarity around the experience and expression of hostility, and,
from the symbiotic character disorder to character style, there is a
consistent lack of well-modulated, goal-directed, sustained aggression.

Winnicott (1971) has been particularly instructive in emphasizing
the role of aggression in the individuation process. Winnicott seemed
to literally believe that the child discovers what is *not* him by trying
to destroy it and finding he cannot.

More recent developmental research would certainly challenge
this more radical object relations position. Still, aggression is a separating force. It establishes the existence of difference. Furthermore,
it is reasonable to conjecture that a child might easily fear damage
to himself or the other as a function of his own aggression (i.e.,
retaliation or destruction of the object). To the extent that the child
operates with the illusion of "omnipotent responsibility," he may
believe that his aggression literally has the power to injure or destroy.
So, what is necessary to separate can easily create a danger situation
in the classic analytic sense, thereby providing a conflict. The impulse or wish to aggress stimulates a complex of fears. To the extent
that the parental figures can withstand and sustain themselves
through this aggression, they literally desensitize the child's fears and
enhance the accurate reality perception that his aggression does not
necessarily injure, destroy, or lead to traumatic retaliation. This is
what Winnicott means when he writes, "In the unconscious phan-

tasy, growing up is inherently an aggressive act. . . . If the child is to become an adult, then this move is achieved over the dead body of an adult (unconsciously)" (1971, pp. 144–145).

The problem for the symbiotic character is that the necessary aggression is disallowed, and the fantasy, that aggression is inherently harmful and dangerous is either created or reinforced. The creation of the adult through aggression is thereby prohibited, and there is a resulting developmental arrest.

For purposes of clarification, it is probably necessary to underline the meaning of symbiosis as used here: This term does not refer to the illusion that "Mommy and I are one" (Silverman & Weinberger, 1985). Rather, it refers to the experience of this character structure that the self is essentially void without enmeshment in another.

In healthy development, the child's aggressive responses are both optimally indulged and optimally frustrated. He is allowed to discover that aggression is permissible and even encouraged, but within limits. As a result of this continuing process, he learns to modulate aggression appropriately and is thereby able to increasingly express it within a middle range and evaluate his aggressive responses appropriately. When this is not the case, a polarity response around the expression and evaluation of aggression will result. In the symbiotic character of the middle to high range of structural development, the aggression will typically be overcontrolled, with excessive fear of damage and retaliation as a result of even minimal aggressive expressions, together with the breaking-through of extremely aggressive fantasies, dreams, or even behaviors which are quite alarming and ego-dystonic. At the low end of the structural development continuum, where a borderline pathology is exhibited, there will often be the episodic lack of control of aggressive impulses which can indeed be both destructive and stimulate retaliation. Concomitantly, the borderline personality may often see the aggression as justified.

Where one's natural aggression is habitually repressed and resentment builds, the aggressive impulse is more and more accompanied by an increasingly savage hostility, which is destructive and which would, if expressed, stimulate retaliation. As this occurs, and the person loses the distinction between aggression and hostility, the illusion of danger is no longer an illusion. The child's illusions about aggression bolstered by the parent's reinforcement of those illusions, together with the progressive change in the aggression/hostility constellation, makes what once was an illusion a reality. And, short of intervention, this snowballing continues. Finally, to the extent that there is a developmental arrest in structure, the individual must deal with the high level of aggressive and hostile impulses with limited resources. This results either in the out-of-control hostile behavior of the borderline or the more adaptive denial and passive aggression of the symbiotic character neurosis or style. In treating the symbiotic character, a great deal of therapeutic direction can be gained by continued attention to the patient's relationship with his aggression and hostility.

When natural aggression is disallowed, normal individuation cannot occur and, as a result, a separate identity or sense of self cannot be established. A true identity is built through a combination of the discovery of self through its expression and the gradual internalization of external figures through optimal indulgence and optimal frustration. When normal aggression is disallowed, neither process can unfold as it should and, as a consequence, a real-self identity cannot be adequately established.

Identity formation, such as it is, occurs through a more primitive incorporative introjection of the self-regulating other. An identity formed in this way is not truly assimilated or owned and, in the case of the symbiotic character, there will always be the need for a significant other for the experience of self-cohesion. As Meissner (1986) has so cogently pointed out, it is this unassimilated, incorporated, alien, and implanted identity that may be projected so readily onto others, because it is not fully one's own in the first place. This is particularly true, of course, of the uncomfortable or undesirable aspects of that identity. In the case of the symbiotic character specifically, this projection often involves the controlling, guilt-inducing, and aggression-inhibiting aspects of the introjected identity.

Concomitant with the processes outlined above, the symbiotic character has not gradually internalized the abilities to care for the self and to self-soothe. These functions remain with the external object, so that the other is needed as a vehicle for projecting the negative aspects of the introjected self as well as an instrument for performing the functions of sustenance and regulation. Thus, in the symbiotic character, the other is absolutely necessary for any semblance of the experience of cohesion, stability, or firm relationship to reality. But, if the other gets too close, the symbiotic person experiences the engulfment of a controlling and hostile force; if the other is too distant, he experiences the panic of loneliness and abandonment with a poverty of internal resources. With this extreme polarization, it is nearly impossible to find, much less maintain, an optimal distance from another. Particularly where ego strength is also quite limited, as in the borderline case, one witnesses the characteristic pattern of extreme dependency alternating with enraged distancing (Masterson, 1976). This pattern exists ubiquitously even at higher levels of structural development in the symbiotic, although its expression is more subtle and more appropriately defended from the underlying feelings.

Etiologically, the symbiotic's difficulty in modulating aggression is related to her inability to modulate distance. Aggression is separating; the symbiotic cannot aggress and therefore cannot separate. The natural impulse to aggress and to separate constitutes a danger situation. So, the individual must create some compromise solution to handle the aggressive, separating impulse, the continuing need for contact, and the increasingly realistic fear of her own destructiveness and the environment's retaliation. This compromise is the symbiotic character expressed along the dimension of ego development from borderline or dependent personality disorder to a more neurotic-like symbiotic character neurosis and style. In whatever expression, this character structure will contain the failure to reconcile two important polarities and maintain a tendency to split along these dimensions. They are aggressive vs. passive and enmeshment vs. distance. These polarities are seen in almost every expression of the symbiotic character, whether they be in the affective, behavioral, or cognitive realms.

The impulse to individuate, which may express itself variously in the wish to explore, in the expression of exuberance, in the desire to succeed, or in the expression of difference, will elicit the internalized negative consequences. Then, the individual will feel anxiety or guilt or some other form of self-imposed prohibition. That prohibition, which interferes with one's natural self-expression, naturally elicits aggression and hostility. But, again, as an expression of one's impulse to differentiate, the aggression and hostility themselves elicit the prohibition, the anxiety, the guilt, etc. There is, then, a whole cluster of impulses and affects that are conflicting, each of which the troubled individual will attempt to avoid. Neurotic-like symptomatology is the typical consequence of trying to find some compromise solution to all of these conflict-ridden impulses. When these compromise solutions work reasonably well and are ego-syntonic, we observe characterological adaptations that are not experienced as problematic but that are nevertheless typical of the individual's overall functioning and might most easily be seen as examples of character style.

As the individual goes through a psychotherapeutic process focused on her symbiotic issues, she begins to experience more and more the various forms of the impulse to individuate, the prohibitions to such differentiation, and the consequences of such prohibitions (i.e., the anxiety, the guilt, the self-sabotage, etc.). There occurs, then, a typical conflict as to how much to identify with or to make ego-syntonic the originally prohibited ideas and affects. At this stage of the game, the individual may become even more neurotic in that she represents a house more consciously divided—for example, one part being more interested in adventure or success and the other part more afraid of or guilty about such impulses and ambitions. As the individuation process continues, the individual typically becomes more aware of her anger and hostility at the prohibitive injunctions and affects and, at the same time, becomes aware of the anxiety that this anger and hostility engender. In the most highly developed individuals in which this pattern is typical, analytic and reconstructive working-through can be of immeasurable assistance.

The structural development continuum is useful here in helping us understand other problematic feelings of the symbiotic character and what to do about them. At the lower end of the continuum, there is more open access to the primitive fears that make the symbiotic so emotionally vulnerable. Because the defensive structure doesn't work very well, the individual can tell you of her rage at anticipated abandonment or her terror of rejection and loneliness. The problem is in the transference acting-out of all this in her life, as well as in the therapeutic relationship, and the extent to which the powerful feelings overwhelm and disorganize her.

The person functioning at the lower structural level needs the security of an interpersonal relationship in which the boundaries are firm and caringly set with a confrontation of the destructiveness of the acting-out. At the higher end of the continuum, where things are more neurotic, the person does not have full access to what his often mysterious symptoms are all about. He may feel obliged to be ever-caring and attentive to others yet, paradoxically, show an absence of normal thoughtfulness, an absence of spontaneously generous feelings, or evidence of clearly hostile dreams or fantasies. Because the impulses to distance, separate, or aggress are unacceptable, they have become unconscious and result in behaviors that are experienced as mysterious or dystonic. Similarly, preservation of dysfunctional relationships, attitudes, and even behaviors may serve the function of allaying fears of separation, but this is also a secret. In these latter cases, the interpretation of this underlying emotional pattern can be therapeutic because it brings these "irrational" feelings into the conscious sphere where they may be understood, evaluated, and directly experienced by a person whose ego resources are capable of a reordering. The person suffering the symbiotic character style needs to know what the symbiotic borderline knows all too well— the chaotic feelings of the immature child caught in the conflict of the fear of abandonment or the fear of engulfment.

The dysphoria of the symbiotic person often relates, in one way or another, to the fundamental void in the experience of self. In the more borderline individuals, this is often acted-out in blaming others for failing to provide that necessary direction or meaning or for taking over the weakened self. As one moves up the continuum, one finds a more responsible expression of sadness at the emptiness and meaninglessness of life, either chronically or periodically. In the process of psychotherapy, the person with a symbiotic character will encounter this grief at the void in his own life in the same way as does the narcissist. This realization and the grief it brings are important to experience as a true experience of a real self.

Cognition

Central to understanding the cognitive aspects of the symbiotic character is his confusion about self-other boundaries. The experience of the self and other as fused may be held consciously or may be totally disavowed or repressed. But whether conscious, partially conscious, or unconscious, the underlying assumptions of the cognitive errors in the symbiotic have to do with this self-other fusion. There is not a realistic perception of who is responsible for what in lower functioning "borderline" structures, so there is a greater tendency for the individual to hold others responsible for her actions or states of mind. The "borderline" tends more in therapy as in life, toward transference acting-out and "turning passive into active" (Weiss & Sampson, 1986). Transference acting-out refers to the pathological reaction in which the individual sees the other as the original frustrating figure but without acknowledgement of the transference process, so that, unaware of the projective nature of the stimulus, he acts-out as if the other were as truly frustrating as he is experienced. Turning passive into active refers to the process in which the individual frustrates the other in the way that he himself was earlier frustrated. For the present character structure, this might be manifested by the individual expressing extreme disappointment in and rage at the other for failing to adequately understand, antici-pate, and remedy his needs.

At higher levels of functioning, however, the tendency toward merger more often expresses itself in the excessive responsibility taken for the well-being of others. For the symbiotic characters in the neurotic range and higher, the concepts of separation guilt and survivor guilt (Modell, 1965, 1971) will prove particularly useful. In these cases, the child's natural tendencies toward "omnipotent responsibility" have been reinforced rather than gently disabused, so that the individual believes that his individuation will literally hurt the one he loves and on whom he depends. The belief is that separa-tion really hurts the other and that one is responsible for that hurt. Nor far removed from this is the magical notion of survivor guilt: the belief that the positive experience of life itself will be purchased at the expense of the other. Having anything good in life is, in this inaccurate model of reality, the result of taking it away from some-one else. Weiss (in Weiss & Sampson, 1986, p. 43), writes, "the child may develop guilt . . . not only about motives such as incest and murder, which are generally considered reprehensible, but also about reasonable and generally accepted goals, such as becoming stronger or deriving greater enjoyment from life. Indeed, a person may suffer from guilt or anxiety about relaxing, or about feeling healthy and happy."

Many individuals with this characterological issue were told dis-creetly and repetitively that they were indeed responsible for their parent's well-being and that separation in any form—from adventure to difference of opinion to self-expression in which the parent could or would not engage—was injurious to that parent. This "How could you do this to me, your parent?"message reinforces what appears to be the child's natural tendency to err in the direction of "omnipotent responsibility." Furthermore, this kind of conditioning occurs during developmental periods in which it is vitally important for the child to maintain solidly positive ties to the parent, and during which he will sacrifice almost anything to do so. So it is no wonder that the child will accept and identify with the parent's construction of reality and then see himself as bad to the extent that he does not live up to it.

If the symbiotic individual could have separated gradually and with support, the other would have become gradually less vital and central to her sense of identity. However, because that did not occur, the other remains vital to the symbiotic character at an emotional level, as is normal for a young child between one and two years of age. This is an extremely debilitating set with which to enter adult life, particularly in modern Western cultures. The solution constructed maintains symbiotic contact with the other while, at the same time, living an adult life with all its autonomous contacts.

Underneath the complexity of highly neurotic solutions, one will often find the script decisions or "pathogenic beliefs" of the following nature: "I am nothing without you. I owe you myself. I don't deserve what you can't share. I deserve punishment for my success. I can't be happy unless you are. I am responsible for your unhappiness," etc. These beliefs are often unconscious for a number of reasons. They may have been verbally disavowed by the very parent who promulgated them nonverbally; they may have been disavowed by the individual in order for him to survive in the world, they may be seen by his rational conscious mind as inappropriate, etc. Underlying all this, one often finds the belief, often based on threats or on actual experience, that the assertion of one's autonomy will result in abandonment. Particularly to the extent that this is true and to the extent that one faces adult life with the emotional organization of a child, this is very effective in keeping the individual from truly emerging. As these sorts of beliefs are uncovered in psychotherapy, the intricacy of what Modell has termed "mental bookkeeping" can be truly remarkable. For example, an individual might pay for his success by not enjoying it or in some way sabotaging himself. Because of the internalization, it's often the case that the individual will replicate the more self-destructive patterns of his parent in this bookkeeping effort.

As with the other structures where the primary psychic trauma occurs in the process of individuation (i.e., narcissistic and masochistic), the central objective of psychotherapy is the resurrection and development of the true self. This process first involves the discovery and then selective removal or modification of those aspects of self that are solely the product of incorporative introjection, inappropriate indoctrination, self-destructive identification, and inappropriate decisions. While this "false self" is not as obviously false as in the narcissistic personality, it is, nonetheless, artificial, adopted, and imposed. The erosion of this malignant self will leave a void and an emerging need for the discovery and development of a true sense of self, a realistic self-concept, and a set of behaviors that defines the self. In higher functioning individuals, the void may be more easily filled, as the individual takes ownership of that part of his life with which he can truly identify and uses his considerable skills to develop additional areas of self-functioning. In lower functioning individuals, the entire process will take longer because there is greater requirement for the remedying of deficits and some substantial filling of a real void. In either case, there will be periods of the experience of the void and a need for the therapist to deal with this phenomenology in the patient.

Psychotherapy of the symbiotic issue involves taking ownership of the self and rebuilding it where it has been enfeebled. Fortunately, however, the *feelings* of enfeeblement are usually more regressed than the actual development of the self. Indeed, one popular compromise solution for the symbiotic character involves the development of the capacities of the self while denying such capacities. Once the right to ownership of the self is reclaimed, a relatively speedy recovery is possible for these individuals.

THERAPEUTIC OBJECTIVES

Affective Objectives

The central affective therapeutic objective with the symbiotic character is to assist the individual in expressing himself more freely, particularly expressing those affects that have been inhibited and disallowed. Most often, this involves the expression of assertion, aggression, and hostility, though often other more benign affects are also involved. To effect this, the therapy for all those other than the acting out borderline must reduce the individual's sense of obligation to others, his generalized guilt at self-expression, and particularly, his fear of hurting others through self-expression or succeeding at others' expense. Somewhere along the way, the therapy will have to involve accessing the client's real hostility at others, usually at the imagined or real restraint or intrusion that they are seen to impose.

Frequently, the psychotherapy of the symbiotic character will involve dealing with affective states that grow out of identification with the affective states of others—usually the parent. It is not uncommon, for example, to see individuals in this category who experience life as overwhelming, extraordinarily unfair, depriving, abusive, etc., not so much because this was their *direct* experience, but because it was the experience of their immediate and even extended family. These "adopted affects" need to be understood for what they are and returned to their original owners. Often, the patient's family has encouraged this kind of maladaptive identification and indoctrinated the patient with the notion that to be good is to feel for others, particularly the family, in these ways. As all these negative affects and discriminations are elicited, the individual will need to be carried through the fears of her own destructiveness and the fears of abandonment and retaliation which all this can elicit. Such a patient can be helped to see that such fears are the result of earlier conditioning, the kinds of cognitive errors that are typical of young children, as well as of the accumulation of her own aggression and hostility.

A second common conflictual theme involves closeness vs. distance. Often, the therapist will need to normalize and give permission for the client's natural impulses—particularly those involving the need to distance. The therapist can also help the symbiotic individual understand similar impulses in others, thereby affecting the client's fear of abandonment. An overall theme of the therapy of the symbiotic character will be the modulation of the self-other boundary. Particularly as the person is developing the capacities for increased closeness, she will experience enhanced fears of engulfment, of "losing herself" in the needs and personality of another.

The personal growth of the symbiotic person will be suffused with loss—loss of the compensatory characteristics of the self, realization of the historical loss of the real self, and not infrequently, loss of significant others who have been, like the parent burdensome to the patient. Furthermore, to the extent that the person has not completed grieving for the losses of loved ones, this empathic grief must be finally worked through.

Finally, the symbiotic individual needs permission for pleasure in life. In particular, he needs to develop the ability to enjoy and take pride in his self-expression and its results. He may need to learn that not only is it OK to be powerful, but it's OK to enjoy being powerful. Adventure, indulgence, and accomplishment are all a part of his birthright, and he is entitled to their enjoyment. In short, the symbiotic character needs to learn that it's OK to be himself; it's OK to be different; it's OK to have pleasure; it's OK to be proud of himself; it's OK to be satisfied, even if others can never be satisfied, and others' satisfaction in life is not his responsibility. Except for obvious modification for the acting out borderline, the following are the affective objectives for the symbiotic character:

1. Increase self-expression of feelings.
2. Decrease guilt for all self-expression.
3. Decrease sense of obligation to others.
4. Decrease fear of hurting others or succeeding at others' expense.
5. Decrease harmful affects which are the result of identifications with family or with family-imposed role.
6. Access aggression and calm the anxiety at its expression.
7. Access and correctly aim hostility, particularly at restraining and intrusive others.
8. Encourage pride and enjoyment in self-expression, power, adventure, accomplishment, success, indulgence, etc.
9. Assist in modulation of "optimal distance" through allowance and acceptance of impulses for closeness and distance.
10. Reduce fear of abandonment.
11. Reduce fear of engulfment.
12. Access and work through grief at the loss of the real self, the compensatory self relinquished in therapy, and destructive relationships relinquished during therapy.
13. Work through the grief for the losses sustained by parents or family.
14. Enhance the sense of self.

Cognitive Objectives

Perhaps the central theme of the psychotherapy of the symbiotic character will be the repeated uncovering and correction of patho-

genic beliefs, script decisions, and inappropriate introjects and identifications. Almost always, this will involve the uncovering of a belief
that self-expression will harm others—particularly parents or their
psychic equivalents in current life, and the belief that the good things
or feelings of life are acquired at the expense of these others. The
fusion of the symbiotic self with a significant other is typically maintained in numerous and often marvelously intricate ways. The analytic therapy of the symbiotic character will, to a great extent, involve interpretations that highlight the preservation of this kind of
internal fixed relationship. This can involve the incorporation of
affects, belief structures, and behaviors that are really authentic attributes of another. Repeated insight into this adopted identity in all
realms of experience will be necessary for the relinquishing of the
symbiotic's compensatory self. A well-developed understanding of
the symbiotic's history and arrested cognitive development will be
necessary to extricate him from the family of origin and his pathogenic role in it. Repeated help in reality relatedness, particularly in
the area of social obligation and responsibility, may be needed to
correct the symbiotic's tendency toward creating social enmeshment
and expecting it from others.

Insight into the particular nature of compromise solutions to essential symbiotic conflicts will be required. In other words, how has
the individual been able to solve the problems of being aggressive
while denying it, of being successful while failing to acknowledge or
enjoy it, or being adventurous while being anxiety-ridden in adventure, etc. Uncovering the "games that symbiotics play" with particular emphasis on the passive-aggressive maneuvers they employ will
often be productive.

The symbiotic's arrested development in the issues of rapprochement often leads to the maintenance of splitting in adult life. Others
are typically seen as good when they are indulgent and bad when
they are not, while the self is seen as good when indulging others as
demanded and bad or guilty when not. Awareness of this ambitendency and maturation to ambivalence about the self and others is
often a very necessary aspect of the treatment, particularly at the
lower ranges of structural development. Finally, perhaps the most
basic theme of the symbiotic's successful psychotherapy will involve
the identification, development, and accurate labeling of a concept
of self. This involves finally answering the questions, "Who am I?"

in terms of one's ambitions, abilities, aptitudes, skills, preferences, tastes, etc. Sometimes the realization by the client that she really likes or dislikes something very simple but idiosyncratic signals or symbolizes the accomplishment of self-identification. The cognitive objectives for the symbiotic character are:

1. Access pathogenic beliefs underlying separation and survivor guilt.
2. Develop insight into patterns that serve to preserve a fused relationship with parent(s).
3. Develop insight into patterns based on excessive or pathogenic identification with parent(s).
4. Develop insight into the nature of one's real self (i.e., tastes, skills, aptitudes, etc.).
5. Develop memory for and understanding of the family and the history that produced the symbiotic self.
6. Assist with the realistic perception of the social environment (e.g., spouse, parents, coworkers, etc.).
7. Assist with the realistic assessment of social responsibility and obligation.
8. Decrease splitting and increase ambivalence in perception of self and others.
9. Increase awareness of compromise patterns such as passive aggression and "game" interactions which express while denying aggression, hostility, success, etc.
10. Confront manipulative behavior which seeks to maintain merger and externalize responsibility.

Behavioral/Social Objectives

It is really in the context of the client's current social environment that he must extricate himself from an identity based on fusion and establish an identity that is more his own. It is often the case that current relationships replicate and thus preserve historical, pathological ones. These must either be changed or dropped. Where the weight of a pathological history is compounded by the weight of a pathological interpersonal present, many changes will be hardwon. Yet, it is these very contemporary relationship problems that often enhance the reconstruction of the original ones. Where the patient's reactions are more purely transferential and the environment is not cooperating in the patient's current imprisonment and, particularly where the positive changes will be welcomed by the social environment, the therapeutic gains can be more easily and rapidly achieved.

As distinct from affects and thoughts, it is important in the behavioral-social arena for the therapist to support, encourage, identify, and even directly instruct the client in those social behaviors that express individuation and effectively modulate closeness and distance. Though more traditional psychodynamic therapists may have difficulty with such direct interventions in the social sphere, I believe that it is appropriate to assist the client in understanding and managing his social environment. This is particularly true with the symbiotic patient, who is likely to be required to deal with significant others who are intrusive and binding in their communications. It is not uncommon for these patients to need some more practical and concrete assistance in extricating themselves from these aspects of relationships, if not the relationships themselves. This means practical assistance in the behaviors required for mobilizing, expressing, and modulating aggression and hostility.

Finally, we define ourselves—we know who we are—by our behavior, by our social relationships, by those with whom we choose to identify, and by those qualities we choose to internalize and make our own. The symbiotic character is helped immensely by understanding all of that and orienting to those behaviors and those others who will, in these ways, help him define himself. The building of identity is an active process, and sometimes a very active therapy is necessary to assist in achieving it. The following are some behavioral objectives for the symbiotic character.

1. Support behavior that expresses individuation from significant others.
2. Identify and support behavior that represents true self-defining expression and thereby furthers the experience of a real self.
3. Directly instruct or support social behaviors that smoothly modulate closeness and distance.
4. Assist in the behaviors for the mobilization, expression, and modulation of aggression and hostility in the client's "real" world.
5. Assist the client in using the past and present social environment for useful identifications and internalizations.

CHAPTER 6

Insights from Psychoanalysis
and Family Therapy

THIS CHAPTER IS THE MOST theoretical and difficult of the book. In spite of my efforts to translate and simplify object relations theory, some of it remains necessarily dense. The work of Fairbairn, in particular, will require some careful study and contemplation. For the depth of understanding that is possible, one will need to study the original sources. But it is worth it. The material reviewed and synthesized here is, in my view, among the most important available for executing therapy that truly transforms character. Though reviewed in the context of the symbiotic issue, these ideas apply to all character structures.

All of the contributions offered here concern the processes used in internalizing structures that contribute to health and pathology. This knowledge is then used to guide us in exorcizing that pathology and strengthening that health. What follows is no mere intellectual exercise. These are the most essential building blocks of a model that, for me, best represents the reality of psychopathology, health, and change.

OBJECT RELATIONSHIPS

Before getting dense, let's make it simple. Object relations theory, which can be so esoteric and confusing, can also be profoundly simple in its suggestion that we conceptualize psychological symptoms as relationships between internal structures, selves, ego states, etc. In this, object relations theory has a lot in common with the often simpler notions of transactional analysis and gestalt therapy. But, after having studied all of them, it appears very clear to me that the psychoanalytically derived object relations theory gives a far more complete and generative model of the phenomena in question. For example, someone who is perfectionistic can be seen as having internalized the critical, exacting, hard-to-please parent. When perfectionism rules, the individual is treating himself as he was treated. Another relationship to self is typically expressed when the individual procrastinates, flares in temper, or sulks and withdraws in response to an external critic or becomes extraordinarily anxious at the prospect of some external criticism. Both types of relationship to self and objects are developmentally arrested in that the perfectionism tends to be quite absolute and uncompromising, and the various reactions to it are typical of a child who feels powerless and unable to appropriately control resulting emotions.

To understand these symptoms as expressions of relationships between internal structures, to explain them in terms of "who's on" at the moment, and to explain mysteriously alternating symptomatology of this sort can be extremely valuable to therapist and client. The insight itself is, of course, worth a lot, but, in addition, it guides the therapist in structuring interventions and the client in structuring his life to be emotionally corrective. This chapter is really about discovering the intricacies and details of developing this understanding. To the extent that this material is confusing, I would suggest the return to the simple notion of symptoms, or any form of self-expression for that matter, as a reflection of internal self-object relationships. Seeing human behavior from that perspective is for me what object relations theory is really all about.

FAIRBAIRN'S CONTRIBUTION

It was perhaps Fairbairn who first gave voice to the oft-noted phenomenon of the extreme attachment of abused children to their abusive parents. Indeed, it was his work with this population that first led him to a theory that could explain this extremely strong attachment to undeniably "bad" objects and, by extension, explain much of human psychopathology. Fairbairn also noticed the difficulty these children had in recalling instances of abuse and the high level of denial they exhibited in dealing with it. These observations figure heavily in Fairbairn's theory of psychic structure, which emphasizes our denial and repression of the badness of primary objects, our profound attachment to them, and our internalization of them.

Fairbairn's observations on internalization came out of his experience with schizoid patients and patients with "war neuroses." In both classes of psychopathology, Fairbairn repeatedly observed patients who were "haunted" or "possessed" by self-hating and self-destructive internal forces. From these and other observations, Fairbairn (1952) cataloged the evolution of his theory of psychic structure in his only book, *An Object Relations Theory of the Personality* which contains his work from 1940 to 1951. He later summarized and updated his work in a single page containing 17 basic points (Fairbairn, 1963). This approach relies on his unique view of the processes of the internalization of objects and the splitting and repression of "bad" objects that I will outline.

One of Fairbairn's earliest and most central propositions is that "libido" — that hypothetical, innate form of mental energy — is *object seeking*. In other words, the most basic objective of the organism is not, as in classical Freudian theory, to reduce tension but rather to establish connection with others.

The second basic underlying theme of Fairbairn's work involves the processes of *internalization* through which the individual is believed to adopt the qualities and functions of significant others. Though he vacillated, over the years, in his beliefs about whether and how individuals internalize the good components of others, he was consistent about and gave most attention to his theories on the internalization and repression of the bad components of objects. Essentially, Fairbairn proposed that when others are experienced as frustrating or pain inducing, they are internalized in these negative functions. This internalization is motivated by several factors. First, the child internalizes what is bad in order to achieve control over it. Second, he internalizes what is bad in order to remove the badness from the object on whom he is dependent and thereby maintains a sense of security in the external world, albeit at the price of internal insecurity. Fairbairn also suggests, particularly in later writings, that internalization of the other's characteristics may simply be an endogenous characteristic of humans.

The remainder of the theory involving the internalization of bad objects relies on the phenomena of *splitting* and *repression*. Fairbairn suggests that the bad objects that are internalized are split by the child into what he has termed the "rejecting" and the "exciting" object. The rejecting object is, of course, that part of the original primary object that was punishing and frustrating to the individual's libidinal attempts to make connection. This structure operationalizes the individual's negative expectation of others and is the ground from which such negative projections spring. The exciting object, by contrast, represents the individual's hope for the gratification of his original organismic needs. This structure operationalizes the individual's often idealistic and infantile expectations of others for primitive gratification and is the basis of this kind of "positive trans-ference."

To review briefly, these original organismic needs include the need for safety, holding, nurturance, recognition, sexuality, etc. But now, this painful drama, in which the self is excited by the promise but rejected and disappointed by the reality, is internal. In response to the pain this disappointment, the individual does two things, accord-ing to Fairbairn: She splits and represses. The split involves (1) the individual's need for the object and (2) the painful rejection of the self by the object. The need of the self for the potentially gratifying aspects of the other represents one side of the split (libidinal self relating to libidinal object as in Figure 1). This self needs, both libidinally and primitively. It is arrested. It reaches for this libidinal object who is expected to gratify completely and unconditionally. The rejection is represented in the other side of the split (antilibidinal self to antilibidinal object, Figure 1). This rejected self is, according to Fairbairn, experienced as unconditionally or intrinsically bad. This rejecting object represents the internalized block to the life-supporting needs of the person.

In this model, both of these split self-object relationships are re-pressed together with the "libidinal" impulses that join or attach them. Such libidinal impulses include the object-seeking need, love, and attraction to the potentially gratifying other, as well as the natu-ral aggression and hostility of the rejected self toward the rejecting other and the natural attachment of the rejected self to the reject-ing other. In other words, a bad object is better than none and, therefore, yields an attachment. Remember, even the most abused children often want to return to their parents.

Fairbairn suggests that the repression achieved here is accom-plished by the aggression of the core self toward these structures. Fairbairn also hypothesizes that it is the aggression on the part of the rejecting object *and* the rejected self that keeps the libidinal self-

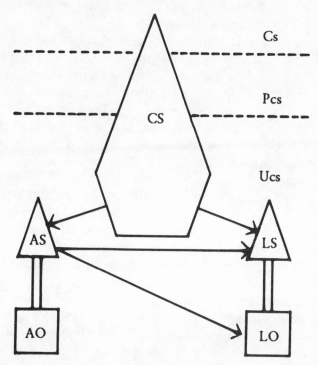

Figure 1
FAIRBAIRN'S MODEL OF PSYCHIC STRUCTURE
(After Fairburn, 1958, p. 105.)

CS, Core Self (Central Ego); AS, Antilibidinal Self (Internal Saboteur); LS, Libidinal Self
(Libidinal Ego); AO, Antilibidinal Object (Rejecting Object); LO, Libidinal Object (Exciting
Object); Cs, Conscious; Pcs, Preconscious; Ucs, Unconscious.
————>, Aggression; ══════, Libido

expressions repressed. Fairbairn does not see repression as a consequence of the oedipal complex but as a much earlier phenomenon
derived through this process of internalization, splitting, and mobilization of aggressive energy against the structures and their associated
libidinal and aggressive impulses.

This process of internalization, splitting, and repression results in
patterns of internal object relations or "role relationship models," à
la Horowitz (1979), which may then be carried out internally and/
or transferred to external situations. Anyone familiar with the work

of Masterson, which I will review presently, will see the almost identical configuration in his system.

The only remaining feature to be considered in Fairbairn's model is the internalization of the "good" object. As noted, Fairbairn vacillated on this point but began and ended with the following position. First, he hypothesized that we all internalize a "pre-ambivalent" object in the early days of life, prior to splitting. Second, he hypothesized that we split off and internalize the good aspects of the object and retain them as an ego ideal (relabeled here as the ideal self).

I have reconstructed Fairbairn's 1952 model in Figure 1, with some renaming of the structures as indicated, in hopes of making the whole theory a bit more contemporary and comprehensible. Essentially, I have merely replaced "self" for "ego," because I consider the construct of self to be more holistic and comprehensive. This designation of self is akin to Berne's "ego states" or to Horowitz's "states of mind," in which there tends to be a characteristic set of self-schemas, self-concepts, affects, underlying belief structures, etc. Thus, the libidinal self, as designated here, would be that repressed and arrested constellation wherein the oral character might be needy and reaching for more-or-less primitive forms of need gratification, or the narcissistic character might be reaching for mirroring and the idealizable other. The object representation of the potentially gratifying object would, in each case, be that "exciting" image of the totally gratifying other, the perfect mirror, or the ideal selfobject whom one might emulate.

The *antilibidinal object* is that internal experience or expectation of the frustrating, punishing, disappointing other. The *antilibidinal self* or "internal saboteur" is that internal self-frustrator who unconsciously reproduces the original prohibitions, frustrations, and punishments. Any of these unconscious structures or the role-relationship models that can be derived from them create potentials for projection. I have retained the word "libidinal" as a shorthand for the original self-expression seeking contact. To reduce rather than enhance confusion, I have also included Fairbairn's original labels in parentheses in Figure 1.

With regard to the formation of the ego ideal or ideal self, Fairbairn asserts that among the motivational factors affecting the operation of this structure is the fact that it realizes the possibility of a conditional goodness of the self. The internalized bad objects are, in his words, "unconditionally or libidinally bad," i.e., they reject the core self and its true self-expression. The ideal self, like Sullivan's "security operation" or Winnicott's "false self," represents the hope that the person can earn back that unified state of grace that was presumably present before the split of the self. In this sense, Fairbairn's original concept of the central ego representing an originally unified structure is identical to Kohut's concept of the "core self" which I have substituted here.

Whenever we are faced with a model as complex as this one, I think we are obliged to ask ourselves how useful it is in helping us understand the phenomena. For myself, I have struggled quite a bit with the necessity for these dual self-object structures. It has always been obvious to me, as Reich (1949) pointed out long ago, that we join the environment in contracting against our own impulses when they are significantly frustrated or punished. But why complicate this simple and profound insight by invoking an internal model of a natural self being rejected by an *internalized* other *and* by an aggressive "antilibidinal" self? And why further complicate it by a model of coalitions held together by libidinal forces, i.e., antilibidinal object coalesced with antilibidinal self and libidinal object with libidinal self (see Figure 1)?

After much deliberation, I have decided that there are very real and multiple advantages to this more complicated format. In general, this format provides the basic map for role-relationship models (Horowitz, 1979), which usefully capture the individual's multiple relationships with himself and others. As Berne (1964) so clearly pointed out in *Games People Play*, individuals often seem quite adept at playing all the various roles in these stereotypical games that structure their lives. "Victims," for example, turn the tables repeatedly and become "persecutors." The persecutors then become victims, and the victims become "rescuers," etc. These internal role-relationship models, which Fairbairn's theory elaborates, help us and our clients to understand more significant aspects of intrapersonal and interpersonal labyrinths. The model also provides a tool for understanding what many have observed to be a ubiquitous phenomenon: Individuals tend to fall in love with, or be "excited" by, others who in some significant way replicate the frustration or rejection of the original primary object. Simultaneously, however, the excitement usually has to do with the experience of promised gratification.

Thus, I believe this more complex model of self-object relations is worth the considerable effort required to understand it.

What is perhaps the most salient point in Fairbairn's generally applicable theory for the symbiotic issue is the utility of the model for explaining resistance to change, the negative therapeutic reaction, and the maintenance of the pathological "internal closed system" of self-object relations. According to Fairbairn, it is the binding nature of the repressed libidinal self-expression seeking the repressed object promising gratification, as well as the libidinal connection of the antilibidinal self to the antilibidinal object, that holds this structure together and maintains stasis. Further, it is the aggressive forces outlined in the model (see Figure 1) that maintains the repression.

Let us remember now where we started—(1) the observation that abused children tend to deny and forget their abuse while remaining very attached to their abusing parents, and (2) traumatized adults (i.e., schizoids and those suffering "war neuroses") tend to be plagued by internal malevolent forces. Fairbairn writes,

> A peculiar situation arises when the object has been internalized and repressed; for, in these circumstances, we are confronted with a situation in which libido is seeking a repressed object. . . . The phenomenon to which I desire to direct attention is that, in the circumstances mentioned, libido is, for practical purposes, operating in the same direction as repression. It is captivated by the repressed objects; and, owing to the lure of the repressed object, it is driven into a state of repression by the very momentum of its object seeking. *When the object is a repressed object, accordingly, the object cathexis operates as a resistance; and the resistance encountered in analytical therapy is thus maintained, not only by the agency of repression but also by the dynamic qualities of libido itself.* (1952, p. 73)

It is crucial to note something here that Fairbairn did not emphasize as much as we might now while taking a more developmental perspective on object relations. All of these structures are arrested developmentally. The libidinal self seeks a gratification appropriate to a child. The perceived libidinal "exciting" object is one who promises to provide that primitive gratification. The antilibidinal self and object are similarly arrested with all the primitiveness and simplicity which that implies. So, both the libidinal and antilibidinal structures are alien or not truly representative of the contemporary self. The antilibidinal structures are unintegrated adoptions from the environment, and the libidinal structures are immature or primitive forms of the real self.

These patterns of internal object relations, then, are inevitably played out in a person's relationships, therapeutic and otherwise. One popular form of this occurs when the individual experiences the self as libidinally needy and the other as libidinally gratifying (libidinal self to libidinal object). An alternative (and often alternating) state of affairs is maintained when the individual experiences the self as libidinally needy and the other as libidinally rejecting or frustrating (libidinal self to antilibidinal object).

The clearest example of these alternating self-object relations is in the lower functioning person's vacillation between idealization and devaluation of the other. Where defenses have been developed to any significant degree, devaluation is typically accompanied by an intensification of the antilibidinal turning against the self, such that the individual cuts off or denies his own libidinal needs and presses on in this defensive posture. This antilibidinal-self pattern can be seen clearly with the oral character who defends by denying his own needs in the unconscious assumption that no one will ever meet them. This same pattern is seen in the narcissist, who mobilizes his grandiose false self in reaction to disappointment. When this compensated false self relates to those who are believed to need him and who are seen as only reinforcing this compromised self, you have another example of the antilibidinal self relating to the antilibidinal object.

What is fascinating to me about Fairbairn's model is the many ways in which it codifies and explains these maneuvers, both in internal experience and in interaction with others, such that the repressed, and thereby closed, internally determined system, is maintained. At bottom, the preservation is due to the developmentally arrested need, love, and attachment of the self to the bad object. This "libidinal" need, love, and attachment to what has been internalized prevent, in a very real way, the need, love, and attachment from being directed outside the self, where there is at least the possibility of gratification and maturation of these natural impulses. Essentially, Fairbairn's notion of maturation involves the evolution of the individual from a mode of object relations that is oral, "taking," and incorporative of an undifferentiated other into a mature dependence in which the object is experienced as differentiated from the self and is related to primarily through giving.

This evolution, which is essentially the same as that posited by Kohut, emphasizes the transition from relating to others as primitive self-objects to using others for their realistic self-object functions while seeing them as external, "real" objects in the world. Accordingly, Fairbairn's prescription for the therapist is similar to that of Kohut, though the emphasis in language may differ. "The release of bad objects from the unconscious is one of the chief aims which the psychotherapist should set himself out to achieve, even at the expense of severe transference neurosis for it is only when the internalized bad objects are released from the unconscious that there is any hope of their being dissolved. The bad objects can only be safely released, however, if the analyst has become established as a sufficiently good object for the patient. Otherwise, the resulting insecurity may prove insupportable" (Fairbairn, 1974/1952, pp. 69–70). Elsewhere, Fairbairn (1958, p. 381) states,

> For such a change to accrue, it is necessary for the patient's relationship with analyst to undergo a process of development in terms of which a relationship is based on transference becomes replaced by a realistic relationship between two persons in the outer world . . . it also represents the establishment of an open system in which the distortions of inner reality can be corrected by outer reality and true relationships with external objects can occur.

Thus, while the transference is necessary for eliciting the various unconscious structures and role-relationship models, both Fairbairn and Kohut stand with the camp of analysts who see the necessity for a real "good enough" external relationship with the therapist to produce the "strengthened context" in which the bad objects may be released from unconsciousness as well as from cathexis and then be replaced by real external relationships in which gratification and maturation of need are possible.

What I find particularly useful about Fairbairn's theoretical model is the unique personification of the particular self-schema and associated role-relationship models that explain an individual's various states. Associated with this is the great explanatory and therapeutic potential of the libidinal and aggressive forces which preserve the closed and fixed pathological system of relating to oneself and others.

Fairbairn is remarkably correct, I think, in asserting that therapeutic change consists of the release from repression of bad objects and their associated affects so that there may be a realistic gratification and a maturation of these libidinal self-expressions in the real external world involving an uncertain but open system. That he developed these insights in the isolation of Scotland, through the modification of classic psychoanalysis in the early 1940s, is even more remarkable. Although it is true that Wilhelm Reich came to some essentially similar conclusions before him, Fairbairn added an object relations orientation and model that make unique contributions to providing the necessary understanding, uncovering, and repair.

MASTERSON'S CONTRIBUTION

On the basis of his work with both adult and adolescent borderline patients, James Masterson has contributed a useful description of one type of borderline etiology and its resulting symptomatology. Masterson's model of the borderline's internal object relations is very similar to that of Fairbairn's, relying, as it does, on the concept of a split self-object role-relationship model to explain the borderline's disturbed perceptions and behaviors. While Masterson's contributions concerning this internal structure are of interest, I believe that his most salient contributions to the problem at hand is this: He clearly outlined the environmental contingencies that can result in intense problems in mastering the symbiotic issue. Masterson (1976, pp. 37–38) writes,

The mother of the borderline patient usually suffers from a borderline syndrome herself. . . . Having not been able to separate from her own mother, she fosters continuation of the symbiotic union with her child, thus encouraging dependence to maintain her own emotional equilibrium. She is threatened by and unable to deal with the infant's emerging individuality and therefore clings to the child to prevent separation, discouraging moves toward separation by withdrawing her support.

Masterson was the first to formulate so clearly these contingencies wherein the parent is more or less nurturing and responsive to those behaviors that keep the child close, dependent, fused, or similar to the parent, but the parent is anxious, withdrawn, punitive, and otherwise libidinally unavailable when the child moves away, demonstrates opposition or dissimilarity, or in any way individuates and becomes autonomous.

This is the essential etiology of what I term the symbiotic character. I use this terminology because current research on those diagnosed as borderline suggests that there are at least five distinct types of borderline condition (Andrulonis, 1982). Some of these syndromes have a functional etiology, while others have a more organic one. Furthermore, not everyone with this symbiotic etiology becomes truly borderline, yet they do usually have issues concerning autonomy. While this etiology does appear to be common in functional borderline syndromes, other etiological constellations can certainly result in "borderline" functioning. In particular, the schizoid, oral, and narcissistic issues can result in behaviors which are characteristically "borderline."

It makes more sense to me, theoretically and practically, to classify psychopathology by the characterological-developmental issue that it represents. "Borderline" has been a very necessary and useful "garbage can" category, and it is only recently that it has been sorted out into at least some of its many subcategories. Also, it has always seemed to me an oxymoron to label someone a high-functioning borderline. But a person with a symbiotic issue may be quite high functioning, albeit with difficulties in maintaining self-other boundaries and autonomy. I tend to use the term "borderline" for describing functional pathology characterized by low levels of structural development. With that orientation, one may speak of a borderline schizoid, oral, narcissistic, or symbiotic individual, thereby communicating that that person may have a high probability of ego breakdown under stress.

Be that as it may, Masterson has made it very clear how an individual with this kind of symbiotic etiology can develop into an adult who seeks to preserve, both intrapsychically and interpersonally, a regressive dependency and fusion with the gratifying other. In his earlier works, Masterson termed this relationship of the gratifying internal self-object to the gratified self as the "rewarding object relations unit" or RORU. This is perfectly analogous to Fairbairn's "exciting" object and libidinal self, as Masterson acknowledges (Masterson, 1976, p. 62). Employing the concept of splitting, Masterson then outlined and described the alternate role-relationship model of the bad self relating to the rejecting or abandoning other. This was termed the "withdrawing object relations unit" or WORU. In this latter state, the other is experienced as attacking, critical, hostile, angry, and withholding, while the self is experienced as inadequate, bad, helpless, guilty, ugly, empty, etc. (Masterson, 1976, p. 58).

These two states of mind, which include characteristic affects, role-relationship models, experience of self, etc., are distinct states from one another and tend to alternate. Thus, many borderlines alternate between states in which they feel good, at least temporarily, as they act-out or otherwise aggressively indulge a childlike dependency, while denying the self-destructive reality of what they are doing. Alternatively, when others fail to be coerced, when the gratifications of acting-out fail to satisfy, or when the negative reality consequences of such behavior catch up, these individuals enter the other polarized state with its self-concepts, role-relationship model, characteristic affects, etc.

At this point, it is probably necessary to outline the fundamental differences between Fairbairn and Masterson in this conceptualization, although a full understanding of it may require the reading of the original works. For this, the reader is referred to Masterson (1976, pp. 55–68) and Fairbairn (1952, pp. 82–136). With a balanced understanding of both of these theoreticians, I am convinced that these theoretical differences will make very little practical difference. However, like any differences, they can be exaggerated and used to justify therapeutic positions based on countertransference. Because of this, understanding the difference may be critical in helping us resolve a classic argument concerning psychotherapy technique, i.e., the advisability of abstinence and neutrality vs. authenticity and support.

The essential difference between Fairbairn and Masterson arises from their initial presuppositions about the nature of the human infant's earliest functioning. Masterson joins Freud in assuming that the child's initial cognitive functioning is "under the domination of the primary process . . . motivated by the pleasure principle" (Masterson, 1976, p. 59). In this mode of functioning, it is assumed that the child attempts to maintain satisfaction through "hallucination," which is "abandoned only in consequence of the absence of expected

gratification" (Freud, 1911). This manner of functioning is then replaced, according to this view, by the reality principle, "because of
the disappointment experienced, the mental apparatus has to decide
to form a conception of real circumstances in the outer world and to
assert itself to alter them" (Freud, 1911).

Masterson's split into RORU and WORU is based on the presup-
position that "a large part of the patient's ego structure fails to un-
dergo this transformation; therefore, there is not a splitting of a
previously formed structure but a failure to coherently develop the
reality principle. This leaves a portion of the ego's structure under
the domination of the pleasure principle rather than the reality principle" (p. 60).

By contrast, Fairbairn's view postulates a functional and unified
structure prior to the split, wherein instinctual impulses are best
understood as object-seeking rather than pleasure-seeking. The experience of pain and frustration result in the splitting of a prior unitary
self. Further, Fairbairn hypothesizes a very early childhood capacity
to repress these split structures, whereas, as is consistent with Freud,
Masterson sees splitting as a more primitive defense which developmentally predates the repression that is a consequence of the oedipal
situation.

Masterson's view then leads to an emphasis on therapeutic confrontation with reality, particularly the reality of separation, the
denial of which "allows a persistence of the wishful reunion." This
illusion of reunion serves as the primary defense against what Masterson has termed the abandonment depression—a catastrophic re-
visiting of the helplessness, void, and despair of a totally dependent
infant cut off from the supplies needed for his survival. Masterson's
therapy for this symbiotic borderline condition involves a therapeutic
alliance between the therapist's healthy ego and the patient's "embat-
tled reality ego." This alliance can sustain the client through the
necessary, but painful and delayed, shift from the dominance of the
pleasure principle to the dominance of the reality principle.

Fairbairn's approach, by contrast, emphasizes more the continued
libidinal need of the self for the object in both its "good" and "bad"
expressions. It is the "aggression" in the internal system of selves and
objects that keeps the nature of all this repressed and out of the
patient's awareness. The objectives of treatment, then, are (1) the
release from the unconscious of these internalized "bad" split objects

and their associated affects and self-representations and (2) the breaking down of "libidinal bonds" or attachments to these internalized structures. In presenting advice on technique, Fairbairn suggests:

1) that situations should be interpreted, not in terms of gratification, but in terms of object relationships (including, of course, relationships with internalized objects); 2) that libidinal striving should be represented to the patient as ultimately dictated by object love, and as, therefore, basically if not superficially, good; 3) that libidinal "badness" should be related to the cathexis of bad objects; 4) that guilt situations should be related by interpretation to "bad object" situations; 5) that caution should be exercised over interpretation in terms aggression except perhaps in the case of depressives who present a special problem for analytic technique. (1952, p. 74)

So, if one wanted to differentiate these two, one would note Masterson's greater emphasis on confronting the borderline individual with his or her denial of the self-destructive consequences of pleasure-seeking behavior. Consistent with this difference, Masterson concentrates more on the need to avoid gratifying the patient's "pleasure ego," because this would maintain the pathology, while Fairbairn concentrates more on providing the patient with a good and real object who can assist the client through the turmoil of release from the oppression of the bad internalized objects. Fairbairn puts much greater emphasis on interpreting all psychopathology as the internalization of bad objects that were, and still are, desperately needed.

But, before taking sides in this imaginary battle, it is important to remember that Fairbairn was not, at least so exclusively, working with borderlines who required limits and reality confrontation. Furthermore, Masterson repeatedly emphasizes the importance of the therapeutic alliance and "communicative matching" and demonstrates the capacity to be a real object in the therapeutic work he reports. Fairbairn, like Masterson and Freud, sees the primary developmental transition from childhood to maturity achieved through the ability to live and relate in external reality rather than in internal reality based upon historically introjected models of the self, others, and the world. I think a balanced reading of both of these contributors yields a great deal of convergence in point of view.

Controversies of this kind often serve simply to provide a focus for a great deal of intellectualized aggression, on the one hand, and support whatever kinds of countertransference errors we are prone to, on the other. In other words, Masterson can be misread to justify what is really a fear of real encounter—a pedagogical, distant, superior, parental approach to clients in the name of the necessary "confrontation with reality." Similarly, Fairbairn, like Alexander and French, Kohut, Rogers, Winnicott, and others can be misread to justify a countertransferentially-based response to clients which is rescuing, infantilizing, colluding, possessive, co-dependent, and enabling in the name of genuine and "good enough" therapy.

Even in deciding which, if any, of these models to use in understanding and conducting psychotherapy, it is most important to remember that these are just models. They are useful fictions which somebody made up to represent reality. As Kegan (1982) has suggested, it is important to rent our theories, not buy them. Buying leads to reification and the kind of investment that makes our own resistance to change pathological.

The current developmental research as interpreted by Stern (1985), Mitchell (1988), Lichtenberg (1983), and others would certainly give more current credence to Fairbairn's model of an initial unitary functioning in the infant with good reality testing and the necessary equipment for good self-other and other-other differentiation. This same research certainly emphasizes the "hardwired" propensity of the infant for social interaction and strongly reinforces Fairbairn's notions about the object-seeking nature of instinctual impulses. Further, Fairbairn's emphasis on the attachment propensities of the individual certainly does seem to lend a beneficent therapeutic reframe to reconstructions, explanations, and interpretations which might otherwise lead the client to decide that the therapist thinks him "bad" in relation to his aggression and other potentially unseemly impulses.

Masterson, however, is consistent with others in recognizing the universality of the transitions of maturation, from predominantly internal need-based object relations, to predominantly external, reality-based object relations. Furthermore, Masterson has contributed greatly to the recognition of the need, when working with borderline patients, to confront what they so persistently deny. Most critical for current purposes, Masterson has cogently outlined the etiology of the symbiotic character all along the continuum of structural development, from personality disorder through character neurosis to character style.

THE CONTRIBUTIONS OF FAMILY THERAPY

The area of family therapy, like that of psychoanalysis, can serve a basic research function for the practice of adult psychotherapy, because the family therapist directly observes the very phenomena that the adult therapist seeks to reconstruct, interpret, and work through. While all of the family therapy case studies and theoretical explorations are of interest here, the family therapists' experience with anorexia nervosa is particularly significant for the study of the symbiotic issue. Whenever family therapists of any school have investigated this problem they have found the anorexic family to be characterized by (1) a high level of enmeshment with insufficient intergenerational boundaries and (2) cross-generational coalitions from which the anorexic child finds it extremely difficult to extricate herself (e.g., see Bruch, 1978; Minuchin, Rosman, & Baker, 1978; Selvini-Palazzoli, 1978). The consistency of these observations across schools and even cultures is quite impressive, and the picture presented is entirely consistent with the etiological constellation of the symbiotic character as conceptualized here.

I have found Selvini-Palazzoli's (1974) description of these cases to be the richest, though, in most respects, it is completely consistent with the observations of other investigators. I will draw primarily from her descriptions to sketch briefly the typical anorexic family. She characterizes the parents in these families as self-denying and martyred and notes that the children often model this way of being. Members of these families view themselves as serving others in the family and tend to avoid direct expressions of their own needs, either stating them indirectly or projecting them onto others. There is, in other words, an absence of direct communication, particularly where needs and wants are concerned, and an avoidance of direct conflict by everyone in the family.

The second distinguishing feature of these families, noted by all investigators, is the presence of cross-generational alliances, which are kept hidden. These alliances involve often subtle communications between the mother and the anorexic daughter or between the father and that daughter which establish, yet hide, that cross-generational dyadic alliance so as to not directly threaten the excluded parent. Not infrequently, the anorexic girl is trapped in a situation where she is expected to have such hidden alliances with both parents simultaneously.

Anorexia, then, develops in this family system when it is time for the child to move toward greater autonomy. Directly asserting independence is extremely difficult because it violates the central family rules: (1) Behave only to satisfy the needs of others, and (2) avoid direct confrontation or conflict. The anorexic symptoms are totally consistent with the family predisposition for self-deprivation. Furthermore, to become anorexic is quite assertive and hostile, yet that can be denied by attributing everything to "the illness." Finally, anorexic behavior has the important function of keeping the daughter a child within the system and thereby preserves the family in its rigid patterns of communication and dyadic alliances.

The more active family therapies of Selvini-Palazzoli and Minuchin are generally short-term and prescriptive with the objectives of breaking up the hidden intergenerational coalitions, establishing intragenerational coalitions, and encouraging direct communication of conflict. This is often done strategically by creating situations that demand the direct expression of wishes in the first person singular.

The typical anorexic case is not, of course, the only family constellation that can give rise to difficulty with separation. These case studies of anorexic girls and their families, however, provide poignant examples of the kinds of complex binds, family rules, and rigid interactional patterns from which many adult psychotherapy clients are still trying to extricate themselves. In the latter cases, the parents are usually no longer available for direct, therapeutic intervention. In a very real sense, the rigid, closed system that the family therapists have documented is now internalized and, as Fairbairn has asserted, held in place by the "libidinal connection" of the individual to her internalized objects. Self-starvation is merely one of the forms people employ to hold the family system together, whether it exists in the current external world or in the intrapsychic world.

Family therapists have still another important lesson on intervention for the adult psychotherapist. In executing their active and prescriptive family therapy, both Selvini-Palazzoli and Minuchin rely a good deal on what the former has labeled "positive connotation."

This refers to a method of interpretation that emphasizes the positive motivation or intention of the people involved. Thus, an enmeshed family may be described not as confining but as unusually loving; or a daughter's anorexia is described not as hostile but as preserving the unity of the family and providing the mother with a job.

This "positive connotation" is also a very significant part of the reframing process in neurolinguistic programming as outlined by Bandler and Grinder (1982), which has its roots in the hypnotic work of Milton H. Erickson. This emphasis on positive intention or motivation is quite consistent with Fairbairn's model, wherein resistance and negative therapeutic reactions are seen to be motivated by the preservation of the libidinal (i.e., loving) ties of the individual to his parental objects. It is, as I have stated earlier, an additional reason for preferring Fairbairn's construal of these phenomena over Masterson's.

It is interesting to note that in the family therapy literature the most ubiquitous interpretation for anorexic, as well as other, problems is that of emphasizing the given problem's role in preserving family unity. While the nature of this interpretation is influenced by the principle of positive connotation, it is also emphasized so frequently because these family observers feel it to be true. It is identical to Fairbairn's interpretation of the literal pull of libidinal ties which preserve a rigid internal system of self-object relations. In both of these cases, then, it is the preservation hypothesis that has been central to the therapeutic reframe or interpretation. The individual, adult psychotherapist may also learn from the active, interpersonal, prescriptive family therapists who, among other things, often construct rituals that serve to communicate interpretations to all members of the family with a drama and power difficult to achieve through consulting-room verbalizations alone.

UNCONSCIOUS GUILT

We are now approaching the last few pieces in the study of the historical origins of the symbiotic characterological issue. The issue is existential, lifelong, and held together by two counterbalancing forces—the strong and innate pull of the interpersonal matrix against the instinctual need of the individual for autonomy, self-expression, and involvement with a wider world. It is clear that what human

beings want is to feel valued and secure in the matrix *and* to venture
out to a wider world to express their individuality. It is also clear
that pathology results when the individual feels he has to choose
between these two objectives and thereby deny an essential part of
the self.

Selvini-Palazzoli argues that the norm in more traditional agrarian
cultures is to emphasize the family, clan, and village. Clearly, the
industrial revolution increased the strength of the opposite pole, resulting in greater pursuit of the needs of the more autonomous self.
In any case, a balance is always required, and when the individual
feels he or she must forsake one pole to have the advantages of the
other, there will be problems.

Niederland (1961) was the first to label one form of such trouble.
In studying survivors of the Holocaust, Niederland found a number
who experienced "a deep and pervasive sense of guilt accompanied
by unconscious or conscious dread of punishment, for having survived the very calamity to which their loved ones succumbed" (1961,
p. 238). Niederland called this "survivor guilt" and hypothesized
that it was based on the unconscious belief that surviving what their
loved ones did not amounted to betrayal. Subsequently, others (e.g.,
Horowitz, 1986; Modell, 1965, 1971) have made the same observations in a much wider context. Modell has described more subtle
forms of "survival" in which "survivors" are plagued by similar forms
of unconscious guilt-motivated behaviors and attitudes which are
self-sabotaging and effectively undo success, happiness, and the ability to thrive. Sometimes, individuals with this issue will consciously
express the guilt, but more often they will simply engage in behaviors
or adopt attitudes that are motivated by it.

Modell has described two types of such guilt. "Separation guilt" is
based on the belief that separation, as defined by leaving home,
being different, opposing the parent, or thriving in ways unattainable
by the parent, etc., will do damage or actually destroy the parent.
The other highly similar form of "survivor guilt" is the belief that "if
one has something good, it is at the expense of someone else being
deprived" (Modell, 1971, p. 342). Friedman (1985) has named this
second form of guilt "depletion guilt." Modell believes that survivor
(depletion) guilt is a potentially universal phenomenon based on the
human being's inborn empathic potentials. This universal empathic
response would, according to Modell, enhance survival of the spe-

cies. Irrespective of how innate this capacity is, it is interesting to note that this ethic appears to be more characteristic of agrarian cultures, as well as the more rigid and self-denying families who can produce anorexic children. Asch (1976) and Lowenwald (1979) have cited the anorexic patient's loyalty to parents and guilt over "abandoning" them, either literally or symbolically, as central in the maintenance of symptoms, the production of negative therapeutic reactions, and the general resistance to positive change.

Weiss and Sampson (1986) also utilize separation and survivor guilt as central constructs for their "control mastery theory" of psychopathology and psychotherapy. They suggest that in order to avoid intense survivor guilt, individuals adopt two strategies which lead to psychopathology: (1) They identify with the suffering parent from whom they cannot separate and manifest similar pathology and suffering, or (2) they comply with what is *perceived* to be the parent's expectation that they will fail to succeed, be happy, coupled, independent, etc. In both cases, these maneuvers maintain a unity with family mediated by pathology. It is, then, the individual's misdirected or exploited empathy that is seen as underlying many forms of self-defeating psychopathology.

However innate this tendency, the literature is consistent in demonstrating that parenting that is associated with anorexia and certain forms of borderline pathology is characterized by a high level of parental dependence on children for fulfillment, together with a high level of unhappiness and disordered communication. The patients' acceptance of the family ethic concerning their obligation to fulfill their parents, combined with their inability to do so, makes it most difficult for them to lead a fulfilling life. That is so because such self-fulfillment would require giving up the assigned task and pursuing activities viewed as selfish, all of which amounts to desertion and betrayal. Friedman (1985, p. 35) emphasizes the role of survivor guilt in the anorexic cases he has treated: "My patients were not motivated as much by their need for maternal care and love as by their need to protect their mothers from real or imagined harm, depression, loneliness, envy, disintegration and so forth."

So, it is here in the psychoanalysis of the interpersonal origins of pathology that we find convergence with the observations of the family therapists. Human behavior can be understood in an interpersonal context. Closed systems exist in families and exist intrapsychically through their internalization. Awareness of the rules of the closed system, appreciation of the powerful motivational force of human connections, and the possibility of opening closed systems underlies both approaches. In particular, providing new avenues for the maintenance and expression of this human connection provides the basis for therapeutic change strategies. Reliance on the object-seeking nature of human impulses is the ground from which the therapeutic strategies are born.

UNCONSCIOUS PLANS: THE WORK OF WEISS AND SAMPSON

Weiss and Sampson (1986) put forth some very optimistic propositions concerning our natural tendencies towards correcting those beliefs, models, and predispositions that bring us anxiety, shame, inhibition, or guilt. Their theory is often referred to as "control mastery theory," in line with their major theoretical proposition that "there *are* powerful unconscious motives, namely, ego motives, which cannot be described as impulses, defenses, or products of conscience. . . . they are directed to solving of problems. . . . they tend to reflect thought, to take obstacles into account, to be reasonable, moderate and adaptive" (Weiss & Sampson, 1986, p. 91). In other words, the ego controls events in the process of seeking mastery. For purposes of understanding psychotherapy, the most important unconscious plans involve those directed at disconfirming pathogenic beliefs—those ideas and models that bring pain. These writers echo Freud in suggesting that the repetition of traumatic experiences in dreams has as its purpose the mastery of trauma. This same kind of repetition is seen in the adult's repetitive talk, which relives the trauma, and the child's analogous repetitive play, which is assumed to have the same purpose. The well-known play-therapy tactic of effecting an alternate outcome of the traumatic event is an example of achieving such mastery, at least symbolically. Adults frequently achieve this same kind of mastery through discussion and future planning.

In the sphere of psychotherapy, therefore, Weiss and Sampson postulate that much of the patient's behavior is motivated by the desire to control and master prior trauma. Thus, the patient's transference reactions may be produced with the unconscious hope that the therapist will *not* react in the same way as the injuring parent.

Rather, there is an unconscious hope that the therapist will do or say something that will disconfirm the patient's pathogenic expectations or role-relationship models based on earlier traumatic experiences. All such maneuvers are viewed as "tests" by Weiss and Sampson—"tests" that the patient unconsciously hopes the therapist will "pass," thereby weakening the pathogenic beliefs and reducing anxiety about making them conscious.

The single-subject research that supports these essential hypotheses is perhaps the most exciting current research in psychotherapy. Their data (Weiss & Sampson, 1986, p. 267–276) show that when a patient's intense transference is followed by the therapist's maintenance of neutrality, the patient's behavior becomes both more relaxed and insightful. Specifically, clients may then recall repressed memories, produce relevant and insight-enhancing associations, confess to repressed feelings, or show enhanced awareness of underlying pathogenic beliefs. In Weiss and Sampson's model of the psychoanalytic process, patient tests repetitively passed by the therapist will lead the patient to progressively deeper self-understanding and disconfirmation of his pathogenic beliefs.

The tests are of two types according to these authors. *Transference tests* occur when the client believes, inaccurately, that he is being treated in the present as he was in the past or assumes that he will be so treated if he acts in a particular way. The most powerful transference tests of this type occur when the patient acts in such a way as to provoke this historical reaction in the therapist. The patient may, for example, become seductive, obsequious (in order to be dominated), limit testing (in order to be dominating), etc. The therapist passes the test by resisting the pull to react in the expected ways and by responding differently, thereby providing disconfirming evidence for the underlying pathogenic beliefs derived from the original experiences. Such pathogenic beliefs or script decisions might include, "I am loved only for my sexuality," "I am too stupid to make my own decisions," "I can control whomever I wish," etc. Technically, in Weiss and Sampson's (1986) definition, pathogenic beliefs include an action statement in an "if/then" format: "If I act smart, then I'll be rejected." Such a statement is more behaviorally precise and indicates what the test will look like. I use this label more generally here and elsewhere simply to refer to pathogenic cognition.

Alternatively, the patient may test by "turning passive into active." As outlined earlier, this test involves the patient treating the other in the way she was originally treated. Thus, someone who was excessively devalued may devalue, one blamed may blame, one dominated may dominate, etc. Again, by responding differently than the patient responded originally, the therapist indirectly challenges the pathogenic belief that resulted from the prior experience. One learns that domination can be resisted, for example, or that undeserved blame can be rejected, thereby challenging one's own prior acceptance of such blame. In Weiss and Sampson's work, this different response generally involves the analyst maintaining neutrality. While this is perhaps the safest way of responding differently and is consistent with analytic practice, it is by no means the only way of responding therapeutically, passing the client's tests, and working to disconfirm the unconscious beliefs.

By outlining this process, Weiss and Sampson have delineated perhaps the single most important active ingredient of "the corrective emotional experience." I think this process is widespread in successful psychotherapy, and that most good psychotherapists pass such tests daily but often with a level of unconscious matching that of the client.

Conceptualizing the therapeutic process in this way provides us with a simple conscious plan for conducting therapy and inoculates us against the naturally occurring human errors that cause us to fail these tests — to be seduced or dominated, infantilizing or dominating, etc. Furthermore, laying this template of pathogenic beliefs and unconscious plans over the templates of character helps to predict a good deal about the course, themes, and tests of psychotherapy. For each characterological issue, we already have a good idea of the constellations of pathogenic beliefs, together with the associated role-relationship models, concepts about self, schemas of the world, etc. Further, for each case, we have a constellation of probable etiological factors that go a long way in predicting the likely transferences and the expected forms of "turning passive into active."

Our knowledge predicts not only the patient's most salient interactions with the therapist but also those with significant others and the objects and requirements of his world. As Weiss and Sampson (1986) have stated, but not fully developed, we all test out these pathogenic beliefs in our lives. Much of our behavior, particularly that with intimate others, can be understood more fully by employing this model. While it is probably most essential to pass the client's tests in the therapeutic process, it will also be extremely useful to point out the patterns of testing in the patient's life more generally. This will be even more therapeutic when the patient tends to test those beliefs on others who do not have the resources to pass them. In these situations, the patient's extra-therapy experiences will be counter-therapeutic and can become therapeutic only insofar as the therapist can help the patient to "stop barking up the wrong tree."

Weiss and Sampson's model achieves an important fourth dimension when we lay it over an object-relations view of pathogenic beliefs. Using Fairbairn's model, we can see that the pathogenic beliefs of the libidinal self are often those developmentally arrested hopes and dreams of child-like gratification that have not been optimally frustrated and that, as a result, have not matured. Such arrested, immature "beliefs" would include the oral's unconscious expectation of complete, unconditional, and nonreciprocal need gratification appropriate to an infant. It would also include the narcissist's unresolved beliefs in his grandiosity and entitlement and the symbiotic's dream of the seamless and perfect merger that will define him. When operating in these infantile ways, the individual will see the other as that "exciting" object who can fulfill these infantile needs.

The pathogenic beliefs that reside in the antilibidinal self, on the other hand, come out of the "internalization of bad objects." Here, the individual is at the mercy of the "internal saboteur" who sabotages, rejects, disappoints, frustrates, and exploits the core self. Operating with the role-relationship model of the "antilibidinal self— antilibidinal object," the individual expects rejection, sabotage, disappointment, frustration, and exploitation from others. This expectation justifies the maintenance of defense. Herein lies the basis of negative transference.

The ability of the client to turn passive into active is consistent with this internal self-object relationship model, wherein the individual can shift from one position to another either in relation to the self or in relation to the other. Weiss and Sampson (1986) postulate that turning passive into active, by virtue of being a more aggressive stance, is safer. They hypothesize that it will generally be seen more in those situations in which the patient feels unsafe. Less safety in psychotherapy can be a function of a more severe original trauma or a relatively less-developed therapeutic alliance. As I stated earlier, in justifying the complexity of the Fairbairn model, its power in explaining these positional shifts is one of the primary reasons for its adoption.

The remainder of this book will be devoted to making all of the ideas presented thus far more concrete by illustrating how they apply in the lives of clients, how they enhance the therapeutic encounter, and how they inform therapeutic techniques. I hope now to make good on my promise by illustrating how the most heady concepts translate into practical work.

PART III

TREATMENT OF THE SYMBIOTIC CHARACTER

CHAPTER 7

Therapeutic Themes

I WAS RECENTLY IN AN AIRPORT and observed a practicing (i.e., 14-month-old) child exploring this crowded and strange environment. She was making many friends, while her mother, who was enjoying her own interactions with strangers, was keeping a watchful-enough eye on her. The mother at times enjoyed the child's playfulness as she tottered around and between the pillars made by people's legs, yet there was no overprotection or intrusion. She was there when necessary but otherwise very much in the background. This stimulating world and the child's emerging abilities served, as they do for every child, the only necessary invitation to autonomy and adventure. This good-enough mother provided support, permission, and, had it been necessary I think, encouragement. She was available for the inevitable "round trips" that all children make as they engage in the process of separating from the former context and emerging into an ever-expanding one. If this mother's behavior in the airport is representative, this child does not have to choose between her own need for individuation and her mother's love.

This unfair choice is the dilemma underlying every symbiotic character. To elucidate and explicate how this occurred in the symbiotic individual's life constitutes that part of the treatment I have labeled "getting the story straight." The initial invitation to autonomy in therapy involves uncovering this illegitimate choice and labeling it as such. While this unresolvable dilemma permeates the symbiotic's life, it is often unconscious and its legitimacy has gone unquestioned. This depriving choice is even more negative than represented because the symbiotic child never *really* gets the mothering love or true connection desired. What is billed as love in these families is actually a kind of exploitative and possessive attachment. It is better than nothing, of course, but it is at once too little and too much.

135

THE SYMBIOTIC CHARACTER AND THE CORRECTIVE
EMOTIONAL EXPERIENCE

The essence of the "corrective emotional experience" for the symbiotic character is to experience such self and world discovery in all
its forms (i.e., adventure, aggression, separation, differentiation,
etc.) within a relationship that, at least, stays constant and, at best,
strengthens and deepens as a function of the interaction. With the
symbiotic person, a good-enough therapist will allow, encourage, or
require, as necessary, the client to be fully herself while simultaneously uncovering all the unconscious internalized demands which
have prevented that outcome. This uncovering comes largely in the
interpretation of transference, both in and outside therapy. The symbiotic character will expect significant others to act like the binding
parent or parents and in relation to others will accommodate or
resist, often finding neurotic compromises of these polar responses
in cyclical vacillation. He may assume that separation or difference
will be threatening to others, that success may inspire envy and
retaliatory rage, that the sharing of failures will ensure a close relationship, etc. The inaccuracy or possible inaccuracy of these assumptions must be brought to the attention of the symbiotic client again
and again in all the various contexts in which he makes them.

While such intervention is useful with respect to every one of the
client's relationships, it is probably most crucial in the therapeutic
relationship itself. In this here-and-now immediate context, the client
can learn over and over again that the therapist does not need to be
enmeshed, to own, or to set limits on the client's self-expression or
other relationships. Further, the client learns she has the freedom to
leave this relationship, to experience the other as less than perfect,
and to criticize without destroying the other or provoking retaliation, etc. In other words, the client can learn that all of these binding,
enmeshing, impinging characteristics of her role-relationship model
are specific only to that relationship in which they were constructed.
Other types of relationships are possible and can be chosen. Finally,
the internal relationship, which consists of aspects of the internalized
negative object relating to aspects of the arrested self, can slowly but
surely be eradicated and replaced by a maturing one based on healthier external relationships.

In many ways, this liberation from others in the external world, especially the therapist herself, is easier to effect than the liberation from the internalized negative other. As Fairbairn has pointed out, there are more degrees of freedom in the outside real world than there are in the internalized object relationships of the symbiotic person. So, when you see the symbiotic client, it is important to have your antennae out for any example of a projected restriction, restraint, envy, or guilt where the client's reality perception can be productively corrected.

In making these interventions, the therapist need only introduce the possibility that these reactions are projected and that another kind of relationship is possible. Because symbiotic individuals frequently involve themselves in enmeshed relationships with enmeshing others, their projections are often justified and confirmed by how others behave. They can, however, often understand that other kinds of relationships are possible, and wherever the therapist can provide such a relationship herself, supporting evidence for that possibility is given. The choice is not between contact and autonomy. It is possible to have both, and, indeed, it is possible to have far more of both than the symbiotic individual has ever experienced before. Indeed, it's quite possible that more autonomy can create more and deeper contact, but this fact must be learned experientially.

I believe that without this externally available alternative there cannot really be a transformation of the internalized self-other relationship that has become a self-self relationship. The role-relationship model cannot be reformed without an alternative relationship. So, "corrective emotional experiences" involving as many others as possible are essential to reforming the individual's relationship with self. The therapist's job is to provide one such relationship and to help the client create others. At the same time, it is often the therapist's task to help the individual to at least distance and, at times, completely separate from, those enmeshing relationships that only serve to continue the symbiotic binds to others and reinforce their internalization.

For the symbiotic character, the therapist is essentially a liberator. He must work through the binds that restrain the client in her historical, current, and internalized relationships, while inviting her to embrace the wider world of adulthood that has seemed frightening, forbidden, guilt-laden, etc. In this latter scenario, the therapist really plays the role of the father figure (as in classic psychoanalytic theory) by representing the external wider world and advocating the excitement, gratification, and mastery available there.

It is not the cozy symbiotic safety of the therapeutic hour that this kind of client most requires. Part of the invitation to the external world is to a real and equal intimacy with others which is characterized more by a collaborative give and take than the mutual dependency that characterizes the symbiotic relationship. In such relationships, the therapist can feel free to show her genuine pleasure in the client's new or deepening relationships, successes in the world, appropriate assertion and aggression, etc. What is often important in this show of approval, however, is avoiding anything that will communicate that the therapist owns or takes sole credit for accomplishments that are almost entirely the client's. Of course, the therapist needn't deny her contribution, but, because of the client's history, it is important to be careful about preempting these accomplishments.

SYMBIOTIC TRANSFERENCES AND TESTS

The central theme of the symbiotic's transferences and tests has to do with acting on or rebelling against those pathogenic beliefs that we have labeled symbiotic. The extent to which such patients will see their therapy as something that is for you, their therapist, rather than for themselves is remarkable. They may show reactions of guilt, fear, censure, or withdrawal if they have to be late, cancel an appointment, go on vacation, etc. These transference functions are, of course, expressed in more subtle ways, but I focus here on therapy time issues because they are simple and universal parameters which often serve as lightning rods for these phenomena. Similarly, clients may unconsciously test the therapist by being late, canceling unnecessarily, carefully noting the therapist's reactions about vacations, etc.

I frequently see therapists, as psychotherapy clients, many of whom are involved in outside training groups and other accoutrements of a psychotherapy career. For such clients with the symbiotic issue, however, these outside involvements constitute a test concerning how I will react to these alternative and potentially "rival" sources of therapeutic help. The symbiotic client typically expects my disapproval, and, more than once, I have heard reports that such clients' former therapists failed such tests and overtly or subtly punished for disloyalty. A client with a symbiotic issue may be among those who need to cut back psychotherapy, or even stop it for a while, primarily in order to experience separation with support rather than censure.

For therapists who are secure and who have enough business, these will be easy tests to pass. But they can be passed with even more therapeutic product when they can be recognized as tests and when the patient's feelings about these maneuvers can be brought to awareness. For therapists who are less secure or busy, these maneuvers may well be challenges, but when they are recognized as tests, they confirm the therapist's competence for the therapist and for the client. When these maneuvers are recognized as tests, the therapist will have an easier time reminding herself of the responsibility to continue to encourage the client's self-ownership and freedom from obligation to binding relationships.

On occasion, I have had clients so exaggerate their responsibility for my welfare that they literally believed that their stopping or reducing therapy would significantly jeopardize my livelihood. Typically, these clients come out of situations where their importance in the family was extraordinarily exaggerated, and they project that model on any significant relationship. They are then bound by their own importance to serve the other. The simple message "you are not that important" is frequently experienced by these individuals not as insulting, but as incredibly relieving.

Following similar pathogenic beliefs, the symbiotic client will often hide her successes, accomplishments, other relationships, or material acquisitions, in the unconscious belief that any of this may threaten the therapist and stimulate envy or retaliation. Alternatively, the client may flaunt such things in order to test the therapist's reactions—to which she will be extraordinarily vigilant—tending to project the negative reactions that she fears. Consistent with their unconscious plans, clients will often arrange for and welcome getting caught in such maneuvers, particularly when the therapist can pass the test by not being threatened, envious, or retaliatory, but rather by appropriately celebrating the client's wins, while being careful not to own them.

Turning passive into active, symbiotic clients will test by insisting that we take excessive responsibility for them. Patients labeled "borderline" are masters of this with their suicidal threats and gestures, late night phone calls, and other coercive demands. Limit setting in these cases is often therapeutic because it corrects the pathogenic belief that such demands must be met and models a response that these patients often need to have in their own lives with respect to parental or other figures, real or internalized.

Again, the value of these tests and the passing of these tests can be even more enhanced when this entire process is recognized and brought to the client's attention. What is important in all this is not only that the therapist pass the test, but also that he help the client become aware of his assumptions about other people, (i.e., his role-relationship models). For, while others have presumably passed such tests before in relation to him, the client continues to assume that others are enmeshing until proven otherwise. So people with this issue may go through life knowing that one, two, or even a handful of individuals in their lives do not treat them in these binding ways, without realizing that their underlying unconscious assumptions about people in general contaminate their relationship to life.

Along with hiding their successes, individuals with a symbiotic issue may cling to their symptoms or some vestiges of them as a way of maintaining the therapeutic relationship, taking care of the therapist, and perpetuating the kind of mutual dependence that characterized their earliest primary relationship. In a number of cases, I have had clients reassure me that they weren't going to get better quickly, in a manner that I experienced as an attempt to reassure me. Alternatively, clients may prematurely show the disappearance of symptoms in order to test how you, as therapist, will react to the possibility of their autonomy and separation from you (i.e., transference cure as transference test).

Just as the therapist of the narcissist has to be the unflagging advocate of that individual's real self, the therapist of the symbiotic needs to remain the steady advocate of the client's grounded emergence into an autonomous adulthood. Much of the client's pathological behavior patterns in relationships can be best understood as attempts either to obey the demands of an enmeshing relationship or to rebel against it. The emerging healthy behavior of the symbiotic, on the other hand, is based on more realistic assumptions about adult-adult relationships which recognize boundaries rather than assuming mutual ownership. As this occurs, support, which is not engulfing, can be given and intimacy, which is not invading, can be accepted. Prior to this, true intimacy was not possible because the individual was too busy obeying and rebelling against the assumptions of a pathological role-relationship model.

It is for this reason that symbiotics often have difficulty truly utilizing therapeutic intervention, because either they are taken over by your ideas, or they are afraid of such a takeover. It is difficult for the symbiotic individual to internalize external input by assimilating it into her own structure or by accommodating that structure in such a way that it is still her own but modified by what you have given. She can either swallow whole, and thereby be taken over by you, or resist you.

In the symbiotic, the process of transmutation of self through external influence is disrupted. In various ways, this kind of client needs to be given permission to take what you have and make it her own. She needs to be reassured that she is not hurting you by taking your gifts, transforming them for her own purposes, and using them to live a better life. She needs to be reassured that she is not leaving you in the dust, as it were, nor thriving at your expense. She needs to learn that you will be OK, that you can rejoice in her successes without owning them, and that you can derive pleasure from your contribution to her life rather than demand binding loyalty for it. She needs to know that she may even excel beyond you and that this excellence can give you pleasure. She also needs to know that she can succeed in any number of areas where you have had absolutely no input or influence, and that this excellence, too, can be equally appreciated and celebrated. Now this is not a neutral stance. It is the corrective stance, essential for the successful transformation of the symbiotic character.

THE SYMBIOTIC CHARACTER AND COUNTERTRANSFERENCE

Anyone who has been in the practice of psychotherapy very long has seen clients who have a history with at least one other therapist who in some sense would not let them go. Subtle forms of this exist when the therapeutic work is determined more by the needs of the therapist than by the needs of the client. Wherever these other kinds of issues are predominant, the transferential expectations of the symbiotic client will be realized. Wherever it is the therapist's self-esteem or the therapist's commitment to a certain philosophy or type of psychotherapy that is on the line, wherever the therapist's income is more important than the therapeutic outcome, or wherever the therapist truly needs the client as a self-sustaining element of his environment, the client will be reinjured, not liberated.

The first thing to understand in considering this issue is that we all have some such needs. We all have some of the characterological issues outlined in Chapters 1 through 4. Some of us need to maintain a commitment to a philosophy, a religion, or a scientific belief in order to sustain ourselves. Some of us need to remain co-dependent. Some of us are prone to enmeshing relationships which give us security. Some of us need to aggrandize ourselves in a narcissistic maintenance of false self-esteem, etc. There is always a legitimate concern that these personal needs will overcome our professional judgment. The symbiotic character will be among the best at sensing these needs, subjugating himself to them, and then rebelling against them. It is not our job not to have such needs. Rather, it is our job to be aware of them and, in each case, to keep them secondary to professional therapeutic objectives.

Countertransference that is nontherapeutic involves failing the kinds of tests outlined above. But the projective identification pulls from the client provided by such tests give extremely useful information. When we find ourselves identifying with the client's projections and having human reactions in the direction of holding on to, infantilizing, feeling jealous of extra-therapy relationships, or feeling oppressed by the demand to be responsible for them, we are cued into the kinds of issues with which they are dealing. Additionally, as we ourselves feel bound to be inordinately careful about offending or frightening the client, we have additional information about how the client herself may have felt in primary relationships. These reactions, particularly if they are independent of our own issues, often result when the client is "turning passive into active," i.e., treating us as she was treated. In these situations, the therapeutic task is to model an alternative, healthy, and conflict-free way of responding to these kinds of binding communications.

The binds that borderline patients present to therapists provide the most obvious illustrations of the kinds of pulls for countertransferential errors that are available. The symbiotic character confuses the allocation of responsibility. He either takes responsibility for meeting our needs as therapists, or he attempts to manipulate us into taking responsibility for him. In more subtle forms, clients will lead us to believe they are more dependent and less capable in the world than is really the case. This serves the dual purpose of validating our need to be needed and to minister to their regressed needs.

For all these binds and boundary crossings, I have found the "analytic attitude" (see Schafer, 1983) to be the most generally useful response. This stance, which is characterized most by an interested but detached curiosity, prompts one to explore all that is going on with both parties. It is not necessary for the therapist to retain a kind of inhuman perfection concerning any contribution that he might be making to the interaction. While it is good to be aware of the potential dangers of countertransferential disclosure, awareness by the therapist can do no harm, and disclosure can often be very therapeutic. Indeed, I have found that most clients will welcome this kind of interpersonal processing. The symbiotic character, in particular, will notice the mutual give-and-take interactive quality of the discussion, which so differs from the originally injurious relationship.

The therapist's exploration of her own human fallibility may be threatening or frustrating to the client, but, if done properly, it can be optimally so, because the client really needs to work through what McArthur (1988) has labeled "the impinged adult's myth of self-righteous perfection." The challenging of this myth, about both the client and the therapist in processing an interactive snarl, can be a profound antidote to the symbiotic's interpersonal history.

THE SYMBIOTIC CHARACTER AND
THE THERAPEUTIC ALLIANCE

A good deal of the early work with the symbiotic character, as with all others, involves understanding symptoms and difficulties in living as expressions of the underlying characterological issues. Wherever possible, I believe in sharing this emerging understanding with the client as fully as possible. But, even where these interpretations cannot be immediately shared for some reason, such an understanding greatly informs the therapist's intervention. I favor most a collaborative approach to psychotherapy in which both patient and therapist are highly active, moving from dialogue that is ever more precisely descriptive of the client's behavior, attitudes, and feelings, to interpretative dialogue that reframes those patterns and opens the way for change.

For the symbiotic character, this "working together" is highly valued and uniquely therapeutic when differences occur and are resolved. The therapist's willingness to be continually informed, corrected, and influenced will obviously be a corrective emotional experience for this individual. Further, the client's continual effort to describe precisely his own experience, together with the enhanced precision added by the therapist, will serve to increasingly define the undefined self. I have become increasingly convinced of the therapeutic value of simply helping the client to find exactly the right words to express himself, his experience, his behaviors, the attitudes of others, etc. Even if it is only descriptive, knowing exactly what is going on, in language that represents reality as closely as possible, renders that reality optimally accessible to the problem-solving resources of the self. Paradoxically, such a full understanding can often result in letting go more readily of conscious problem-solving when this is called for. For, when understanding has clearly achieved all it can, we may let go of understanding more easily and allow our more unconscious resources to operate on a problem. This is one of many reasons I keep asserting that a comprehensive theoretical understanding of each of these characterological issues and their various expressions is essential to the contemporary psychotherapist. Understanding can provide release from the search for understanding and thus open other possibilities.

EXPERIENTIAL THERAPIES AND
THE PROBLEM OF GENERALIZATION

The test of any intervention is, of course, whether it makes a difference. The most profound insight, the deepest catharsis, the most intense interpersonal encounter, the cleverest behavioral prescription—all need to be utilized somehow by the client before they represent good therapy. In psychotherapy, it is the problem of generalization that must ultimately be solved. I have always been attracted to experiential therapies because it has always made sense to me that we learn (and unlearn) through experience. Yet, just as I have seen the most accurate analysis of a problem fail to produce change, I have seen the most profound experiences in the therapeutic hour fail as miserably.

What causes an intervention to "take"? We may never fully know the answer to that question, but I propose these variables in explaining experiential interventions that fail. First, most experiential therapies share the risk of producing experiences in the therapeutic hour that are isolated both from the corrective interaction with the therapist as well as from the day-to-day experience that they seek to affect. The processes of hypnotic, body, gestalt, and other affective therapies, for example, often lend themselves to unusual experiences which can be difficult to integrate. Just as some people are affected more by unusual dream experiences, so do people show differences in their ability to integrate unusual therapeutic experiences. In general, I would suggest that those interventions that are more naturalistic and interwoven within the interactive process of therapy will be more effective. This is why, at least in part, the working through of transference in that real, here-and-now interaction with the therapist can be effective — it is truly experiential.

Second, many experiential therapists regard cognitive understanding as superficial and merely defensive, which, of course, it can be. Yet it is the human being's unique capacity for cognitive and self-reflective work that has allowed the mastery humans enjoy. To ignore that channel seems foolhardy.

Third, people do seem to have differing capacities to learn in different modalities. Experiential therapies, which are excellent for some, may not match the accessing or change modalities of many others. As my integrative work as a therapist has matured, I find my strategies have changed to accommodate these phenomena. I find myself integrating the principles of many experiential techniques into more ordinary forms of interpersonal interaction. I use specific strategies that are clearly marked off from the more ordinary flow of therapy, but not often. I find myself checking repeatedly the cognitive understanding of a learning — whether it be in the affective, behavioral, or cognitive realm. I find I am increasingly attuned to the "channels" my clients use, have used, or could use to learn, unlearn, or cope. Results continue to shape me in these directions.

Therapeutic Channels

This notion of therapeutic channels was suggested to me by Bruce Johnston, when he made an observation that entirely fits my own experience: Transference onto the therapist represents a kind of

channel, dominant in the therapeutic encounters of many, but relatively minor or absent for many others. Some people see their therapists relatively clearly, do not tend to project their issues onto them,
and do not find exploration of possible transference to be a particularly useful forum for exploring their problems. Yet, it is extremely
important for any therapist to be aware of how to communicate in
this particular channel, to recognize transference when it occurs, to
use his own reactions to such transference therapeutically, to understand the working-through process, and to understand the dimensions of character and ego functioning so that his interpretations and
other interventions are appropriate to the person with whom he is
dealing. By the same token, to assume that everyone is going to
transfer and that it is the interpretation of that class of behavior that
constitutes what is really important in psychotherapy is erroneous.

For some individuals, what I will label the *dissociative channel* is
extremely useful in both accessing and intervention tasks. In these
cases, the individual is usually more "at home" in altered states of
consciousness and more than usually ready to receive messages found
in dreams, fantasies, trance, or various other altered states. While
all language is metaphorical and metaphor is active in everyone's
psychotherapy, metaphor is often particularly useful with individuals
who operate well in this dissociative channel.

The idea of therapeutic channels is very similar to the concept in
the hypnosis literature of "pacing," wherein the hypnotist joins the
client's behavioral and cognitive ways of being and knowing. Such
pacing is thought to melt the boundary between hypnotist and client
so the therapist may enter and then lead the client to other ways of
thinking, perceiving, or feeling. I believe that all good therapists
naturally do a great deal of this pacing or joining, often using the
client's metaphor, speaking in his idiosyncratic language, seeing
things as he sees them, even literally getting into his postural position
to increase the empathic response and the subsequent therapeutic
influence. The analogous notion of therapeutic channels is a bit
broader, suggesting the kinds of therapeutic strategies or techniques
that would be useful in any given case. This proposition also argues
the necessity for the therapist to switch channels and, therefore, to
be conversant in a number of ways of doing things.

A useful therapeutic channel may be not only one in which the
client is initially conversant, but, quite the contrary, one that he
needs to acquire. Thus, someone who is highly intellectual but out

of touch with feelings may best be dealt with initially in channels that are more cognitive, but eventually she will have to be led to forms of encounter that emphasize feelings. Therapists who only know one channel will be greatly hampered, in that they can join but not lead or lead but not join. It is naive to expect that all therapists will be equally talented in all channels, and, of course, all therapists will have different talents and predispositions for executing the art form of psychotherapy. My experience strongly suggests, however, that all therapists must be conversant in affective, behavioral, and cognitive realms to be generally effective.

The *insight channel* involves those therapeutic strategies that assist the client in being more aware of his motivation and perception, often with an emphasis on the historical origins of these motivational and perceptual errors. Also related to this cognitive channel is one I will label *educational*. Therapists often have to educate their clients in some general principles of how the psyche works, how others perceive them, how emotions can be expressed or contained, the current and historical determinants of behavior, the role of defenses, etc. These sorts of explanations and reconstructions of past history are essentially educational; while they may lead to insight, it is productive to separate these two highly related cognitive channels.

The *feeling channel* is most easily accessed by those who are more in touch with their feelings, who communicate in the language of feelings, but who may need to learn better affective modulation or may be prone to affective defenses. Typically, these people do not need elaborate affective therapy procedures to get to feelings but may be easily paced by this type of therapy. It is generally true that an individual's preferred access channels are more likely to be overused and used defensively. Indeed, for clients who are most comfortable with the feeling channel, therapy that remains exclusively focused on this channel may make them feel good temporarily but do little else.

Similarly, the *behavioral channel* will be most useful for individuals who know by doing. While many of the strategies of behavior modification, strategic, and family therapy will obviously be included in this category, there is much more to the behavioral channel. This is the channel of action and feedback. Indeed, in many cases, work in this channel will ultimately decide the real value of intervention through the others.

The channel of *internalization* cuts across a number of others already mentioned. Like the metaphor channel, the internalization channel is really operative in nearly every case. That is, in almost every case, individuals need to build or repair some part of their structure to really change. This channel becomes particularly central, however, when there has been extensive structural damage and the primary therapeutic task is to repair the damaged structure. In these cases, internalization of others, including, but not limited to, the therapist, is really necessary before anything else substantive can be consummated. Therapy that supports reality relatedness and functioning is only one example of this.

I know that all of the therapeutic channels are not included in this brief introductory list. Indeed, the concept is a rather loose one, in that the channels overlap a bit and the levels of abstraction they represent differ a bit. Nonetheless, I have found this to be an extremely useful concept in cataloging what must be done or what has been done in a given case. I have found it to be a particularly useful language for case presentation and supervision. So, in many of the cases and presentations of techniques that follow, I will be repeatedly attending to the therapeutic channels that worked for each client in accessing what was needed and changing what was problematic.

Symptoms Modeled as Internal Self-Object Relations

Throughout the remainder of the book, one organizing principle of case presentations will be the analysis of symptoms as expressions of internal object relations. Because I find this perspective to have high therapeutic utility, I will be repetitive in explicating it theoretically and by example.

The forthcoming analysis sees symptoms as highly relational, even if they appear isolative, because it is assumed they were originally developed in relationships, and those relationships now exist internally. In an object relations analysis of symptoms, we ask (1) Who is relating to whom in this expression? and (2) What rules for relationship are being followed? In Horowitz's language: What is the role-relationship model? Who is on, who is the object, and what is the purpose of the activity? This analysis is predicated on the belief that people tend to stick to the rules they have learned about how relationships are structured. Intimacy, for example, may be found only in the sharing of mutual unhappiness or through physical, psychological, or sexual abuse. Aggression may be disallowed or allowed only through passive, deniable expressions. Loyalty may be expressed only through self-denial. True love may be experienced only as total abandonment of reason in romantic surrender, and so on. Thus, the modeling of symptoms suggested here is relational, focuses on internal relationships (often projected), and utilizes libidinal connection and aggression as central explanatory forces.

At this juncture, I intend to provide a general overview of the most common categories of symptomatic expression as conceptualized from the object relations viewpoint. I will use a redefined version of Fairbairn's model in this analysis, and the symptom prototypes outlined here are graphically portrayed with this model in Figure 2. My analysis of many cases and the symptoms that they

Figure 2
SYMPTOMS MODELED AS INTERNAL
SELF-OBJECT RELATIONS

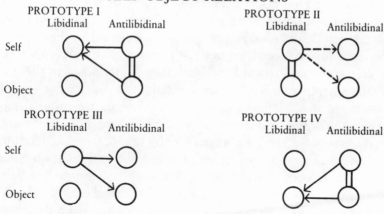

==== Libidinal Connection
——> Aggression
- - - -> Aggression Possible

I. Antilibidinal self coalesced with antilibidinal object wherein aggression is directed at the libidinal self. Resulting symptoms are maintained by the bond of antilibidinal structures.

II. Libidinal self to libidinal object with concomitant *possibility* of aggression directed at antilibidinal structures.

III. Aggression from libidinal self to antilibidinal self and object. The pattern is maintained by the irrepressible nature of the libidinal impulses, as well as by the bond of the libidinal structures (not pictured here so as to distinguish this analysis from prototype II).

IV. Antilibidinal self and object to libidinal object wherein the aggression is directed at the libidinal object. The pattern is maintained by the bond of the antilibidinal structures.

of symptoms so conceptualized. The most common of these (prototype I) involves those symptoms that are clearly antilibidinal for the
individual, in which there is a clear collusion between introjected
antilibidinal self and the introjected antilibidinal object. In other
words, the individual does himself in as he was done in. For example, he may criticize himself and project criticism of self onto others.
Or he may become depressed and wallow in that depression, expecting others to sympathize with him, join him in depression, or even
humiliate him for that depression. Here, he may unconsciously believe that to be happy or above criticism would be threatening to
others, in some way damage them, or lead to his censure or abandonment. Characteristic of prototype I are these or similar antilibidinal
pathogenic beliefs. This prototype is designated by I in Figure 2
wherein libidinal connection is illustrated by the lines connecting the
antilibidinal self and object and aggression is illustrated by the
arrows from these structures to the libidinal self.

Central to the clinical utility of this conceptualization is the
object-seeking intention of the symptomatic behavior. Not only is
this a therapeutic interpretation of the symptomatology, but it also
leads to therapeutic prescriptions of behaviors that are healthier and
likely to result in beneficial ties with others in the external world.
There is aggression toward the libidinal self embodied in these self-
defeating symptoms, which are conceptualized as a coalition between these antilibidinal forces. Indeed, Fairbairn's original labels
for these unconscious internalized forces was nicely descriptive. The
"internal saboteur" and the "rejecting object" are seen as colluding to
reject and sabotage the organism's natural libidinal self-expressions.

The second common prototype involves the symptomatic behaviors that can be usefully seen as expressions of the libidinal self to
the libidinal object. In this situation, the developmentally arrested
libidinal self reaches, with primitive needs and desires, toward an
object expected to gratify these desires completely and unconditionally. Initially, it is often the individual's exaggerated excitement
about the new person, activity, idea, or drug that may provide the
tip-off that this is the internal constellation being activated. This, I
believe, is why Fairbairn labeled the object in this role-relationship
model as the "exciting object." Masterson has been the most articulate in his repeated explication of this phenomenon in borderline
patients. Such patients are prone to throw themselves into dangerous

acting-out with, among other things, drugs, sex, money, or gambling, denying the danger of their behavior as they pursue primitive gratification.

The more obvious occurrences of prototype II symptoms in this constellation do, indeed, occur with lower functioning or borderline individuals. At higher levels of structural functioning, we may see this in the idealization that individuals show, particularly toward parent figures, therapists, lovers, or philosophical or religious beliefs. When one relates from the primitive arrested self to the "exciting object," salvation is at hand. It is this phenomenological stance that defines symptoms in this constellation.

This prototype is designated II in Figure 2, emphasizing the importance of the libidinal connection between libidinal structures. It is also true that these symptoms sometimes additionally represent aggression from libidinal structures to antilibidinal ones, but this is not always the case. The therapeutic utility of the prototype II modeling revolves around the need to mature the libidinal self by providing "good-enough" objects for connection while enhancing the individual's reality perception of the ultimately disappointing "exciting object." Wherever aggression is involved in the expression, this can be made more conscious and more realistic.

The third and very common constellation involves that aggression expressed by the libidinal self toward the antilibidinal self and object for their life-denying restraint. This is most obvious when the individual directly expresses rage at those on whom he has projected such restraint. More common, however, are those symptoms that are really passive-aggressive expressions, such as procrastination, forgetfulness, or other irresponsible behavior, the intention of which can be denied in order to preserve the perceived existing human connections. Prototype III, depicted in Figure 2, highlights the aggressive expressions of the libidinal self toward the restraining and defeating antilibidinal structures.

Symptoms of this kind, which often become increasingly more obvious in their aggressive expressions, are typical of higher functioning individuals as they get better in therapy. These individuals become more aggressive toward the antilibidinal forces that restrain them in an attempt to separate from these negative introjects. The most useful therapy is that which encourages this healthy aggression, assists in maturing its expression, and helps the individual seek out others with whom the autonomous self may be expressed. The initial step involves making the aggression conscious and legitimate.

The fourth symptom prototype is seen somewhat less frequently than the other three and, like prototype II, is more common in individuals functioning with a lower level of structure. This symptom constellation is descriptively similar to Weiss and Sampson's concept of "turning passive into active." It occurs when the individual treats others in a rejecting or antilibidinal fashion just as he was treated. This, too, represents a coalition of the antilibidinal self and object. There is simply a reversal in the self and object roles in the role-relationship model. In other words, someone has to be abused, and someone has to be the abuser in this model of relationships, and it is now you rather than I who is abused. The physical or sexual abuse of children by adults themselves abused as children expresses this antilibidinal self and object to libidinal object prototype. As with the flip side of this paradigm (i.e., prototype I), these behaviors preserve the original family relationships and provide connection to the object, often in the only way in which the individual has learned to have human connections. A therapeutic regimen that introduces the client to other ways of achieving connection and reinforces them, often for long periods of time, is necessary to remedy symptomatic behaviors of this kind.

In the next two chapters, each client's major symptoms will be analyzed from this internal object relations perspective. I hope the therapeutic utility of this object relations model will become increasingly evident with its explication in treatment.

CHAPTER 8

Symptoms as
Internal Object Relations

FOR THIS BOOK, I HAVE CHOSEN to tell the stories of two people who were able, in large measure, to escape the bonds of family ownership and be free. Both exemplify character neurosis and, as such, lend themselves to analysis of symptoms as representations of internal object relations. Indeed, the hidden and convoluted nature of symptoms is often typical of psychopathology in the character neurosis range, and uncovering the underlying conflicts is most interesting here. Thus, I will attempt to tell their stories fully, giving you a feel for their particular bondage and a report of the detailed sleuthing required to uncover their conflicts. I will supplement this analysis with some explication of active techniques for further encouraging change in their therapy and that of others.

ALICE

Alice entered therapy at 45 as she was separating from her first husband. Alice, who was the mother of three grown children, had lived all but the last few years of her life in highly symbiotic relationships—first with her mother, then with her husband. Because she was in the throes of a marital separation, the first few sessions of her psychotherapy were naturally devoted to this current massive stressor, though she had come seeking a more characterological psychotherapy oriented toward her core issues. It was obvious, from her description of the marital relationship in the very first session, that symbiotic issues were at play here. As an aside, one of the many advantages of this characterological view is that it can often provide a very early reading of an individual which will predict the basic themes of psychotherapy.

Shortly after graduating from college, Alice had married a man 10 years her senior, a doctor and business partner of her own physician-father. From the beginning, she subjugated herself to his will and was employed as a wife and mother until her children were in their adolescence. A striking symbol of her overall subservient status in the relationship was that this upper middle-class family of five was to be maintained on a monthly grocery budget of $50.00. For a number of years, Alice prided herself on being able to accomplish this rather impressive task, yet resented the fact that her husband would spend relatively large sums on opera tickets, occasional dinners out, etc.

Her first step out of the house occurred when she became a school crossing guard. Doing this in opposition to her husband's wishes, she marked her first step toward independence. A little later, she went to school in an advanced degree program, again against the wishes of her husband. Upon graduation, she obtained an office and began practicing professionally. Her husband never wanted to see her office or in any other way be confronted with her outside life.

Separation and survivor guilt were problems in that each of these separations, and particularly the final one, deeply hurt her husband. In many ways she was thriving while he was suffering. Though he attempted to punish her by withholding appropriate spousal support during the pre-divorce period, she came close to surrendering all her remaining assets to him because she had earlier promised to commit these funds to needed home repairs. It was necessary for me to question the wisdom of this almost masochistic commitment to consistency before she would see how inappropriate and self-damaging it was. Indeed, a good student of this model will be correct in seeing some of the descriptions given so far as potentially coming out of an oral or masochistic adaptation. As it turned out, Alice's overall structure can best be understood as symbiotic, this illustrates that initial cues as to character structure, though potentially quite valuable, should be held loosely and that there are very few single-issue clients.

In the course of exploring her character and symptomatology, a history emerged that was replete with signs of the symbiotic issue. Alice was born two days after the death of her mother's father. The labor was induced the day after Christmas because the mother was so distraught by her own father's death that she "just had to get rid of this baby." Because the date of her birth was so close to Christmas, it was deemed a "bad day" for her birthday; so, as a child, Alice always celebrated it on her mother's birthday, which was a couple of weeks earlier. She was given the nickname of Baboo because that was how her older sister pronounced baby, and that nickname held until she changed it at age 40.

As the theme of enmeshment began to emerge, Alice had memories of a number of occasions where her mother would "seize my experience and make it her own" and others "when she always wanted me to feel what she felt." Anything that mother could not participate in with Alice, or with any of the other children for that matter, was discouraged. For example, if mother could participate in a diet with Alice, she would encourage it. If Alice tried to diet on her own, her mother would very much discourage it.

She spontaneously reported a recurring dream from childhood in which "a grandmother would slit open my stomach and take my insides out." It is the experience of having one's insides taken away that exemplifies the symbiotic character. Indeed, mother had successfully blocked a number of Alice's earlier attempts at independence and achievement. The most striking occurred in Alice's adolescence when she was found to be a good enough swimmer that training for the Olympics was a realistic possibility for her. Mother vetoed this opportunity.

Alice's relationship with her father was also strongly restricted by her mother. Her father was an idealized and somewhat distant figure for the entire family, and mother kept it that way. Communications from children to father were channeled through mother, and Alice reported that if her father tried to become more involved with the children, Mother would humiliate him for the awkward way in which he did it.

Other memories led to the characterization that mother was hurt whenever Alice's feelings and thoughts differed from hers. These memories and characterizations were confirmed in a contemporary visit with her mother wherein mother continued to complain about the purple in Alice's wardrobe. As Alice steadfastly stuck to wearing the clothes she had brought, maintaining her preference for the color purple, her mother found a purple flower in the garden and put it under her watch as a kind of nosegay. When Alice remarked on the purple flower, her mother said, "Yes, I am trying to get used to it." This story illustrates, I think, the pervasiveness of the pressure for merger which characterizes individuals with the symbiotic issue.

The symbiotic etiology apparently affected Alice's sister even more severely. According to Alice, that sister has yet to escape the same kind of immersion with both her original and contemporary family. The sister is seriously overweight, depressed, without personal goals, and hampered by the typical symbiotic history of ceasing autonomous activity just before attaining a goal. It was this sister who failed to graduate from college because she quit three weeks before her final term was up. That pattern of quitting shortly before the attainment of a "separating" goal is characteristic of individuals with the symbiotic issue, (e.g., see McArthur, 1988). As we shall see when examining Alice's symptoms one by one, this pattern also pervaded her experience, although at a less serious level than is reportedly true of her older sister. Alice, of course, felt survivor guilt in relation to her sister.

There was a family legend about Alice and her father which I find quite telling. Apparently she was an active and exuberant child, and one day, when the father was climbing up a staircase in their home, Alice excitedly rushed down the stairs into his arms. This nearly knocked father over backwards and "almost killed" him according to the legend. Alice apparently took the legend quite literally, and took from it the belief that her exuberance, energy, and power might really overwhelm and "kill" her father if it got out of hand. Alice offered the interpretation that this belief had generalized to other important men in her life.

Consistent with this theme, Alice learned that it was very important to her mother to maintain father as the smart, academic, achieving one of the family. There were consistent but subtle messages from mother, but not from father, to keep the brakes on achievement, particularly academic achievement. Alice remembers "I worked hard to get B's and not A's in school. There was room for only one genius in the house, and that was Dad." In this context, recall the sister's dropping out of college, and allow me to foreshadow again Alice's difficulties whenever success, particularly academic success, appeared anywhere on the horizon. Threatened success often led to experiences of anxiety, mild dissociative fatigue states, and a "fuzziness" of mind, all of which resulted in her repeatedly quitting a task before it was completed.

Alice's case, like almost every other, has a characterological sub-plot that must be understood to comprehend the whole picture. The historical data strongly suggested that Alice's mother really needed to be the center of attention both with her children and her husband. Alice's conclusion in reviewing her family history was that mother needed to be the "pretty one" in the family. She subtly encouraged her children to overeat and thereby become rotund and less sexually attractive. Mother discouraged immediate contact with father and the acquisition of intellectual skills, which would have created a bond between him and his children that she herself could not attain.

Throughout her children's upbringing, mother also actively discouraged the use of makeup and any dress that could be considered overtly feminine. She propagated the belief that it was sinful to attract attention, particularly for one's femininity. She herself, however, tried to remain thin and was quite concerned with her physical appearance. In summarizing her history, Alice said, "I was the Golden Girl until I was in adolescence; then I lost it. It was okay to be attractive as a child, but not as a woman." Makeup, lingerie, dancing, and striking dress or colors have all presented problems for Alice. Each makes her anxious, guilty, and somewhat confused, at least initially. Still, Alice remembered, with a mixture of fondness, arousal, and uncertainty, episodes of "roughhousing" with her father which have an unmistakable sexual quality. Furthermore, Alice remembered that her father was, indeed, proud of her and that the two of them probably could have had a strong intellectual connection which would have excluded her mother.

All of this, coupled with the memories that point to the unmistakable child-like need of her mother to be the center of attention, strongly suggests oedipal issues as contributing to her character. Becoming a successful, intelligent, attractive, sexual adult woman not only threatened a separation from mother but also signaled the kind of rivalry that this parent clearly found difficult to handle. Thus, Alice's problems in all of these areas were multiply determined, as I shall now illustrate.

An Object Relations Analysis of Symptoms As Treatment

Having reviewed the historical highlights of this case, it is now possible to analyze each of Alice's difficulties by focusing on the extent to which the symptoms represent internal object relations. In other words, I want to exemplify how each symptom can be seen as representing an interaction between internalized structures.

Using Fairbairn's model of the libidinal self and other, and the antilibidinal self and other can provide added clarity for the therapist and, when translated, for the client. Such an understanding can also lead to more precise knowledge concerning how a therapy or a life might be choreographed so as to constitute a "corrective emotional experience."

Let us begin with that symptom constellation that is almost always present with any person who could be most clearly understood by her symbiotic issues. This is the experience of the "loss of self"—the experience of being so fused with the other that one's own sense of self, awareness of likes and dislikes, security in the solitary experience of oneself is diminished or absent. Alice had had these kinds of fusion experiences to varying degrees with both her mother and her husband. During the therapy, when she began dating, she had them in her primary love relationship. In these latter episodes, she would become obsequious, continually deferring to her partner. She also became overly solicitous and found herself "asking stupid questions" to keep the conversation going. She reminded herself of her mother in this regard and would display the same kind of shallow, Polly-annaish behavior she remembered as characterizing her mother.

Interestingly, this obsequious state would usually vacillate with another marked by strong and difficult-to-control anger with her partner, accompanied by a desire to get away from him as soon and completely as possible. She found this analogous to a child-like rage reaction which she tried, with mixed success, to control.

In analyzing this symptom constellation, it may help to remember that the natural libidinal self of any individual desires contact and support in the expression of autonomy. As we have reviewed earlier, the symbiotic character is forced to choose between contact and autonomy. Yet the contact provided is wanting because it is not directed at the real libidinal individual, but rather at an idealized merger-object. When separation, individuation, autonomy, difference, adventure, etc., are repeatedly blocked, the individual internalizes that block and copies the environment in doing to herself what was done to her. *This self-restraint constitutes the antilibidinal self.*

Through such restraint, the individual achieves the least conflicted form of contact available with the other. The other may then be seen as one who wishes such subjugation, self-restraint, and merger. This is the antilibidinal-self to antilibidinal-object relationship with aggression toward the libidinal self, wherein the best form of contact available is maintained by self-restraint and perceived external restraint (prototype I in Figure 2, p. 149). In other words, the proper self-other relationship in this model is one in which I give myself up and over to you to obtain the bliss of merger. It is also important to note that there is developmental arrest in this state and role-relationship model, such that the individual feels herself to be dependent, in need of supplies, and in need of an all-gratifying caretaker as would a small child.

In this repressed state, the individual experiences these archaic feelings irrespective of the degree of adult autonomy she may have really attained. The expectations of such fusion must be, by the very nature of adult life, frustrated. They are, however, less frustrated when the real other justifies one's antilibidinal projections and shares this view of the relationship, because some such gratification is often forthcoming and, in any case, there is a shared view of the relationship and its obligations. This state is always frustrating because it denies the natural libidinal press for individual self-expression. Alice's current boyfriend was healthier than either her mother or her ex-husband, and found much of this obsequious, child-like, and passive behavior both puzzling and irritating.

It was all this frustration, of course, that triggered the polarity state of hard-to-control rage. Alice hated herself for behaving this way, hated the person who made her this way, and, at the most primitive level, wanted to get rid of that other person. This hatred of the antilibidinal object (boyfriend) and her "wussy" (antilibidinal) self was a natural expression of her libidinal self. This enraged state, then, could be characterized as the relationship of the libidinal self to the antilibidinal self and object (prototype III in Figure 2, p. 149). The enmeshing restraint was projected onto the boyfriend and then resisted.

In general, as therapy progresses, awareness of the internal nature of this entire process increases. This awareness includes recognition of the projections of antilibidinal restraints onto the external object, recognition of the self-imposed restraints, and rage at the antilibidinal self for collaborating in all this. People often experience this antilibidinal self as a "demonic force" or, in Fairbairn's words, a cruel "internal saboteur." This kind of rage at the self is often an early signal that the desired separation is taking place. Prior to this, individuals often experience the antilibidinal self as a part of themselves and as syntonic to a very great extent. Finding the antilibidinal self to be alien and the object of one's own rage is an experience of separating it out or, in Fairbairn's language, releasing it from the unconscious.

Yet, it is extremely important to understand that the libidinal self expressed here in rage is also developmentally arrested. The rage is primitive, murderous, "blind," and all-encompassing. The individual typically finds it very difficult to contain and, unless borderline, inappropriate to the situation, "crazy," and, in all these senses, extremely ego alien. Indeed, it is almost always experienced as more ego alien than the antilibidinal tendencies that are well ingrained, socialized, and have a history of approval.

As the antilibidinal forces are brought into the open, separated from the self, or "released from the unconscious" (Fairbairn, 1952), they become increasingly more alien, and the client begins to wonder about her identity and may experience states of void and pain. The familiar antilibidinal restraints are certainly increasingly unacceptable but so is the increasingly intense rage at oneself and others who maintain the straitjacket on self-expression. So, essentially what we have here is an antilibidinal self that needs to be exorcized—identified as separate, as an internalization, and as alien to self-expression and one's contemporary reality. One's libidinal self also must mature to be more present time, more capable of appropriate self-expression in the current context, and more able to get currently available supplies by relating through giving from a more spontaneous expression of the core self.

Therapy for this prototype III constellation of the symbiotic issue essentially involves helping the client to understand and complete this process. Understanding the process typically helps a great deal, but it is not the process itself. However, understanding does provide a road map for the territory to be covered. The interpretation of the "internalization of the bad object" (the "that's not you, that's your mother" interpretation) begins the process of extrication essentially by labeling the tumor which has invaded and permeated the most important aspects of self-functioning.

Similarly, labeling Alice's primitive and hard-to-control rage at self and other as real and fundamentally healthy self-expression, albeit arrested, brings control of as well as acceptance for a force so powerful and ego alien that it could continue to be repressed without such intervention. In the process of working through this issue, Alice would often come to therapy sessions confused and agitated by these episodes. She would respond to the interpretation, which was typically arrived at through the alliance, with obvious relief and relaxation. Often, this would be followed by an expressed intention, on which she consistently followed through, for greater self-expression and/or the repairing of breaches in the love relationship which may have been caused by the outbreak of the anger. Alice was particularly fortunate in having a relationship partner who understood and helped further the necessary processes of change.

Whenever this therapeutic process is undertaken, it is also necessary for the individual to be exposed to and internalize healthier ideas about freedom and obligation in relationships. Many individuals know what these healthier attitudes are and even try to live by them. Yet the arrested internalizations harbor other very powerful notions which control the individual and lead to arrested states of guilt, anxiety, and rage in spite of the fact that the person knows so much better.

To speak to this dual awareness, I often say, "You already know this, but it's my job to tell you . . . you don't owe your life to your mother" or "the better part of your father really wants you to succeed." In this way, I hope to speak to the arrested child without infantilizing the observing adult. Psychotherapy often leads to altered states for the client (and therapist as well) in which these kinds of often simple and obvious ideas can be delivered quite productively to the structures which maintain the problematic, immature states. Therapeutic strategies that enhance this phenomenon can also be quite useful.

Alice's life was also diminished by a constellation of symptoms that expressed conflict over various forms of self-expression. First, she was fairly self-conscious about the use of makeup. Mother overtly disapproved of makeup and characterized women who used it as cheap. In discussing instances concerning the purchase of feminine lingerie, dressing in colors that drew attention, or the occasion when she had her personal colors analyzed, Alice expressed a good deal of embarrassment, guilt, and generalized anxiety. In discussing these things, she recalled again that it was okay for her to be attractive as a child but not as a woman. Similarly, she remembered that she was characterized by her family as the "golden girl" until adolescence, at which time she felt she "lost it."

The mother's public statement was that it was all right to look good naturally but somehow wrong to artificially enhance this, to dress so as to call attention to oneself, or be overtly sexual in any way. However, all of this did not come from a puritanical, self-denying woman. Quite to the contrary, Alice's mother was attractive, invested in her looks, and paid more than the usual attention to enhancing them, including the use of makeup. In discussing all of this, Alice recalled a number of instances when her mother had spoken in a very child-like manner or did inappropriate and demanding things which would call attention to herself if she felt she had lost center stage.

Alice had the same conflicted reactions during the very few occasions when she went dancing. She liked to dance, was good at it, got attention for her abilities, and yet she went very infrequently and, when she did, felt very self-conscious. She always held back from dancing initially and really had to push herself through the inhibition, public self-consciousness, and guilt to participate. Though there wasn't the same kind of indoctrination about dancing as there had been about makeup and dress, it was clear in exploring this topic that the reaction was identical and the origins were similar. This kind of exhibitionistic, energetic, sexual activity could threaten her mother and potentially overwhelm her father. Dancing, like makeup, attention-getting, or feminine dress, constituted a "danger situation."

This conflict is essentially more the expression of the oedipal than the symbiotic issue. These expressions of competition and sexuality would have been particularly threatening to this mother. The inhibiting effect of this is perhaps more profound because of the symbiotic nature of the mother-daughter relationship which enhances "oedipal guilt" (Malan, 1979).

This dual-origin analysis of these difficulties underlines an important point about characterological issues. Almost all clinical cases can be best understood by using the combination of issues that are expressed in the presenting symptomatology. Alice's work is characterized primarily by symbiotic issues and secondarily by oedipal ones. Understanding most individuals by employing only one issue will usually leave significant issues or symptoms beyond understanding.

The final issue in what I will term the oedipal constellation of Alice's symptoms had to do with her conflicts around reading. This was the woman mentioned in Chapter 5 who couldn't read more than a few pages without getting preoccupied by the people who would enjoy or benefit from the particular material being read. Further exploration of her reading pattern revealed that Alice was greatly stimulated and gratified by reading yet failed to do most of the reading required for her professional program. Not infrequently, her arousal at reading would lead to masturbation, which would terminate the reading after a short period. She reported that her father, who was an educated man, was also quite interested in history and "read constantly." She also remembered that her mother read to her and it was quite pleasurable. Furthermore, she had read at length to her own children and this, too, was pleasurable. In her current relationship, there were other instances of gratifying reading together. So, it emerged that reading alone was problematic, but reading with others was not. In exploring her feelings around reading academic material, she accessed the feeling of rebellion against the requirement to read. As we shall see in other symptom constellations, this rebelliousness served in maintaining other problematic behaviors. This part of the symptom picture was difficult to understand for some time because in this instance, as well as others, she seemed to be rebelling against something which gave her pleasure.

After several sessions that circled around this rebellion issue, Alice finally recalled how rebellious her own mother could be. Her mother particularly enjoyed shocking guests in their home who were in any way stuffy or proper. The family lived in a rural section of town where they were able to keep a few animals. Whenever pretentious guests were invited to the house, mother would bring a goat or ram into the living room to meet the guests. On other occasions, she would delight in similarly rebellious activities against rules and convention — particularly interesting in light of her somewhat Victorian stance on makeup and dress. In any case, when it became clear to Alice that this rebellion was based on identification with mother, she could begin to see how this tendency was used by the internalized mother to prohibit her from doing what it was she really wanted to do—in this case, to read, be an academic success, and enjoy scholarly and solitary achievement. This rebelliousness was also self-sabotaging to Alice with respect to her most troubling symptom, as we shall soon see.

Now, we understood that the inhibition to read was in the same constellation as her inhibitions concerning dress, makeup, and dancing. First, reading involved a solitary activity, which this engulfing mother found threatening if only for its propensity to separate her from her daughter. Second, Alice's reading, and all that it could bring, would threaten mother's reality—namely that there was only room for one intellectual in the house: father. Finally, for Alice to read would have opened a channel to her father which mother did not have. Like makeup, feminine dress, and dancing, reading tapped the oedipal issue that was doubly threatening, both to mother and to Alice, due to their enmeshment and consequently exaggerated need for one another. In this light, reading also became a "danger situation," producing the kind of overstimulation that led to masturbation and the defensive pattern of altruistic thoughts of benefiting others that were so much more comfortable.

A final theme, which served to unlock Alice's self-depriving patterns regarding reading, came to light as she was involved in some postgraduate paper-writing that required reading. She recalled that in her graduate work she had been able to pass tests and even hand in well-graded papers without reading the necessary material. She continued to "get away with this" in her current postgraduate work, and, as she discussed this, her hostility toward and disrespect for her instructors were evident. When I pointed this out, she acknowledged it and fondly remembered an instructor in junior high school who had not allowed her to get away with such deceptions. She felt that I, too, would be a "tough instructor," and it was obvious from her remembrance and her projection onto me that she longed for such a teacher who would pay enough attention and be tough enough not to be fooled.

Following an informed hunch, I asked if her mother had been similarly hostile to her father. This question was welcomed with a rush of associations. Yes, mother felt there were two kinds of people in the world—thinking people and feeling people—and one must be in one camp or the other. Father was a thinking person, while mother was a feeling person, according to mother, and much of mother's rebelliousness and hostility were expressed in pulling the wool over father's eyes and manipulating him to go along with her wishes. In this way, according to Alice, mother would prove again and again that feeling people were really superior to thinking people, even though they didn't appear to be as smart. Alice acted out this family drama with her instructors, mostly male, again and again. In addition to uncovering an understanding of all of this, therapeutic intervention included supplementing her own good judgment that one could be both thinking and feeling, and simultaneously successful at both.

As we discovered this, Alice recalled another confirming memory that told us we were on the right track. When Alice learned that she had a very high IQ, her mother characteristically discounted and took credit for this at the same time. She said Alice's IQ was as high as it was because she (mother) had worked so extensively with her on school work. Alice promptly put the fact of her high IQ out of her mind, and though she did not technically become amnesic to it, that fact never was incorporated into her self-concept, and she rarely "remembered" it.

The final symptom constellation involved the repeated occurrences of Alice's feeling particularly successful followed by lethargy, exhaustion, and mild states of fugue and confusion. This phenomenon is very common in the symbiotic. Individual success of thriving constitutes a "danger situation." There does not need to be an oedipal issue operating for this symptom to emerge. The success simply threatens a separation from the enmeshing other—internalized, external, or both. It is just that in Alice's case, success would also open the channel to father, which threatened mother from sexual and competitive points of view.

All the symptoms reviewed above represent, in relational terms, the libidinal self-expression triggering the internalized antilibidinal self and object role-relationship model (prototype III, Figure 2, p. 149), resulting in restraint wherein the self is experienced as bad and the other as injured or punishing or, more often than not, both. In other words, the natural expression of curiosity, sexuality, competition, separation, etc., are found threatening by the antilibidinal self and object. It is this self-object relationship model that produces the anxiety, guilt, self-consciousness, embarrassment, confusion, and fugue states that follow.

Theoretically, the more libidinally expressive self would be relating to that more "exciting" or gratifying object, who would unconditionally support such self-expression (prototype II). The typical symbiotic's actual phenomenology at the middle level of structure (i.e., character neurosis) and above is often quite different in my experience. People like Alice often forget about the other's reaction when expressing themselves. They are so accustomed to having no support for autonomy that they don't anticipate it and are often quite surprised and even deeply moved when they get it. It is more as if they manage to forget for a time the anticipated injury to the other and the punishment from the other that usually keeps them in line. The resulting self-expression then brings on the sabotaging-self forces and projected-object forces that fuel the symbiotic symptoms. Therapeutic change comes, then, not only from eroding negative expectations but also from building positive ones. When neurotic symbiotics are injurious or thoughtless to others it is often because they have had to "forget" about them in order to be themselves for a time.

The last symptom constellation to be reviewed, and the one that held out the longest to interpretation and change, was Alice's recurrent pattern of compulsive overeating. Like reading, eating was done appropriately as long as she was with others. However, when she was on her own, and particularly right after separation from her boyfriend, this compulsion came on with a vengeance. Alice was encouraged to do a great deal of self-study through detailed observations of her patterns. She found that when she was with her boyfriend, the two of them would enjoy planning the meal that they would prepare together. Then they would engage in the preparation and, Alice particularly, would delight in creating the presentation of the food. She would then eat healthy foods in appropriate quantities, enjoy them, and feel completely satisfied. When alone, and particularly after separation, she would be much more likely to dive into a bag of cookies and finish the entire bag to the point of feeling overfull or even nauseous.

When asked to track who was symbolically present at these times, Alice once again discovered this rebellious feeling and, on the heels of that, remembered the many times her mother would mischievously bring out and pass around a bowl of M&M's or similar treat, which she would urge on her children as a sort of naughty indulgence, while often abstaining herself. Alice also discovered her own irrational rule concerning food: She must get rid of the "bad" food (i.e., cookies, ice cream, etc.) before beginning to eat the "good" food, which meant a rather strict and depriving dietary regimen. In contemplating this idea, she realized that the rebellion was aimed at the strict regimen and fueled by anger at her partner for leaving (i.e., for the separation). It was as if she couldn't have the healthy relationship with the boyfriend so she would have the familiar relationship with the internalized mother. At these times, it was as if her irrational thinking told her that she was trying to stay thin for her boyfriend, so because he wasn't around, it didn't matter. This is, indeed, the kind of symbiotic thinking that characterized both her mother and herself, but it did not at all represent reality. She enjoyed the healthier form of eating, which was neither depriving nor particularly fattening.

In further pursuing these thoughts, Alice also realized that she unconsciously did not feel worth the effort required for the planning and presentation engaged in with her boyfriend. This thinking represents the typical symbiotic notion — "I am nothing outside a relationship." As she explored these thoughts further, she was then reminded of the recurrent childhood dream in which she experienced the grandmother figure taking her insides out, leaving her empty and in terror. For the first time, she owned the thought, common for eating-disordered individuals, that she was trying to fill the emptiness with food. At this moment, she remembered that her mother had instructed her to eat something when she felt empty, depressed, or scared. She did not remember this in the same class of challenge or rebellion that her mother made concerning forbidden desserts or other things but, rather, as a sincere effort on her mother's part to give her a strategy to remedy discomfort. There is little more discomforting to a symbiotic individual than being separated from her primary love object, especially, as was the case for Alice, when not always knowing when the *au revoir* would come. After cognizing these controlling factors, Alice had increasing periods of being able to eat more appropriately — fixing herself these more elaborate and well-presented meals. Whenever she did this, she felt much better, not only physically healthier and less neurotic emotionally, but more separate and autonomous, vis-à-vis her boyfriend.

The boyfriend traveled a good deal in his work, and the trips were often unpredictably extended. As we discussed this, it occurred to me that the here-today–gone-tomorrow quality of her relationship might in fact be very good for her autonomy building, because she had periods of frustration during which to internalize the healthier object relationship—for example, that surrounding the issue of food.

It was during one of these alone periods of feeling better and eating healthier that she urged her boyfriend, in an atypically assertive way, to "just stop" the kind of compulsive overwork that kept them separate more than necessary. That night Alice had a dream. She dreamt that she was back in a high school math class taking a test, when the teacher added a pop quiz for which she might have been unprepared. Alice freaked out. She couldn't think straight, became panicky and agitated, and went to another woman teacher and cried in order to get her pity and assistance. That teacher kindly but firmly suggested that she go back to the class and complete the test and quiz.

Alice woke up at this point in a very agitated state and couldn't let go of the feelings associated with the dream. She couldn't soothe herself. The reassurance that it was only a dream didn't seem to work, and she couldn't get back to sleep. In working on this dream, I asked Alice what her contemporary "test" might be. She said, to stop overeating, to shed this compulsion which, like many compulsive overeaters, she had come to realize was a kind of companion. Then she recalled that conversation with the boyfriend in which she firmly told him, just like the teacher in the dream, to "stop it." She then remembered that it was the day after the dream when she had thought, "If I can tell him to just stop it, I can tell myself the same." Furthermore, she reasoned that her stopping her compulsive behavior might serve to stop his. She discredited some of that idea on the basis of its merging qualities. I pointed out, in the context of this dream interpretation, the realistic elements of that proposition. I suggested that she might very well have subconsciously begun to give herself this "stop it" instruction at about the same time she delivered it to her boyfriend, that stopping the compulsive eating was probably the test and that it freaked her out for the reasons Fairbairn has so nicely outlined. In this case, to "stop it," is to separate from the mother, to cut those libidinal ties, and to live more in the healthy relationship that, in the area of food, is represented by her communion with the boyfriend.

I conceptualized the overeating as an expression of the antilibidinal-self to antilibidinal-object relationship. By overeating, Alice was staying with mother, modeling her rebellion to rules, accepting her prescription for dealing with upset, and taking the unwanted food that mother mischievously offered. Furthermore, the overeating was done alone (i.e., with internalized mother). The fat and self-defeating feelings that it produced kept her less competitive, attractive, sexual, and autonomous than she actually was. At one point in delivering this kind of analysis, I suggested, a bit tongue in cheek, that if worse came to worse she could apparently cure her overeating problem by never eating alone. What needed to happen, and what in fact ultimately did happen, was that Alice transformed herself through exorcizing one internalization and replacing it with another more appropriate one. Alice's compulsive overeating did change, albeit more slowly than other problems, in response to this kind of analytic, fine-grained analysis of her behavior, feelings, motivations, and dreams.

The kind of free-wheeling, actively shared exploration of her thoughts and feelings, as typified by the foregoing example, was typical of the kind of psychotherapy I engaged in with her over a period of two years. Though I did employ very brief bioenergetic processes on a couple of occasions, Alice was an ideal candidate for this kind of active, collaborative, analytic psychotherapy. This was the channel that worked for her. I don't believe she would have been a particularly good hypnotic subject, and much of the possible gestalt and bioenergetic analysis was not appropriate for her simply because she didn't need it. Her own access to feelings and fantasies was quite sufficient. Furthermore, the transference channel, which is typically thought so important for analytic work, was not really that important for her. Unlike clients where this is an extremely useful channel, Alice saw me very realistically, her object constancy for me was very high, and there was not the kind of projection that one sees when this particular channel is rich in possibility.

What Alice's case does illustrate so well is the often overdetermined nature of symptoms that do not yield until (1) all unconscious maintaining elements have been uncovered and (2) the external interpersonal ties are strong enough and healthy enough to allow relinquishing the internal object ties.

Because Alice's therapy was largely of the analytic variety, I will now present her central symptom constellation as it occurred in other cases and was treated by more active interventions. Illustrating these techniques will make some of the therapeutic strategies used with Alice more concrete. Indeed, it is often such concreteness that renders these techniques effective when more abstract interventions would fail.

ACTIVE THERAPEUTIC STRATEGIES FOR THE "LOSS OF SELF"

Carol

The experience of the loss of self is, in one form or another, a nearly universal phenomenon in those who suffer from the symbiotic problem. Alice's extreme capacity for accommodating to the point of losing touch with herself was paralled in Carol who suffered an almost identical manifestation of this problem. Her background, however, had been one that combined the symbiotic and schizoid issues. In other words, her upbringing was more characterized by coldness and lack of appropriate attunement by both parents. She was literally used by her family as a nurse for her chronically ill, passive-aggressive, demanding mother. Her siblings, particularly her older brother, were more harsh, rejecting, and distant than either of the parents and contributed to Carol's aversion to social contact.

Carol's contemporary need for others continued to be mediated through her caretaking, accommodating, "nursing" role. In the close interpersonal relations that she came to quite a bit later in life, Carol would also frequently feel taken over and invaded. At these points, she would be much more likely than Alice to develop a deep, fugue-like confusion and panic which, as she became more aware, yielded to intense feelings of rage. Like Alice, Carol was helped by a cognitive understanding of this phenomenon. She benefited from a deeper understanding of her history and from an accurate description of her process arrived at through the alliance. She felt more control because of this understanding, and she was able to catch on to the patterns earlier in the sequence. However, because of her more disadvantaged childhood, she had a less well-developed structure than Alice and needed higher levels of support for such development. Furthermore, she was much more amenable to the dissociative channel. She had done a good deal of meditative practice in her life and had had extensive hypnotherapy prior to the work reported here. As a result of all this, she was very trusting of her own unconscious processes.

In Carol's treatment, I used a very simple trance utilization which, with various modifications, I have used in other cases. In a trance state, I assisted her in accessing the early sequence of events leading to the experience of loss of self or personal boundaries. Then, following the metaphor that made most sense to her, I suggested that she visualize and experience a kind of Plexiglas boundary that she could voluntarily raise in order to shield or define herself. This was a boundary that she could raise whenever she found herself in a threatening situation or whenever she felt the fusion that was the initial sign of fugue and confusion. Then, I simply "future-paced" her use of this boundary-construction strategy by helping her rehearse, in her imagination, situations in which she would raise and/or lower the boundary. Of course, the individual tailoring of such a trance procedure involves attention to the different settings in which the boundary will be needed, the cues for raising or lowering the boundary, the type of boundary used (i.e., a fence, a shield, etc.), and the nature of suggestions, both direct and indirect, concerning the use of such a device.

In later explorations of this issue, we found that, with her husband, Carol was much more likely to slip into this state without knowing it. However, she began to notice that she had odd physical sensations when this was occurring, predating the kind of rage that began to arise as she became more aware of herself. These early signals included the room shrinking, a fuzzy sensation in her perception of reality, and a "floaty" sensation which seemed to represent a loss of grounding or good sense of differentiation. Her ability to isolate these early cues led us to develop a more conscious strategy for establishing more solid perception, grounding, and differentiation. My own contribution to this strategy comes out of my training in neurolinguistic programming or NLP (e.g., Diltz, Grinder, Bandler, Bandler, & DeLozier, 1988).

In further exploration of this phenomenon, we discovered that the de-differentiated state was often elicited and maintained by instructions or direction from her husband. In initiating or maintaining this state, Carol would frequently obey the instruction without thinking. Her behavior was analogous to a reflex arc, in that it seemed automatic and without reflection. She was doing someone else's bidding and lost herself in the process. This awareness led to the first step in the new strategy: noting any direction or instruction from her husband. Then she was to ask herself the "difference" between herself and her husband. That is, what was her different perception, how would she do the thing differently, did she want it done at all, was this the way she would approach the task or subject, etc.?

The third step of the new strategy required her to do or say something. This could include such obvious things as telling her husband to butt out, moving her body in some way that she would initiate independently, or simply breathing and self-consciously seeing things about her. A particularly effective cue turned out to be moving her arms in an outward direction in the symbolic gesture of removing the invading other prior to returning to her awareness of herself, her desires, her perceptions, etc. Even though the development of these insights and the associated strategy was highly conscious, it was followed by a brief trance induction and utilization, including future pacing. Once again, I suggested that, in her imagination, she enter into a number of situations with her husband that were likely to initiate the problematic de-differentiation and re-access the new strategy leading to differentiation.

Allen

Allen was a man of 36 whose history suggested primary schizoid issues mixed with narcissistic and, to a lesser but significant degree, symbiotic issues. He was in business with his older brother and, especially in this context, would often show the profoundest signs of loss of self. This occurred particularly when it was necessary to make a business decision that contained some element of risk or that could potentially challenge him beyond the limits of his known abilities. There was, in his case, a combination of the schizoid risk of security, in the deepest sense, with threats to a somewhat shaky self-esteem. When confronted with such a situation in which the brother was making a persuasive case for a new business risk, Allen would become quite symptomatic, with some vague sense that it had to do with the business deal. Typically, he was quite unclear about where he stood, what he felt, what his independent decision would be, etc. Rather, he became anxious, showed some dissociative symptoms involving memory and his ability to organize his activities, and would attempt to self-soothe by withdrawal.

What seemed to help Allen most was a more careful and well-mirrored exploration of what he did feel and think about the decision in question. In this exploration, we learned that Allen found it very difficult to mount a coherent presentation of his position, sensing, somewhat correctly, that the degree of terror he felt was way out of proportion for the situation. He felt like a "weak sister" in relation to his brother, whose style was at times somewhat more counterphobic in relation to such business decisions. This was particularly true since Allen was more responsible for the financial end of the business and was the one asked to predict the likely financial consequences of these various decisions. As anyone who is in business knows, such predictions are never made with certainty and, to some degree, business ventures often represent a kind of betting on the outcome of various unknown factors.

In this case, it was useful for the therapist to legitimize Allen's thoughts and feelings, discuss, and even model a more self-possessed presentation of his point of view. Wherever you have this type of prominent loss of self, you have a very real loss of self-respect — respect for one's own thoughts, feelings, needs, etc. With the symbiotic issue, the therapist will often need to point out repeatedly this loss of self-respect and show the client that she has respect for his experience, judgment, point of view, etc. This kind of treatment is a combination of what I have labeled the educational channel and the internalization channel.

The origin of many of these characterological issues involves a failure of parental respect for the client, given through attention, mirroring, or attuned response to the individual's self-expression. This origin needs to be explained and the current patterns deriving from that history described again and again. In that process, the therapist needs to show the respect, mirroring, recognition, or actively attuned response required. The individual will then begin to learn where he stands, how he feels, what he thinks, and what he needs. Perhaps more important, he will learn that his position is as legitimate as that of anyone else. He learns to stop tracking others excessively and begins to track himself first. Particularly when this self-tracking is followed by self-expression that is assertive, there will be a building of structure through "exercise of function" (Greenacre, 1959). In Allen's case, as he learned to recognize and present his case, his sense of self grew, his role in the business relationship was reinforced, and the recognition and respect of his brother enhanced his self-respect.

Robert

Robert was a man of approximately the same age as Allen, whose history and behavior were consistent with the expression of the narcissistic and symbiotic issues. He had a demanding wife and a demanding job. He spent all of his time accommodating himself to these demands. In the course of therapy, Robert began to discover how unself-directed his life was. Descriptions of these patterns and interpretations of their origins were useful but were not enough. What was perhaps most helpful in his case was a mutually agreed upon behavioral prescription wherein he spent an hour a day in self-directed activity.

Initially, this was so difficult for him that parts of several therapy sessions were spent developing a menu of activities for this time. He did like going for walks, so, at first, he simply took daily hour-long walks. After a while, some things along the walk drew his interest, or during the walk he would decide on other things that he would like to do, either at that time or later. The walks led him to decide upon and schedule other athletic activities and, eventually, weekends away with his wife, which he increasingly planned himself.

This kind of exploration and reclamation of the self led him to more assertive behavior at home, which was not always welcomed initially but which, in the long run, significantly improved the quality of his marital relationship. By seeing and feeling what he did, Robert learned who he was in a far more grounded and concrete way than he had heretofore experienced. As with Allen, the support and confirmation of his therapist were extremely important as he, like all symbiotic characters, had lost the self-respect that was his birthright. Robert's case is a simple example of the use of the behavioral channel.

The next chapter details the use of the feeling channel, with a particular focus on the negative therapeutic reaction in the symbiotic character.

CHAPTER 9

Internal Object Relations and
the Negative Therapeutic Reaction

THE PHENOMENON OF THE NEGATIVE therapeutic reaction is simply the exacerbation of symptoms in response to therapeutic intervention. Such intervention may include speaking hopefully to the client or expressing a satisfaction with the progress of treatment (Freud, 1923), interpretations that are expected to alleviate symptoms (Rycroft, 1973), or interventions that achieve actual therapeutic benefit (Masterson, 1976).

Hypotheses concerning the dynamics underlying the negative therapeutic reaction have been many and varied. The phenomenon has been used as evidence of primary masochism (Rycroft, 1973), as well as the expression of the patient's envy, which has remained silent or hidden. More positive construals of this phenomenon, which fit the current object relations perspective, include guilt at separation and/or survival, fears of separation, including retaliation of the original object, and the conflict between the wish for fusion and the wish for separation. All of these latter dynamics may be clearly operative with the symbiotic and masochistic client, including the negative therapeutic reaction as an aggressive or hostile response to the therapist, as Klein and others have suggested.

Given the inhibition of aggression in these character structures and the frequent self-destructive nature of its convoluted expression, the negative therapeutic reaction is clearly prototypical. An analysis of which of these dynamics are operative in any given case can be extremely useful, directly suggesting interventions which will speak to the underlying dynamics. The following case, while illustrative of a number of points, is a particularly salient example of the recurring issue of the negative therapeutic reaction in a personality characterized by both symbiotic and masochistic features.

SIU

Siu looked very much the masochist when we first met. At 46, he reported a lifelong depression characterized most by stasis, in spite of many years of various forms of psychotherapy with several therapists. Siu, a physician, was the son of Chinese immigrants whose family histories were marked by tragedy. His mother had lost her own mother when she was a small child. Her father remarried a cruel, rejecting woman, and Siu's mother lived in mortal fear of her stepmother until she was banished from home in adolescence. She thought her father loved her, but he was completely unable to protect her from what appears to have been an evil woman. She looked for the salvation and protection in her husband, Siu's father, that she could not find in her own father.

Siu's father had already emigrated to America to escape dire poverty and returned to China to find a wife. Though he was from a lower class than mother and was uneducated, he held out the promise of the New World. Mother's conceptions of this world were quite unrealistic: according to Siu, she literally expected the streets to be paved with gold. Her salvation was to be ensured by the marriage. The reality was far more modest—a small Chinese restaurant in a New Jersey town devoid of Chinese. The family was the target of racism, the more frightening because their immigration had not been legal.

Father hoped to return to China with his family, and he groomed his three children for such a future. Father was quite rigid in that aim and, on occasion, was forceful with his children in enforcing his will. Occasionally he would unleash his temper on Siu, and the child was afraid of him. In these interactions with the father, as well as in his exposure to racism, Siu had direct experiences with the kinds of subjugation and overpowering of will that are associated with the etiology of masochism. But these instances were rare and never seemed to wholly explain the recalcitrant symptomatic conditions that he experienced.

Far more salient in his etiology, we came to find, was his relationship with his mother. Having lost her own mother, been severely let down by her father, and disappointed in her husband and new home, she had fixed her idealized hopes for salvation on her son. In reconstructing his childhood, Siu most clearly remembered his mother's almost constant plaintive manner and tone. He had resolved to do anything to help her feel better. But this turned out to be an impossible mission, which he eventually abandoned in practice but not in spirit.

After he left home for college, he never really returned. Indeed, he forgot how to speak his native Chinese, the language with which he had been raised and expected to use exclusively one day in China.

After college he was very active in the anti-war movement, exposing himself to danger and his family to the possible discovery of their illegal immigrant status, which could have resulted in deportation. In that movement, Siu once fasted to the point where death by starvation was at hand. He was repeatedly beaten—more than once beaten unconscious—and jailed for his acts of passive resistance.

This combination of rebellion and self-sacrifice was typical of him, albeit less obvious earlier and later in his life. Psychodynamically, his rebellion seemed more aimed at the authority of the father, while the self-sacrifice joined him with the mother and represented attempts to save her. For example, after college, Siu married a Hispanic woman against the wishes of his family. His father refused to see him ever again, though his mother did visit without her husband's knowledge. Siu was drawn to a series of human rights causes, for which he repeatedly sacrificed himself, sometimes in small and sometimes in major ways. Throughout his two years in psychotherapy with me, he repeatedly struggled with his feelings of obligation to sacrifice himself once again for some worthy cause, against his growing desire to be himself, meet his own needs, and be free.

Siu's presenting complaints included this lifelong, low-grade depression, which periodically would be accompanied by more serious symptoms, including early morning awakening and disruptive rumination. His self-esteem and confidence in his abilities as a doctor and administrator fluctuated markedly. In addition to his conflicts concerning obligation, he knew that at times he was far too sensitive to the feelings of others and could not help but overmodulate his behavior in response to their feelings, either real or imagined. Yet, at other times, he would act out this obligatory self with very limited self-awareness. He was repeatedly conflicted by the sense of obligation to put himself in positions of leadership or responsibility which would be exceedingly time-consuming, place him in uncomfortable situations of conflict, and ultimately result in his having very little time for himself or his family, which consisted of a wife and three children. He also complained of a recurrent tendency to procrastinate and saw himself as overly self-critical. This attitude of staunch critic was also aimed at his children, particularly his son, at his wife, and, at other times, at other Chinese-Americans whom he could see in very negative, stereotyped ways. He was a man who appeared from the first moments of our contact to be consistently uncomfortable. I was taken almost immediately with the sense that here was a person for whom it would be a sin to be happy.

Siu had had a good deal of therapy, including five years of gestalt work, several years of body-related psychotherapy, involvement in a very intensive, short-term therapy program, a year of psychodynamic psychotherapy, and several years of body-related group work. It was difficult to determine whether any of this work had done him much good, but it was clear that this was a man still imprisoned. The history of therapy was marked by a tendency toward dual relationships. One therapist in particular had involved him in aspects of his institute program and had solicited further involvement, which Siu resisted with considerable guilt and discomfort. When Siu resisted this involvement, and particularly when he sought supplementary therapeutic assistance, he was rejected. This therapeutic encounter, in particular, seemed to have replicated some of the injuries that Siu had suffered from both the mother, who was engulfing, and the father, who was so controlling. The therapist, like father, attempted to be overpowering and, when he failed, was enraged and rejecting.

In order to survive as an independent person, Siu had escaped his father and his therapist, but at considerable cost. As with all such personal rebellions, his remained highly object related, and he never left the object of the rebellion behind. Siu never felt entirely good about himself as a result of the hurt he had to inflict or the loss he had to sustain in order to be himself. He was never at peace with his decisions to resist and rebel to gain autonomy.

Given the symbiotic's impossible and somewhat artificial choice between autonomy and contact, Siu had consciously chosen autonomy, but had never really been confirmed in this choice and had never felt really good about it. The guilt remained, and he repeatedly found both mother and father figures in the environment with whom he could replay the conflict. He would repeatedly feel the pull to enmesh and subjugate himself and the corresponding impulse not only to rebel but to retaliate in order to be free.

Siu's younger brother and, to a lesser extent, his younger sister had both capitulated more to their parents' desires. His sister was a workaholic academic who lived not far from her mother and brother, who lived together. The brother, who was the youngest and still living at home, seemed to be a clear example of the infantilized youngest child who can never escape the nest. This young man, now in his thirties, had very little, if any, social life and was bound to his mother as Siu thought he too should be. Siu, of course, felt a good deal of both survivor and separation guilt in relation to this family, particularly the younger brother with whom he could so easily identify. To be happy as well as separate would have cut him off even more from the misery of this family and would, indeed, have been a kind of sin.

The largely active analytic treatment of Siu resulted in our delineating a number of masochistic and symbiotic themes in his character. The masochistic themes came from his interaction with his father, coupled with his identification with his mother. In other words, Siu looked more masochistic than he really was. This was definitely a part of his character structure, but that part of it that came from his identification with the mother and his self-sacrifice for her was essentially symbiotic in nature. This is not uncommon in symbiotic individuals. They can often look masochistic when they have merged with a masochistic parent. Siu's case represents an interesting wrinkle for, while this happened, his more direct experience with his father certainly did have elements of the more typical masochistic etiology in which control is an issue and the patient's will is overwhelmed by a more powerful force. Furthermore, this etiology was reported in several racist incidents in which Siu or his family were suppressed or subjugated.

Let us delineate the masochistic themes first. Symptomatically, Siu had episodes in which he would experience himself as worthless in the extreme, "deformed, fit only to do some degrading form of manual labor; there would be no work too low for me." However, in reaction to that, he began to recognize that his whole history was one in which it was all right for him to fight with determined and controlled rage from the lower position.

He got even by withstanding pain and by secret retaliation. He remembered feeling all of this when he was beaten in the instances of passive resistance in the anti-war movement, as well as during the life-threatening fast. Then, he remembered instances in which he had sadistically and secretly retaliated against those who had been abusive to him. He also remembered instances from childhood in which he had been abused or beaten by older white children. He remembered the thought that he wasn't good because he could be hurt, yet retaining some self-esteem by not letting the pain show and resolving to "show them." He remembered that the older boys respected him for his ability to hold out in these situations, and he resolved to continue to show his strength and worth through this kind of masochistic show of will.

Siu also remembered that his father had quite a temper. He could flare up at customers in the restaurant and show temper with his family. Siu remembered one instance in which his father got into a rage and beat him with an ax handle. He remembered being both surprised and terrified in this situation but could remember no other incident as severe as this and he had very few memories of any other corporal punishment from his father. It was unclear whether there were other instances that he could not remember or whether this fatherly rage only exploded very occasionally. I suspect the latter, but his father's complete abandonment of Siu after his marriage outside the race is extreme enough to suggest that this was a man who could be overpoweringly willful with his children.

In relation to me, Siu often projected racism, rejection, or felt that I must be bored with him and wanted to get rid of him. Initially, he pulled in various subtle ways for me to take a one-up position. Given his high level of acculturation, I found it a bit unusual that he would lower his head to me and then look up at me. I found myself scrunching down in my chair, trying to get at his level, only to be one-downed again by this persistent habit. In his case, I found it useful to share the countertransference pulls I was feeling, as well as to share my efforts at resisting them. In his case, it was particularly useful to repeatedly deny as well as analytically explore the boredom, racism, and rejection that he projected.

On occasion, I would experience a countertransferential pull to justify the projection, together with a strong distaste for doing so and a wonderment at my own reactions, which I experienced as inconsistent with my responses generally and my responses to Siu over time. My forthright sharing of my own phenomenology with him seemed particularly important. I think this was unusually helpful because of his earlier bad experiences with therapists and his history of being used by them. Indeed, Siu felt guilt about sharing his experiences with the more exploitative therapist and felt that in even telling me of this relationship and its problems, he was being bad by "dragging me into the mud." During the exploration of these themes, Siu uncovered the prototypic masochistic pathogenic belief that, among other things, underlies the negative therapeutic reaction: "Suffering is good. It means I can't be doing anything wrong."

Turning to Siu's symbiotic side, one incident presents itself as particularly clear evidence of this constellation. During much of his therapy with me, Siu had continued in an experiential therapy group. The female leader of this group was troubled by recurrent poison ivy, and, in an effort to help her, Siu provided her with a nonprescription ointment that some literature had indicated was quite effective. The leader used that ointment and then dove into gardening in a highly infested area, apparently confident that this medication would protect her. As it turned out, the ointment did not give such blanket protection, and she had a serious outbreak of poison ivy. In addition to the more understandable reactions of anger at the woman for this cavalier approach, given her known affliction, and some guilt at not having prevented this outbreak, Siu himself began experiencing the extreme itchiness of a poison ivy rash. He also took on responsibility for treating the woman's outbreak. He was alarmed at the very enmeshed nature of his own dramatic symptoms.

In sessions surrounding these issues, he remembered fearing that his father had died 15 years ago because he was not loyal. His mother was currently suffering from a painful medical problem for which he took excessive responsibility, feeling that, in some undefined way, she too was ill because of him. Throughout the therapy, there were countless examples of Siu's feeling a loyal attachment to his mother's depressive mood. He became increasingly aware of the pathogenic belief that his being happy would make his mother unhappy. There was, in short, a connection with mother mediated by her unhappiness and his attempts to remedy it. Indeed, to be mother's son was to join in the melancholy present with the mother and to work for a perfect future which was, of course, never realized.

Mother would invoke father's ghost to further enhance this symbiotic guilt, charging that the father's ghost would be displeased in some way with aspects of Siu's current behavior.

Further invasion of Siu's consciousness came from his not altogether believed belief that his mother could read his mind or see across time and space, thereby knowing that he was not engaging in the kinds of housekeeping and cultural practices of which she would approve. He experienced the same kind of guilt and feelings of disloyalty in talking about the former therapist with whom he had been enmeshed, and he experienced a good deal of fear that I would indeed turn on him for talking about that therapist in this disloyal fashion. He also projected that I was threatened by the group therapy work that he was continuing. This was a clear-cut transference test that was easy to pass.

An Object Relations Analysis of Symptoms

As we did with Alice, let us now take each of Siu's symptom constellations and analyze them in terms of the self-object relationship that they represent. The pervasive lifelong depression can be conceptualized most usefully as the expression of the antilibidinal self maintaining contact with an antilibidinal object through aggression toward the libidinal self (prototype I in Figure 2, p. 149). Primarily, it is the object-seeking nature of this self-annihilation that is therapeutically useful. The core objective of the symptom is to maintain contact with both the mother, who is engulfing, and the father, who is controlling. This, of course, results in a very narrow range of self-expression. This killing of the life force keeps Siu working for that unrealizable perfect future but, at the same time, attached to an unhappy family in the unhappy present.

Similarly, Siu's ability to hold out in a kind of masochistic tolerance of pain can usefully be seen as the antilibidinal self in relationship to the antilibidinal object hurting the libidinal self (prototype I). Once again, there is an object-seeking reward in such holding-out behavior. It was admired in his past by those who subjugated him, and it mediated contact with them. This is the long-suffering attitude that typifies the behavior of many members of families and groups who have survived by a persistent tolerance of persecution. For Siu the persecution was no longer present in the external world. But the

internal closed system was kept in place by the power of that continuing self-persecution, which served the function of preserving early
internalized object ties.

Conceptualizing these antilibidinal, self-defeating behaviors and
attitudes in this way is particularly useful therapeutically because it
pulls out the positive intention of the behavior or attitude and potentially redirects the life energy away from archaic internal objects and
toward current external ones. It suggests that one must relinquish
one's attachment to these archaic antilibidinal objects, mourn their
loss, and additionally, mourn never having had those parents who
really should have been there to meet those original needs. In other
words, conceptualizing these as antilibidinal-self behaviors directly
suggests the need for relinquishing, mourning, and redirection of
energy from the internal and past to the external and present.

Siu had a history of seeking out idealized, world-renowned therapists who proved to be, at best, disappointing and, at worst, exploitative and rejecting. This pattern can be viewed as an example of
symptom prototype II, where the libidinal self reaches to the libidinal
(exciting) object with infantile expectations and is ultimately disappointed.

As he got better, Siu experienced the expected sadness at the symbolic loss of his mother, father, and former therapist, and at relinquishing the hope that merger with these idealized gratifying figures
would make his life more comfortable and fulfilled. Experiencing
and mourning that loss did have the effect of making his life freer,
more fulfilled, and open to current gratifying relationships.

There are three symptom constellations that I believe can be usefully represented as expressions of Siu's libidinal self to his antilibidinal self and object (prototype III, Figure 2, p. 149). These are (1)
procrastination, (2) loss of the ability to speak Chinese, and (3)
anti-Asian prejudice. I see each of these as aggression by the libidinal
self towards the demands and constraints of the antilibidinal self and
object. The passive-aggressive rebellions are procrastination and the
loss of the ability to speak Chinese. The infrequent breaking through
of intense rage and anti-Asian prejudice of which Siu was aware,
though highly dystonic, are more directly aggressive expressions.

The more passive-aggressive behaviors are obviously attempts by
Siu to refuse being such a good boy who meets all of his obligations
(e.g., he procrastinates or "forgets"). His loss of the ability to speak

Chinese is a rebellion against the family, particularly the father, who demanded that he stay rigidly in the Chinese-American subculture. I see Siu's prejudice against certain things Chinese—a kind of shamefully admitted prejudice against some Chinese characteristics—as an attempt at libidinal self-expression. This is so because it expresses a wish to separate and differentiate from some of the negative aspects of his own culture and family.

I have seen this same kind of rejection of one's cultural background serving this separation function in several other cases involving other races or religious groups. Again, it tends to be rather absolute, infantile, and shamefully admitted, but, in a very real way, it represents both the desire to separate and triggers the separation and survivor guilt that that wish elicits. Often, patients will show a corollary self-hatred that represents a rejection of elements of themselves which are life denying (i.e., antilibidinal). In these cases, the turning against the self is basically a healthy attempt to separate from internalized antilibidinal forces.

I interpreted Siu's frequent and hostilely felt criticism of his wife and son, and his occasional outbursts of rage at them as examples of prototype IV (Figure 2, p. 149). Here Siu is treating others who become frustrating as he was treated by his father. The original role-relationship model is propagated; the internal closed system is preserved, and there is a release of frustration to external objects that temporarily releases internal pressures.

I believe these distinctions in self-object relations are useful in many ways for conceptualizing and doing psychotherapy. Generally, those symptoms that represent libidinal-self expressions (as in prototypes II and III) may be encouraged, particularly as these expressions can be matured and made relevant to the present. In Siu's case, there can be a rejection of the obligation, the restraint, and the enmeshment with a depressive family. That rejection and separation can be owned and become ego syntonic. That change then can make the aggression, which is now internally directed and therefore debilitating, available for external expression.

Similarly, idealized "exciting" objects may be replaced by "good enough" objects, who naturally provide optimal frustration while maintaining constancy and providing gratification. This will, however, invoke mourning the loss of the exciting object. Similarly, those symptoms that are the expression of the antilibidinal self in coalition with the archaic antilibidinal object (as in prototypes I and IV) can be reframed for their object-seeking quality and then matured and redirected to new objects in the external world. This leads, again, to the prescription of relinquishing, of mourning, and of redirection of this originally libidinal energy from the internal archaic and unsatisfying objects to current, external, and potentially satisfying ones.

The Corrective Experience and The Negative Therapeutic Reaction

I will now catalog some of the therapeutic strategies employed to treat Siu's symptomatology in these two basic areas: (1) encouraging libidinal self-expressions and (2) reframing and redirecting antilibidinal self-expressions. This report will elucidate the negative therapeutic reaction and its treatment. The therapy of the symbiotic character most typically involves oscillation between these two contents, for encouraging the libidinal self means further aggression, separation, and autonomy, which increases pressure on the existing structure to modulate and contain all this. Such change automatically triggers, at least initially, anxiety at the separation and consequent aloneness, as well as guilt over such aggression, separation, or success, which may be felt to be achieved at another's expense. Not infrequently, there is also the fear, which is sometimes well-founded, that the existing structure cannot handle this new level of multiple affective stimulation.

These "negative therapeutic reactions" are quite threatening and elicit strategies that the client has found to be comforting in the past. These strategies are usually symptomatic in nature. The therapist's response to such a return of symptomatology will include analysis, resistance of the client's attempts to create connections through symptomatology as he or she has so often done in the past, and the offering of interpersonal connection for more libidinal self-expressions. Additionally, the therapist may need to reduce the guilt engendered by self-expression by providing more current and reality-based standards for personal responsibility or to reassure the client of his emerging ability to handle the new reality. This combination of encouragement, redefinition, interpretation, extinction of problematic patterns and reinforcement of healthier ones should encourage the client to more libidinal-self expression directed at external objects. And, this in turn, may stimulate a recurrence of symptomatology. In a nutshell, this is the therapeutic process with the symbiotic character. This analysis of the negative therapeutic reaction is, of course, reminiscent of Menninger's "triangle of conflict"—the underlying feeling leads to anxiety, which leads to defense (see Malan, 1979); or Masterson's (1981, p. 133) "borderline triad"—separation-individuation leads to depression, which leads to defense."

In the course of Siu's therapy, his most pervasive depressive symptoms seemed to recur particularly when he was presented with a choice between acquiescing to some new obligation vs. pursuing his own self-interest by refusing it. Similarly, situations that demanded his self-assertion in response to another's incompetence, neglect, or maltreatment of himself or others, conflicted with his tendency to withdraw, accommodate, or take excessive care of the offending party. Occasionally, his rage would break through inappropriately at the incompetence of those closest to him, and he would suffer tremendous depressive guilt about such episodes.

In the situations involving obligation, I would often help Siu see the grandiosity of his belief that others could really not take care of themselves and that he was the only man for the job. I interpreted the genetic source of this irrational idea and helped him discriminate between his mother and the current figures who might well use his assistance but didn't absolutely have to have it. This interpretation of Siu's "omnipotent responsibility" was typically very relieving. He could see that the sense of pressing obligation was usually self-generated. While others may have been asking him to do something, they were not necessarily desperate or coercive in their requests, though this was often his experience.

Most of my work with Siu, as with Alice, was verbal in nature. He had had some bioenergetic and gestalt work in the past, and I used these techniques with him sparingly to assist in accessing the feeling channel. For example, on a couple of occasions I asked Siu to stand before me with his back to me and his arms crossed on his chest. I then gripped him from the back, around the torso, restraining him for an extended period. I instructed him to let the restraint build up until it was very unpleasant and then to throw me off as hard as he could. The first time he did this, his movement was very weak and obviously restrained. The second time, there was a powerful surge of energy and he did throw me off quite effectively. He then became quite concerned that he had hurt me in some way, and this exaggerated worry became a quite productive topic for that session.

On a couple of other occasions, I engaged him in a similar exercise in which he repeatedly said the word "no" as I repeatedly responded with the word "yes" or some other cajoling remark such as "please," "just this once," "I'm not asking for much," "you owe it to me," etc.

On another occasion I used the bioenergetic exercise in which the client lays down on his back with his knees up to his chest and his feet extended in the air. The therapist then places the bottom of the client's feet on his chest and leans over the client, supported largely by the client's legs. The therapist is, in this position, literally in the client's face. Again, the client is asked to allow the charge to build up and the intrusion to become uncomfortable. At that point, the client is to throw the therapist off by pushing him away with all the available force in his legs. Again, the first time Siu did this effectively he was afraid he had hurt me.

This process, which replicates the intrusion experienced by the masochist, is particularly useful for the characterological issues of this type. These kinds of exercises are particularly useful for their concrete and immediate nature and are useful here for the simplicity they provide in the exposition of what transpired repeatedly in Siu's therapy in much more subtle ways. This direct encouragement of aggression and self-expression, together with maintenance of personal boundaries and exploration of the client's positive and negative reactions to such expressions, is really the bread and butter of this therapy. The therapist's permission-giving and rational allaying of developmentally arrested cognitions, which underlie separation and survival guilt, employ the "internalization channel" to effect maturation and healing. In simpler language, the client learns he can relinquish the omnipotently responsible ideas about damaging others through his separation and self-expression and internalizes the therapist's ideas about such matters, which are presumably more mature and appropriate to the present time.

This internalization channel was particularly important for Siu, who had continually been looking for a father figure who could wean him away from the engulfing demands of the internalized bad mother who was so unhappy and so powerless. The real father, who had himself been powerful, had strengthened those bad object ties by his imperial insistence that Siu not acculturate but, instead, continually prepare to return to China. Similarly, the father's rejection of Siu for his interracial marriage severely limited Siu's contact with his mother, and this did indeed hurt her. Separation guilt had been confirmed.

Siu was so troubled by this sort of guilt that he was unable to leave a shop without buying something. Similarly, he had great difficulty returning something to a store, even under the most justified of circumstances. As a part of the therapy, we used the behavioral channel to help Siu learn more about himself, as well as overcome such feelings, by repeatedly getting him to do such things. Again, the discussion of these exercises was perhaps more useful than the exercises themselves for the internalization of new values and the analysis of old ones.

Every recurrence of symtomatology in this repetitive cycle of improvement and relapse led to opportunities for interpretation and redirection. Perhaps the central and most organizing conceptual frame for interpretive themes is the triangle of conflict, particularly as it relates to the symptoms and the negative therapeutic reaction. There will be a period, even without good therapeutic intervention, when things are going well. There is more aggression, autonomy, self-expression, success, etc., when suddenly, the client begins to regress and becomes depressed, obsessive about some minor problem, worried that he has hurt someone's feelings or neglected an obligation, etc. Here one often finds that the individual believes that to be out there in the world as an autonomous self-expressive adult means to be alone. The connection with the bad object is lost, and it returns metaphorically, demanding its due and provoking behaviors that preserve the self's connection with it and produce a sense of comfortable familiarity, no matter how uncomfortable the symptoms may be.

It is critical in delivering this interpretation to emphasize the object-seeking nature of the symptomatic behavior. It is connection that needs to be preserved, and, in giving the preservation interpretation, one must always remember to emphasize that underlying objective. For if that is the class into which the symptomatic behavior falls, there are healthier behaviors that fall into that same class (i.e., seeking connection with others in the external world who will support a healthier, happier state of affairs). Here, we will recall Gustafson's (1986, p. 201) concise statement of Bateson's work: "All the moves *seen* are but members of a class which is *unseen*." Providing current alternative connections strengthens the self and facilitates the relinquishing of these very powerful connections to the bad objects of childhood. Nevertheless, one must still relinquish and mourn the loss of those original objects, the familiarity of this way of being, and the identity that these connections, identifications, and preserving behaviors provide. The "strengthened context" of the therapeutic alliance, as well as of the more sustaining life that therapy has helped the individual build, will support and cushion this process but cannot eliminate it. It is supposed to hurt. The therapist's job is simply to help the individual create a life in which these losses are bearable.

A corollary interpretative theme closely related to the first is this: The "negative therapeutic reaction" symptomatology represents a well-learned path to establish or preserve connection with others and is being used now to do this, not only with internalized objects, but also with external, current objects — including the therapist. Here the object-seeking nature of the behavior is again emphasized, and the individual can explore the extent to which others in his current life collude with that objective and the extent to which they frustrate it. This interpretation may lead to rather simple, yet profoundly effective, changes. There are often other, healthier behaviors in which one can engage that provide contact more satisfying than the familiar, but usually troubled, contact based on the symptomatology.

Special interpretative attention may need to be given to the fear or anxiety angle of the triangle. We know that for symbiotics, self-expression activates fear. Such fear may be the result of internal conflict, internal deficit, or actual external consequences. To explain the conflict-based fear, let us use the language of Freud's original "triangle," the structural tripartite model. Here, we simply hypothesize that the wish for greater autonomy and the behaviors that achieve it elicit a fear of the superego. In these cases, intervention that dismantles such a harsh and inappropriate superego is called for, with emphasis on the internalization of other more appropriate values.

Fear based on deficit refers to those cases in which the individual's structure is overstimulated by more affect, of whatever kind, than it can handle. In other words, the ego is not up to it, or one fears that this is so. The most essential therapeutic discrimination concerning such fear is exactly this: Is the patient one who can handle higher levels of excitation and whose defenses may appropriately be eroded, or is this one whose structure must be strengthened before any of that may be accomplished? Once again, this basically boils down to an accurate assessment of the patient's level of structural functioning in the situations in question. Where there is structural deficit, the safest therapeutic response is to soothe, to slow things down, and to provide a relationship that is containing and reassuring in its maintenance of boundaries and firm holding qualities. Within this context, the structure is built primarily through the internalization channel, wherein optimal frustration is repeatedly experienced in a strengthened context leading to the transmuting internalizations. For me, this is really the essence of supportive psychotherapy.

As I have written in the earlier volumes of this series, clients do not fit neatly into a bimodal distribution in which some need supportive therapy while others need only uncovering-expressive therapy. The more typical case is one in which an integration of both strategies is required. In general, clients with lower levels of structural function-ing need more supportive therapy and require therapy to be more repetitive and longer. Clients with higher structural functioning re-quire less supportive work and more uncovering-expressive work, which can be accomplished over a shorter period of time. Since the first objective of therapy, like medicine, must be to do no harm, a therapist must always be wary of those not uncommon individuals who look better put together than they really are. It is easy to be fooled by a client who appears to function well, particularly occupa-tionally, but whose underlying structure is more often revealed by the paucity of her interpersonal relations. Such people can be dra-matically overwhelmed by any precipitous erosion of defenses and, in that process, can be very damaged.

Once clients know of this question, however, they are often re-markably helpful in discovering the extent to which they really can tolerate higher levels of affective stimulation and to what extent they need more work on the structure. Once again, when the therapist is intensively interested in discovering the answer to that question, but not invested in any particular answer, the client can strengthen her abilities at objective self-perception. It is the experience of all individ-uals with a self disorder (i.e., symbiotic, narcissistic, masochistic) that significant others have often done just the opposite. The parents of such patients have been intensely committed to their offspring being a certain way, while simultaneously being very disinterested in who they actually were. The therapist's job in such cases is to exactly reverse this—to be intensely interested but neutral.

When there is an actual external threat of punishment or abandonment for self-expression, the therapist must attend not only to the internal attitudinal and structural issues as discussed but must also attend to how the client will hold up to such threats or actualities. In these situations, good therapy will often include helping the client to strategically engineer such self-expression and cope with the external blocks to it, both behaviorally and attitudinally. Concrete planning, role play, desensitization, and other such concrete strategies may be called for in these cases.

In Siu's treatment we repeatedly traversed the triangle of conflict or typical "borderline triad." It is obvious from the history and report of the therapy, which I have already given, that the pull of internalized and even external bad objects was extremely strong in this case. Relinquishing them took many repetitions, and the treatment course involved such relinquishing with the mother first and the father second. In both cases, former therapeutic figures, who had been similar to both mother and father, were also relinquished, and their more current contributions to the etiology and maintenance of the problem understood.

To tolerate higher levels of affect and self-expression, Siu required solid and proven external current relationships to withstand those feelings, as well as the onslaught of what I will call bad object reactions. It wasn't so much that his existing structure was all that weak, as it was that the force of such an onslaught could overwhelm even a relatively strong organization.

Much of the deficit in structure in Siu's case had to do with the developmentally arrested cognitions of omnipotent responsibility which were tied to the experience of separation and survivor guilt. This could severely erode his maintenance of a constancy in self-esteem and thereby propel him into a kind of static depression, wherein he would doggedly meet his obligations while enduring internal deadness and misery. In this state, he could neither meet his obligations nor get in touch with his life force, in which there would be aggression, true self-expression, and refusal to subjugate himself. It was within this "stuck" state that most of the troubling symptomatology occurred. Moving him out of that essentially involved working through the triangle delineated here again and again, by encouraging the true self-expression and treating the anxiety and the consequent negative reactions to such expression.

THE BORDERLINE SYMBIOTIC

The cases presented thus far represent examples in the middle range of structural development (i.e., character neurosis). As we move down the structural functioning continuum into the range of personality disorder, we will encounter individuals functioning in a more "borderline" fashion. To the extent that the issues are symbiotic, the basic underlying conflicts are the same. What is essentially different is the structure available to deal with them. Because these individuals have had such bad parenting, very often many of the other existential issues have also been poorly handled and are similarly disorganizing.

These individuals usually have more traumatic histories, where the merger has been more extensive and pathological, with less opportunity for the internalization of positive objects. The underlying impulses to separate and the associated aggression and hostility are more intense and disorganize the fragile structure. Furthermore, there is often more legitimate fear concerning the impaired structure's ability to handle the underlying feelings. Also, there is often more real fear of external reality—that is, of the family of origin actually coercing continued enmeshment.

Because of the degree of difficulty, borderline patients often begin therapy earlier in their lives, when the press from the family of origin is more compelling. Finally, the defenses or self-sustaining measures that the borderline patient takes are usually more coercive and aggressive. One sees far more transference acting-out, turning passive into active, and the coercive borderline states in which the individual's conflicts are externalized and the environment is coerced to remedy them.

In the foregoing explication of these similarities and differences, I have been guided by the triangle of conflict to elucidate the underlying feelings, anxieties, and defense constellations of the symbiotic borderline. The other models outlined throughout this book are also directly applicable to explaining the borderline situation. Fairbairn's model of split self-object relations with their libidinal and antilibidinal structures, the therapeutic channels, the encouragement of libidinal expressions, the interpretation and redirection of antilibidinal expressions, and the internalization of good object ties to replace the bad are all equally useful. The primary difference with the borderline is in the necessary emphasis on treating a deficient structure requiring far more reparative learning of such things as synthetic abilities, perspective taking, objective self and other perception, object and person constancy, etc. Often, the themes of therapy may be more obviously organized along these structure-building lines than along the content lines provided by the symbiotic conflict, though these will never be far in the background.

Although the treatment of the borderline symbiotic will usually take longer, be more repetitive, and usually be far more trying, the dynamics are often more obvious and less intricately woven than is the case with the character neurotic or even those higher in the structural functioning range. It is for this reason among others that I have focused more exclusively on somewhat higher functioning individuals in the extended case reports of this book. Still, the kind of integrative, post-modern art psychotherapy I am advocating here and in my other books is particularly well suited to the borderline individual. Indeed, these are the people who often need the very concrete and specific strategies offered by the more active cognitive, behavioral, and affective therapeutic forms integrated in this format. The first two books in this series (Johnson, 1985, 1987) each have a major case presentation involving individuals functioning in the personality disorder range.

Individuals in the lower structural functioning or "borderline" range will often require more therapeutic contact. One can think of an intervention continuum that goes all the way from restricted inpatient treatment through residential day treatment to outpatient psychotherapy several times a week and so on. A useful guideline for prescription along this treatment dosage dimension is optimal frustration. The optimal amount of treatment for building structure corresponds to that which will produce frustration at an optimal level in such a way that the client will be required, yet able, to internalize the therapeutic functions of the therapy. Where what one can offer is less than this therapeutic optimum, one should refer the client to a setting in which more intensive therapy is possible.

There is in the borderline patient a heightened and almost unbearable conflict between child-like dependency, including the need to internalize the other, and the very real terror of being taken over by the other or by one's needs for the other. As every therapist of borderline patients knows, this will be played out by the individual's succumbing to that great dependency and then rejecting or provoking the therapist to reject. The rejection is often welcomed as a release from the torture of a relationship so infused with dependency and engulfment. The borderline patient needs very much to internalize the therapist in order to remedy the basic self-disorder, while at the same time relinquishing the infantile dependency that never was and never will be gratified.

Modeled as internal object relations, this is a pattern of alternation involving prototypes II and IV (Figure 2, p. 149). In prototype II, the arrested libidinal self reaches for the libidinal (exciting) object, who is expected to be unconditionally available and gratifying. This is the relationship that Masterson has described for the borderline. When the inevitable frustration occurs and the therapist is not available nor unconditionally gratifying, the borderline patient often switches to an internal object relationship that I have labeled prototype IV, wherein the antilibidinal self and object aggress against the perceived exciting object. The form of that aggression often replicates that which the patient has himself received. Analysis, explication, and even prediction of this pattern, its origin, and its real necessity as a part of the therapeutic process, is therapeutically useful.

Through interpretation and firm but neutral boundaries, the patient can learn to tolerate the frustration of not having the therapist available for dependency gratification and, in that way, internalize her. Here again, finding that point where the amount of therapeutic contact and support is optimal is the essential therapeutic problem. That equation must include the level of contact and support that the therapist can tolerate without being invaded by the demands of the client. The therapist's most serious error, as with the oral-dependent client in this dilemma, is to gratify beyond her own limits, building up resentment in that process, and finally withdrawing from the client in an aggressive or passive-aggressive manner. Often, a good therapeutic alliance and "observing ego," built up in the patient through accurate explanation and interpretation, will lead to the patient's assistance in the prevention of such an unfortunate outcome. I have found thorough discussion of such issues particularly useful in balancing these requirements, for it is really the alliance at this level that makes both the frustration as well as gratification of infantile wishes bearable.

It is with the therapy of the more damaged patients that the simultaneous double tracks of the psychotherapy process are often most apparent. On the one hand, this is a reparenting process in which the patient uses the therapist as a self-object to fill in and then repair lesions in the development of self. Simultaneously, however, the therapeutic relationship we are considering here is one of mutuality between two adults. The patient's understanding of the nature of these two tracks will assist him in giving in to the dependency so that he might use the therapist in the ways outlined, without being overwhelmed by the dependency, by his reaction to it, or by its gratification or frustration. The therapist is not really the patient's parent; she is merely an adult who has contracted to, among other things, play that role in the process of the patient's self-repair. Though a good therapist can help a great deal, the most difficult work is the patient's, and that work is largely at a symbolic level. That substantial repair can occur at all in this fashion is a tribute to the human being's symbolic system, the innate desire for health, and the reparative power of human contact.

APPENDICES

APPENDIX A

Psychoanalytic Developmental Concepts: A Selected Glossary

accommodation (Piaget, 1936)—a process basic to learning which involves the "changing or adjusting of preexisting structures (within the person) to accommodate reality." Horner (1979) feels that the working-through process in therapy is an example of accommodation.

agency (Stern, 1985)—the child's sense that he is the author of his acts, which he gradually achieves through the first few months of life. According to Stern, it is comprised of three parts: the sense of volition, which he sees as being present in the second month of life; proprioceptive feedback, present from birth; and predictability of consequences, which Stern feels develops gradually over the child's first few years.

ambivalence—the simultaneous experience of positive and negative feelings within oneself; the ability to be conscious of and to tolerate this experience is the hallmark of child development begun during the rapprochement phase.

antilibidinal object—*see* rejecting object.

antilibidinal self—*see* internal saboteur.

attachment—Bowlby (1969/1983) used this term to describe a process by which the infant bonds with an early caretaker, most often the mother. Bowlby brought in ethnological research to show that humans have innate sets of attachment behaviors which the infant uses to gain this bond.

assimilation (Piaget, 1936)—the process basic to learning whereby new experiences are taken into and modified to fit with a preexisting mental

Appendix A was created jointly by Sue Hully and the author.

199

organization. Horner (1979) cites transference within therapy as an example of this process.

autism (Mahler, Pine, & Bergman, 1975)—the "normal autistic phase occurs in the first weeks of life after birth, during which the young infant appears to be an almost purely biological organism, his instinctual responses to stimuli being on a reflex . . . level." Mahler sees the child as attempting to maintain homeostatic equilibrium by avoiding over or understimulation, by the inability to distinguish between inside and outside, and by finding need satisfaction in "his own omnipotent autistic orbit."

This concept has been challenged by Stern (1985), who cites numerous studies that show that the child is, from birth, both aware of and interacting with the external world. Contrary to the picture painted by Mahler, Stern also feels that the child's maintenance of homeostatic equilibrium is inextricably linked within the primary caretaker, who functions to help the infant accomplish this by regulating the stimulus input to the infant.

boundaries—psychic demarcations of divisions between people (or objects). According to Mahler, the infant learns gradually about these boundaries throughout development.

differentiation (Mahler, et al., 1975)—the first subphase of the separation-individuation process, occurring from five to nine months of age. The infant's total bodily dependence on his mother begins to decrease, and he begins a visual and tactile exploration of mother's face and body. Assured of "safe anchorage" (Mahler, 1968) and aided by locomotion and other maturational processes, the infant begins "expansion beyond the symbiotic orbit." Although the infant remains in close proximity to his mother during this period, he is also developing a primitive, but distinct, body image of his own.

enmeshment—a process whereby the realistic boundaries between people are not recognized or are violated. This involves one person's taking over what would normally be aspects of another's functioning or intruding upon what would normally be thought of as another's territory.

entitlement—the belief that one deserves to be given to without reciprocal expectation. Also believed to be exhibited in early life, with resolution beginning in rapprochement.

evocative memory—that form of memory made possible by the acquisition of object permanence. The individual may internally evoke the visual image or affective memory of an object or person in its absence. Adler and Buie (1979) argue that evocative memory is fragile in borderline patients and may be disrupted by intense affective states. They hypothesize that "person permanence" is particularly susceptible, especially given the borderline's relative inability to retain the affective memory of a significant other when experiencing a disruptive state.

exciting object (Fairbairn, 1958)—that repressed part of the original "bad" object that is split off from the "rejecting object." The libidinal self reaches toward this idealized object for the complete and unconditional gratification appropriate to an infant. The exciting object is, therefore, always ultimately disappointing. In this book, the exciting object has been labeled the libidinal object.

idealization (Kohut, 1971)—a type of archaic experience of the other by the person's "damaged pole of ideals," which searches for a selfobject that will warrant its idealization.

identification—a process of internalizing aspects of another to create psychic structure. The child begins to identify with the mother in the first year of life, and the resulting identifications contribute to ego and superego formation. These later combine with identifications with the father to round out ego and superego development. Identification may or may not include processes of assimilation and accommodation, which make what was another's, one's own.

internal saboteur—the repressed, introjected self that maintains contact with the rejecting object by colluding with it in life-denying or antilibidinal aggression toward the libidinal self. In this book, the internal saboteur is labeled the antilibidinal self.

internalization—a process spanning all of life during which the person takes into himself and makes his own, aspects of his significant objects, first by imitation, later, as he matures, by introjection, and finally, through identification. Through this process, regulation, which had previously taken place in interactions with the outside world, are substituted for by internal regulations. Internalization implies active processes of assimilation and accommodation, which result in making one's own what was once external.

introjection (Rycroft, 1968)—the process whereby the child incorporates the parents' attitudes in the form of multiple memory traces: The functions of the parents are thus taken over by the child's mental representations of the parents. In the analytic literature, introjection is usually seen as a relatively primitive form of internalization, in which the attributes of others are more or less swallowed whole and not effectively made one's own. "Incorporation" is also used to label this more primitive process. In this work, I have used "incorporative introjection" to communicate this idea.

libidinal ego (Fairbairn, 1958) — that repressed and developmentally arrested part of the self that retains the original organismic self-expressions. In this book, libidinal ego is labeled libidinal self.

libidinal object — *see* exciting object.

libidinal self — *see* libidinal ego.

magical thinking — a primitive form of thought based on primary process, lacking a knowledge of reality and true cause and effect. According to Freud, infants begin by thinking in this fashion and increasingly enlarge their capacity for secondary process thought, finally abandoning magical thinking. Stern challenges this developmental theory by arguing that the abilities needed for magical thinking develop later.

merger (Kohut, 1984) — seen as the patient's remobilization of a need from an early stage of development for fusion with "archaic idealized omnipotent selfobjects."

mirror — Kohut describes this as the person's need to be "mirrored," i.e., to be experienced with joy and approval by a delighted, parental selfobject. He describes this as "the damaged pole of ambitions seeking a confirming/approving response of the selfobject."

narcissistic cathexis — cathexis (Freud) is the investment of energy in a mental mechanism or an object. Narcissistic cathexis refers to investment in another person without an appreciation of the other as the source of his/her own initiative.

object constancy (Burgner & Edgecumbe, 1972) — "the capacity for constant relations, the capacity to recognize and tolerate loving and hostile feelings toward the same object, the capacity to keep feelings centered on a specific object, and the capacity to value an object for attributes other than its function of satisfying needs." Or, as Anna Freud (1968, pp. 506–507) put it, "Object constancy means . . . to retain an attachment even when the person is unsatisfying."

object permanence (Piaget)—an achievement of the 18- to 20-month-old child whereby he can believe in the continued existence of inanimate, transiently observed physical objects.

omnipotence/worthlessness—internal polarity experienced by the narcissist involving, on the one hand, intense feelings of power and personal effectiveness and, on the other, equally intense feelings of lack of value. These feelings are thought to persist in the narcissist as a result of lack of resolution of the polarity beginning in the rapprochement phase.

omnipotent responsibility—the feeling on the part of the young child that she has responsibility for others and for the fate of self and others. This belief by the child grows out of her own cognitive limitations—her egocentricity, her incomplete knowledge of true cause and effect, and her need to understand and have some control over her environment.

on the way to object constancy (22–30 months)—optimally, the child now has an idea of his mother as being mostly good, has a concept of self as separate from her and others, and has his own boundaries, self-confidence, and self-esteem. At this stage, he is beginning to be able to tolerate an image of himself and others as containing both good and bad elements.

optimal distance (Mahler et al., 1975)—the physical and psychological space between child and caregiver that best allows the child to develop those faculties that he needs in order to grow and to individuate. During the symbiotic stage, there will be little distance, as the infant molds into the mother's body; during the differentiation subphase, he begins to push away from his mother's chest to better explore her. The practicing infant begins to venture away from his mother in order to explore. During rapprochement, the toddler needs to be able to come and go even farther and to find the mother available on his return.

optimal frustration—challenges to the person's cognitive structure, belief system, and experience of self, other, and the world, which are in-phase and appropriately attuned to the individual's developmental level. The infant/child/person can gradually give up notions such as grandiosity, idealization, merger, etc., through such confrontations.

part–object—Rycroft (1973) views this as an object that is a part of a person, usually a penis or a breast. When the young infant views the mother this way, the mother is not recognized as a separate, whole person but, rather, as a need-satisfying object. This part, then, is all that is experienced, either in toto or in a certain state, when, for example, only the "good" or "bad" mother is recognized or only a certain function of the mother is acknowledged. These aspects are split off from other aspects, which may be experienced in other states.

practicing—the second subphase of separation-individuation, lasting from about 9 to about 14 months of age. During this period, the infant is able to actively move away from his mother and return to her, first by crawling and later by walking. The infant is exploring the environment (animate and inanimate) and practicing locomotor skills.

rapprochement—the third subphase of separation-individuation, lasting from 15 to 24 months of age. The infant rediscovers his mother and returns to her after the forays of his practicing period. The toddler loves to share his experiences and possessions with his mother, who is now more clearly perceived as separate and outside. In optimal adjustment, the narcissistic inflation of the practicing subphase is slowly replaced by a growing realization of separateness and, with it, vulnerability.

rapprochement crisis—a period during the rapprochement subphase occurring in all children, but with greater intensity in some, during which the realization of separateness is acute and disturbing. The toddler's belief in his omnipotence is severely threatened, and the environment is coerced as he tries to restore both the union with his mother and his prior feeling of omnipotence. "Ambitendency, which develops into ambivalence, is often intense; the toddler wants to be united with and, at the same time, separate from mother. Temper tantrums, whining, sad moods, and intense separation reactions are at their height" (Mahler, Pine & Bergman, 1975, p. 292).

real object—the other is seen by the developing child in a fashion that approximates that of an adult, i.e., he sees the object (person) as a whole and as separate from himself, a developmental achievement that follows seeing the other as a selfobject and a part-object, and the experience with transitional objects.

recognition memory—the ability of the human organism to recognize a stimulus by calling on the memory of having experienced it before. Recent child research dates this ability from birth, or even before; as Stern (1985) expresses it, "for some events, recognition memory appears to operate across the birth gap."

rejecting object (Fairbairn, 1958)—the repressed part of the original "bad" object which is split off from the "exciting object." The rejecting object aggresses against the libidinal self and its original self-expressions exactly as did the original bad object. The rejecting object maintains connection or bonding with the "internal saboteur" or antilibidinal self through this antilibidinal aggressive stance. In this book, the rejecting object has been labeled the antilibidinal object.

role-relationship models (Horowitz, 1987)—the individual's expectations of self and others which co-vary with one's states of mind. When one is depressed, for example, one might expect oneself to be weak and ineffectual and the other to be critical and powerful. In elated states, one might see oneself as brilliant and entertaining and others as captivated. These models of self and other may be conscious, partially conscious, or unconscious.

selfobject (Kohut, 1984)—similar to Stern's (1985) concept of self-regulating other, but defined by Kohut as an *internal representation* of that other used by the individual to maintain self-cohesion and identity. In practice, Kohut often uses this label to denote real external objects, but the key to the concept is their function in maintaining and defining the self—hence selfobject.

self-regulating other (Stern, 1985)—Stern sees this concept as similar to Kohut's selfobject, referring to an "ongoing functional relationship with (another) that (is) necessary to provide the regulating structures that maintain and/or enhance self-cohesion." Technically, Kohut's selfobject is an internal representation, but its function is self-maintenance and definition.

self-soothing—the infant's and, later, the child's self-comforting activities, derived partially from the child's internalization of nurturing from others.

separation anxiety—the infant/child's fear of being separated either physically, psychically, or both, from an object important to him. For Fairbairn, it is the infant's first anxiety.

separation guilt (Weiss & Sampson, 1986)—guilt felt by the child due to her belief that for her to separate from the parent (or other important figure) would be damaging to the parent and, thus, to the child's relationship with the parent.

separation-individuation (Mahler et al., 1975)—refers to the overall developmental process, which includes differentiation, practicing, rapprochement, and separation-individuation proper. During separation-individuation itself, the child gains a real identity of his own, can differentiate between self and object representations, and can maintain his ties with objects independent of the state of his needs (object constancy).

signal anxiety (Rycroft, 1973)—for Freud, the ego's response to internal danger. A form of apprehensiveness that alerts one to potentially upsetting and/or threatening stimuli and *signals* the need for an adaptive response.

stimulus barrier (Rycroft, 1968)—that part of the psychic apparatus that protects the person from excessive stimulation: It is directed against both internal and external stimuli. Stern (1985) has argued that this term is no longer necessary, as the infant very early begins this kind of regulation for himself.

stranger anxiety—one of an infant's possible responses to a stranger beginning at about eight months. According to Mahler et al. (1975), the infant in this state can display fear responses, avoid and/or shun the stranger, and may, in severe instances, cry or show significant distress. However, for Mahler, this reaction is not the norm, but rather, one that is more likely where "basic trust is less than optimal."

stranger reactions (Mahler et al., 1975)—"a variety of reactions to people other than mother, particularly pronounced during the differentiation subphase, when a special relationship to mother has been well established. Stranger reactions include curiosity and interest as well as wariness and mild or even severe anxiety. They subside at the beginning of the practicing period, but reappear at various times throughout the separation-individuation process" (p. 293).

survivor guilt (Weiss & Sampson, 1986; Modell, 1965, 1971)—guilt experienced by the individual as a result of the belief that for him to survive (or to thrive) is to deprive another with whom he is identified. The irrational belief is that survival is purchased at another's expense.

symbiosis—the symbiotic phase, which occurs as the one- to five-month-old infant and his mother or primary caregiver interact, is a stage of sociobiological interdependence between the two. Since this occurs before the infant has developed concepts of objects, Mahler believed the infant behaves and functions as though he and his mother were an omnipotent dual unity within one common boundary.

transitional object (Winnicott, 1951)—a blanket or other soft and/or cuddly object favored by the infant of about six months to a year. For Winnicott, it is the first object that exists for the infant neither totally internally or externally, but partakes of both; the infant can also use it as a stand-in for the mother. The transition is thus from infantile narcissism to object-love and from dependency to self-reliance.

transmuting internalization—this is seen by Kohut (1984) as a response to optimal frustration in which the person incorporates merged aspects of the "virtual selfobject" into his "virtual proto-self," thereby transforming the self and resulting in added psychic structure and organization with boundaries and a sense of identity.

twinship—Kohut describes this as the "damaged intermediate area of talents and skills seeking a selfobject that will make itself available for the reassuring experience of essential alikeness;" the other is experienced not as fused with the self but as like the self in essential ways—as being psychologically the same.

A Research-Based
Chronology of Development

Birth to One Month

Emotional expressions of interest, neonatal smiling and disgust, and affective expression of pain: at birth (Izard & Malatesta, 1985)

If breathing accidentally occluded by the breast during a feeding, infant was "breast shy" for the next several feedings: newborn (Gunther, 1961)

Can discriminate the mother's voice from another woman's voice reading the same material: neonate (DeCasper & Fifer, 1980)

Can discriminate between and imitate happy, sad, surprised expressions: 2 days (Field et al., 1982)

Can tell the smell of his own mother's breast milk: 3 days (MacFarlane, 1975)

Can recognize difference between a passage read aloud when infant was in utero and a control passage that the infant has never before heard: 1 week (DeCasper & Fifer, 1980)

Through first four months—vocalizations that can be interpreted as affective states; communicative nature of the occurrence varies with the dyadic states and varies across dyadic states in meaningful ways: 2 weeks (Keller & Scholmerich, 1987)

Ability to perform audiovisual cross-modal matching of the absolute level of intensity (able to find that certain absolute levels of sound intensity correspond with specific absolute levels of light intensity): 3 weeks (Lewcowicz & Turkewitz, 1980)

Shows appreciation of more global (nonfeatural) aspects of human face: animation, complexity, and even configuration: 1 month (Sherrod, 1981)

Appendix B was created by Sue Hully in collaboration with the author.

Gazes differently when scanning live faces than when viewing geometric forms: 1 month (Donee, 1973)

Disposed to react emotionally to signals of distress from another individual: "young infants" (Sagi & Hoffman, 1976; Simner, 1971)

Two to Three Months

Emotional expressions of anger and sadness: 2 months (Izard et al., 1983)

Social smile in place, has begun vocalizations directed at others, mutual gaze is sought more avidly, preference for human face and voice very evident, and infant is undergoing "biobehavioral transformation resulting in a highly social partner": 2–3 months (Emde et al., 1976; Spitz & Cobliner, 1965)

Regulates level of excitation by averting gaze to stop receiving stimulation that has gone beyond desirable level and by using gaze and facial behaviors to seek out and invite new or higher stimulation levels when excitation level below desired level: 2–6 months (Brazelton et al., 1974; Fogel, 1982; Stern, 1974)

Gets extensive experience with caregiver as regulator of excitation levels, as helping with self-regulation — this is best observed in the "fairly stereotypic parent-infant games of this life period": 2–6 months (Call & Marschak, 1976; Field, 1978; Fogel, 1977; Kaye, 1982; Schaffer, 1977; Stern et al., 1977; Tronick et al., 1977)

Much of what child can feel is possible only "in the presence of and through the interactive mediation of an other . . . infant and caregiver also regulate the infant's attention, curiosity, . . . cognitive engagement with the world, . . . and somatic state, . . . gratification of hunger and the shift from wakeful fatigue to sleep: 2–7 months (Stern, 1985)

Differential response to three maternal affective expressions (using face and voice): joy, anger, sadness: 10 weeks (Haviland & Lelwica, 1987)

Ability to match or mirror joy / anger: 10 weeks (Haviland & Lelwica, 1987)

Differential response (looked longer) to attractive faces when presented simultaneously with unattractive faces: 2–3 months (Langlois et al., 1987)

Can "know" that the same face showing different expressions (happiness, surprise, fear) remains the same face: 3 months (Spieker, 1982)

Can distinguish between schedules of constant reinforcement, fixed ratio of reinforcement, and a variable schedule: 3 months (Watson, 1979, 1980)

Will react with mild upset and social withdrawal if parents go "still-faced" in the middle of an interaction with them: 3 months (Tronick et al., 1978)

Discrimination among happy, sad, surprised expressions in photographs: 3 months (Young-Browne et al., 1977)

Discrimination between smiling, frowning expressions from photographs: 3 months (Barrera & Maurer, 1981)

Distinction between one unfamiliar face and another: 3 months (Barrera & Maurer, 1981)

Beginning ability to see that object couldn't exist at point A and then at point B without existing in between A and B — shown possible and impossible events, looked longer at impossible events: 3-and-a-half to 4-and-a-half months (Baillargeon, 1987). However, Piaget (1986, 1954) argued that this happens at 9 months.

Four to Six Months

Emotional expression of surprise: 4 months (Izard et al., 1980)

Ability to scan whole face and, thus, to get all the information that would convey expression: 4 months (Caron et al., 1982; Nelson & Dolgin, 1985) — face perceived as social class of stimulus

Ability to tell two fearful faces, varying in intensity, apart: 4 months (Kuchuk et al., 1986)

Infant takes control over beginnings and endings of direct visual engagement in social activities: 5 months (Beebe & Stern, 1977; Stern, 1971, 1974, 1977)

Behavioral discrimination between different emotions evidenced. For example, reacting more negatively — frowning, crying — to sad/angry face than to happy or neutral face and looking longer at sad face than at angry, happy, or neutral face: 5 months (Nelson, 1987)

Cross-modal matching abilities developed — able to discriminate (in two movies) between car receding and approaching, when noise matched picture: 5 months (Walker-Andrews & Lennon, 1984)

Can recognize a never-before-seen facial profile after a short familiarization with either the full face or the three-quarter view of the face: 5–7 months (Fagan, 1976, 1977)

Can remember a picture of a stranger's face seen for less than one minute more than a week before: 5–7 months (Fagan, 1973)

Recognition memory for hand puppet that made infant laugh over one week before (cued memory): 6–7 months (Nachman, 1982; Nachman & Stern, 1983)

Ability to distinguish between faces on the basis of age and sex, even when physical features are similar: 6 months (Fagan & Singer, 1979)

Beginning of ability to localize a sound along horizontal axis: 6 months (Morrongiello & Rocca, 1988)

Beginning of facial display of fear: 6 months (Cicchetti & Stroufe, 1978)

Preference shown for joyful over angry expression: 6 months (LaBarbera et al., 1976; Schwartz, Izard, & Ansul, 1985)

Seven to Eleven Months

Emotional expression of fear: 7 months (Schwartz, Izard, & Ansul, 1985)

Ability to tell both two fearful and two happy faces of varying intensity apart: 7 months (Nelson & Ludemann, 1987)

Ability to generalize discrimination of surprised faces across models of same sex: 7 months (Caron et al., 1982)

Ability to generalize discrimination of happy faces across both sexes: 7 months (Nelson & Dolgin, 1985)

Discovers that there are other minds in the world as well as their own; self and other now include subjective mental states, and these mental states "become the subject matter of relating": 7–9 months (Stern, 1985)

Ability to display facial expressions of interest, joy, surprise, sadness, anger, disgust, and fear: 7–9 months (Emde et al., 1976)

Beginning of ability to coordinate activities with objects and adults: 9 months (Sugarman-Bell, 1978; Trevarthan & Hubley, 1978)

Taking of active role in games: 9 months (Gustafson et al., 1979; Ratner & Bruner, 1978)

Ability to understand elements of content and structure of games, capacity to engage in object-person interaction, and ability to regulate games by requesting partner to continue to participate: 9 months (Ross & Lollis, 1987)

Some underlying capacity for deferring imitation of certain acts: 9 months (Meltzoff, 1988)

Significant increase in initiating positive expression, vis-à-vis mother: 9 months (Cohn & Tronick, 1987)

Preliminary findings suggest that children notice congruence between their own affective state and the affect expression seen on someone's face: 9 months (MacKain et al., 1985)

Intends to communicate: 9 months (Bloom, 1973; Brown, 1973; Bruner, 1975, 1977, 1981)

Attunement (cross-modal matching) expanded to affective attunement (matching mood or emotional state across modes) shared with mother: 9 months (Stern, Hofer, Haft, & Dore, 1985)

Begins to joke and tease, which assumes guessing contents of others' minds: 9 months plus (Dunn, 1982; Dunn & Kendrick, 1979, 1982)

Able to aggregate facial characteristics of faces shown and able to distill an average from them: 10 months (Strauss, 1979)

One to Two Years

Ability to follow social behaviors with look behaviors before gong on to persist in a task (in contrast to younger children, whose social behaviors are not directly involved with task-related behaviors and don't seem to have same salience in attempting to master the environment): 12 months (MacTurk et al., 1987)

Gaze begins to approximate adult pattern in gazing during mother's vocalizations: 12 months (Rutter & Durkin, 1987)

Ability to interpret and make use of emotional signals from others: 1 year (Campos et al., 1983; Stroufe, 1979)

Quality of attachment relationship at one year is an "excellent predictor of quality of relating in various other ways up through five years": 1 year (Stern, 1985)

Unelicited positive expression: 13 months (Kaye & Fogel, 1980)

Can recall past experience: 1–2 years (Ashmead & Perlmutter, 1980; Daehler & Greco, 1985)

Can repeat and recall sequences of common events: 1–2 years (Mandler, 1983; O'Connell & Gerard, 1985)

More systematic problem-solving tasks attempted, as opposed to just playing: 1–2 years (DeLoache et al., 1985; Spungen & Goodman, 1983)

Beginning of tendency to meet compliance requests of others: 2 years (Golden, Montare, & Bridger, 1977; Kopp, 1982; Vaughan, Kopp, & Krakow, 1984)

First representation of self: 2 years (Bretherton & Beeghly, 1982; Fischer, 1980) — can think of self as objective entity

Reaction to activities in terms of standards of performance: 2 years (Gopnik & Meltzoff, 1984; Kagan, 1981)

Develop ability to think, play symbolically, beginning of language development: 2 years (Stern, 1985)

Increase in imitation of conventional social behaviors: imitation of parents in task/caretaking/self-care behaviors, and siblings/peers more in affective behaviors and miscellaneous noninstrumental behaviors: 16–29 months (Kuczynski, Zahn-Waxler, & Radke-Yarrow, 1987)

Increase in deferred imitation: 16–29 months (Kuczynski, Zahn-Waxler, & Radke-Yarrow, 1987; Piaget, 1954 — dated imitation of novel events at between one and two years)

Gaze begins to approximate adult pattern in giving a "terminal look," a look at the end of own turn (in interaction with mother): 18 months (Rutter & Durkin, 1987)

Easily take on agent role in games, initiate games and play games with peers: 14–18 months (Ross & Kay, 1980)

Can operate at highest level category behavior when faced with a mixed array of objects; for example, begins to sort objects into two spatially distinct groups: 18 months (Gopnik & Meltzoff, 1987)

Can function at highest level of object permanence behavior (serial invisible displacement tasks): 18 months (Gopnik & Meltzoff, 1987)

Can function at highest level of means-ends behaviors; begins to use insight to solve: 18 months (Gopnik & Meltzoff, 1987)

Becomes activity- vs. outcome-oriented (earlier, effect-producing-contingency learning or secondary circular reactions are in close proximity to the child's actions, and the child is outcome-oriented): 18 months (Spangler, Bräutigam, & Stadler, 1984)

Acquisition of first feeling-state words: 18–20 months (Bretherton, Mc-New, & Beeghly-Smith, 1981; Bretherton et al., 1986)

Two to Three Years

Looks patterned in exactly the same way as adults—looking up at ends of own and others' turn: 2 years (interaction with mother) (Rutter & Durkin, 1987)

Spontaneous use of terms "think" and "know": 2 years (Bretherton & Beeghly, 1982)

Self-recognition: 2 years (Bertenthal & Fischer, 1978; Brooks-Gunn & Lewis, 1984)

Becomes agent of action in everyday speech: 2 years (Geppert & Küster, 1983)

Demands to perform activities independently: 2 years (Geppert & Küster, 1983)

Gets pleasure from producing outcomes vs. attractive engagement: 2 years (Hetzer, 1931)

Resistant to compliance: 2 years (Wenar, 1982)

Can derive correct inferences in a number of contexts with sufficient evidence: from narratives (Paris & Lindauer, 1976) and inferences about positions and movements of objects: (Haake & Somerville, 1985; Sophian & Wellman, 1980)

Most are able to talk about feeling states experienced by themselves and other people and have begun to discuss causes and consequences of feeling states (according to mothers' report): 28 months (Bretherton & Beeghly, 1982)

Three to Four Years

Has fundamental concern whether objects can cause themselves to move: preschool (Gelman, Spelke & Meck, 1983)

Reproduces judgments of time intervals in a quantitatively adequate way: preschool (Crowder & Hohle, 1970; Fraisse, 1963; Friedman, 1977)

Has some understanding of internal states: preschool (Bretherton & Beeghly, 1982)

Able to distinguish between mental and physical events: about 3 years (Wellman & Estes, 1986)

Can distinguish between intended and accidental outcomes in judgment of story character's emotional reaction to an outcome, given information about motive and outcome: 3 years (Yuill, 1984)

Reliably accurate inferences about movement potentials for five classes of items: unfamiliar mammals, nonmammalian animals, wheeled vehicles, statues of animals, and multipart, rigid objects (Massey & Gelman, 1988)—correctly judged whether objects were animate or not: 3 years (Massey & Gelman, 1988)

Some use of idea of logical necessity, although applied to small range of cases and not consistent: 3 years (Fabricius, Sophian, & Wellman, 1987)

Some sensitivity to necessity of confirmatory inferences in search tasks: 3 years (Fabricius, Sophian, & Wellman, 1987)

Know the "listener rule," i.e., produce messages sensitive to listener's status, knowledge, and abilities: 3 years (Sachs & Devin, 1976)

Capacity to perceive duration noninferentially, without having to infer from nontemporal clues in the presented problem: 3 years (Richie & Bickhard, 1988)

Can detect comprehension problems once they have chosen to listen simultaneously to two stories: 3 years (Pillow, 1988)

Can understand distinction between a person's knowledge or ignorance of same face: 3-and-one-half to 4-and-one-half years (Hogrefe, Wimmer, & Perner, 1986)

Can give correct relative time judgments if not presented with confusing nontemporal cues: 3–6 years (Richie & Bickhard, 1988)

Four to Five Years

Can use a person's verbal explanations to understand that person's appraisal of a situation: 4 years (Deutsch, 1974)

Can use information about another person's behavior and disposition to infer what that person will do in an uncommon emotional reaction to a later event: 4 years (Gnepp et al., 1982)

Can solve problems integrating two dimensions algebraically for problems of intuitive physics and math: 4 years (Anderson, 1980; Cuneo, 1982; Wilkening, 1979, 1981)

Can consider alternative representations of the same object; understands that someone else may see the object from a different angle and will then see it differently: 4 years (Gopnik & Aslington, 1988)

Five to Six Years

Sensitivity to disconfirmatory inferences as well as to confirmatory inferences in search tasks: 5 years (Fabricius, Sophian, & Wellman, 1987)

Can solve problems involving nonnumerical functional relationships: 5–6 years (Case et al., 1986; Piaget et al., 1977)

Trial and error replaced by anticipatory and inferential strategies: 5–7 years (Davidson, 1987)

Cannot be aware of having two conflicting feelings simultaneously: mean age = 5.23 (sd 1.08) (Harter & Buddin, 1987)

Six to Seven Years

Will only infer if sufficient information leads to a necessarily true inference (able to distinguish between sufficient vs. insufficient information conditions): 6 years (Somerville et al., 1979)

Understands that inference is a source of knowledge; before this, children use information, but don't assume that another person would reach the same conclusion on the basis of the same facts, by simple inference: 6 years (Sodian & Wimmer, 1987)

Perception of story characters' mental states as related to blame judgments: 6 years (Fincham, 1981)

Inner mental experiences described: 6 years (Bengtsson & Johnson, 1987)

Begins to use purely mentalistic strategies to regulate feelings: 6 years (Bengtsson & Johnson, 1987)

Takes moral and conventional events seriously and perceives peers as an important source of conventional regulation: 6 years (Tisak & Turiel, 1988)

Uses intentionality and knowledge in judgments of good and bad outcomes: 6–7 years (Yuill & Perner, 1988)

Realizes verbal message may be interpreted in more than one way: 6–7 years (Flavell et al., 1981; Robinson & Whittaker, 1985)

Realizes that person's interpretation of ambiguous or uninformative visual cues may depend on that person's prior knowledge: 6–7 years (Chandler & Helm, 1984; Flavell et al., 1981; Taylor, 1985)

Realizes that knowledge can be acquired through inferential activity: 6–7 years (Sodian & Wimmer, 1987)

Seven to Eight Years

Blames actors for foreseen vs. unforeseen problems regardless of motive value: 7 years (Yuill & Perner, 1988)

Blames protagonist if she keeps intention to act a secret: 7 years (Mant & Perner, 1988)

More consistently sensitive to both necessity of confirmatory and disconfirmatory inferences in search tasks: 7 years (Fabricius, Sophian, & Wellman, 1987)

Can accept some mixed feelings, simple combinations (brother hits you, you feel mad/sad): 7.27 (avg. age; sd 1.47) (Harter & Buddin, 1987)

Eight to Nine Years

Able to infer personality traits—can recognize consistencies in behavior of others and assume that they represent stable characteristics: 8 years (Livesley & Bromley, 1973)

Inferences about internal plans of actors in stories systematically related to blame judgments: 8 years (Sedlak, 1979)

Can accept two equal-valence feelings brought to bear on two targets (mad if she took one of your rings, sad if she broke one of your pictures): 8.73 (avg. age; sd 1.94) (Harter & Buddin, 1987)

Believes that protagonist who makes no commitment is less reprehensible for not acting than one who does (vs. younger children, who hold them equally reprehensible): 9 years (Mant & Perner, 1988)

Ten Years and Older

Can accept opposite-valence feelings but only toward different targets: 10.08 (avg. age; sd 1.3) (Harter & Buddin, 1987)

Don't endorse Type 1 error (solution that is explicitly denied by premises): 11 years (Acredolo & Horobin, 1987)

Sees beyond first solution to discover other equally correct solutions (get beyond premature closure): 11 years (Acredolo & Horobin, 1987)

Recognizes conclusions based on invalid arguments as uncertain: 13–15 years (Ennis, 1971; O'Brien, 1972; Sternberg, 1979)

REFERENCES

Acredolo, C., & Horobin, K. (1987). Development of relational reasoning and avoidance of premature closure. *Developmental Psychology, 23*, 13–21.

Adler, G,. & Buie, D. (1979). Aloneness and borderline psychopathology: The possible relevance of child development issues. *American Journal of Psycho-Analysis, 60*(83), 83–94.

American Psychiatric Association. (1987). *Diagnostic and statistical manual of mental disorders (3rd ed. – rev.).* Washington, DC: Author.

Anderson, N. H. (1980). Information integration theory in developmental psychology. In F. Wilkening, J. Becker, & T. Trabasso (Eds.), *Information integration by children.* Hillsdale, NJ: Erlbaum.

Andrulonis, P. A. (1982). *The borderline syndrome.* Psychiatry, 11, 23, Side B. Glendale, CA: Audio-Digest Foundation.

Asch, S. S. (1976). Varieties of negative therapeutic reaction and problems of technique. *Journal of the American Psychoanalytic Association, 24*, 383–408.

Ashmead, D., & Perlmutter, M. (1980). Infant memory in everyday life. In M. Perlmutter (Ed.), *Children's memory: New directions for child development.* San Francisco: Jossey-Bass.

Baillargeon, R. (1987). Object permanence in 3½ and 4½ month-old infants. *Developmental Psychology, 23*, 655–664.

Bandler, R., & Grinder, J. (1982). *Reframing.* Moab, UT: Real People Press.

Barrera, M. E., & Maurer, E. (1981). The perception of facial expressions by the three-month-old. *Child Development, 52*, 203–206.

Beebe, B., & Stern, D. N. (1977). Engagement-disengagement and early object experiences. In N. Freedman & S. Grand (Eds.), *Communicative structures and psychic structures.* New York: Plenum.

Bengtsson, H., & Johnson, L. (1987). Cognitions related to empathy in 5- to 11-year-old children. *Child Development, 58*, 1001–1012.

Berne, E. (1985). *Games people play.* New York: Ballentine. (Original work published 1964)

Bertenthal, B. I., & Fischer, K. W. (1978). Development of self-recognition in the infant. *Developmental Psychology, 14*, 44–50.

Blanck, G., & Blanck, R. (1974). *Ego psychology: Theory and practice.* New York: Columbia University Press.

Bloom, L. (1973). *One word at a time: The use of single word utterances before syntax.* Hawthorne, NY: Mouton.

Bowlby, J. (1983). *Attachment* (2nd ed.). New York: Basic. (Original work published 1969)

219

Brazelton, T. B., Koslowski, B., & Main, M. (1974). The origins of reciprocity: The early mother-infant interaction. In M. Lewis & L. A. Rosenblum (Eds.), *Origins of behavior: Vol. 1. The effect of the infant on its caregiver.* New York: Wiley.

Bretherton, I., & Beeghly, M. (1982). Talking about internal states: The acquisition of an explicit theory of mind. *Developmental Psychology, 18,* 906–921.

Bretherton, I., McNew, S., & Beeghly-Smith, M. (1981). Early person knowledge as expressed in gestural and verbal communication: When do infants acquire a "theory of mind"? In M. E. Lamb & L. R. Sherrod (Eds.), *Infant social cognition.* Hillsdale, NJ: Erlbaum.

Bretherton, I., Frit, J., Zahn-Waxler, C., & Ridgeway, D. (1986). Learning to talk about emotions: A functionalist perspective. *Child Development, 55,* 529–548.

Brooks-Gunn, J., & Lewis, M. (1984). Early self-recognition. *Developmental Review, 4,* 215–239.

Brown, R. (1973). *A first language: The early stages.* Cambridge, MA: Harvard University Press.

Bruch, H. (1978). *The Golden Cage.* Cambridge, MA: Harvard University Press.

Bruner, J. S. (1975). The ontogenesis of speech acts. *Journal of Child Language, 2,* 1–19.

Bruner, J. S. (1977). Early social interaction and language acquisition. In H. R. Schaffer (Ed.), *Studies in mother-infant interaction.* London: Academic Press.

Bruner, J. S. (1981). The social context of language acquisition. *Language and Communication, 1,* 155–158.

Burgner, M., & Edgecumbe, R. (1972). Some problems in the conceptualization of early object relations. Part II: The concept of object constancy. *Psychoanalytic Study of the Child, 27,* 315–333.

Call, J. D., & Marschak, M. (1976). Styles and games in infancy. In E. Rexford, L. Sander, & A. Shapiro (Eds.), *Infant psychiatry* (pp. 104–112). New Haven: CT: Yale University Press.

Campos, J. J., Barrett, K. C., Lamb, M. E., Goldsmith, H. H., & Stenberg, C. (1983). Socioemotional development. In M. M. Haith & J. J. Campos (Eds.), *Handbook of child psychology: Vol. 4. Infancy and developmental psychobiology* (pp. 783–915). New York: Wiley.

Caron, R. F., Caron, A. J., & Myers, R. S. (1982). Abstraction of invariant face expressions in infancy. *Child Development, 53,* 1008–1015.

Case, R., Marini, Z., McKeough, A., Dennis, S., & Goldberg, J. (1986). Horizontal structure in middle childhood: The acquisition of dimensional operations. In I. Levin (Ed.), *Stage and structure: Reopening the debate.* Norwood, NJ: Ablex.

Chandler, M., & Helm, D. (1984). Developmental changes in the contributions of shared experience to social role-taking competence. *International Journal of Behavioral Development, 7,* 145–156.

Chowdoff, P. (1978, June 12). *The hysterical personality.* Paper presented at the Joint Session of the American Psychiatric Association & The American Academy of Psychoanalytics, Atlanta, GA. Recorded by Audio-Digest Foundation, 7, 11.

Cicchetti, D., & Stroufe, L. A. (1978). An organizational view of affect: Illustration from the study of Down's syndrome infants. In M. Lewis & L. A. Rosenblum (Eds.), *The genesis of behavior: Vol. 1. The development of affect.* New York: Plenum.

Cohn, J. F., & Tronick, E. Z. (1987). Mother-infant face-to-face interaction: The sequence of dyadic states at 3, 6 and 9 months. *Developmental Psychology, 23,* 68–77.

Crowder, A. M. H., & Hohle, R. H. (1970). Time estimation by young children with and without informational feedback. *Journal of Experimental Child Psychology, 10*, 295–307.

Cuneo, D. O. (1982). Children's judgments of numerical quantity: A new view of early quantification. *Cognitive Psychology, 14*, 13–44.

Daehler, M., & Greco, C. (1985). Memory in very young children. In M. Pressley & C. Brainerd (Eds.), *Cognitive learning and memory in children* (pp. 49–79). New York: Springer-Verlag.

Davidson, P. M. (1987). Early function concepts: their development and relationship to certain mathematical and logical abilities. *Child Development, 58*(6), 1542–1555.

DeCasper, A. J., & Fifer, W. P. (1980). Of human bonding: Newborns prefer their mothers' voices. *Science, 208*, 1174–1176.

DeLoache, J., Sugarman, S., & Brown, A. (1985). The development of error correction strategies in young children's manipulative play. *Child Development, 56*, 928–939.

Deutsch, F. (1974). Female preschoolers' perceptions of affective responses and interpersonal behavior in videotaped episodes. *Developmental Psychology, 10*, 733–740.

Diltz, R., Grinder, J., Bandler, R., Bandler, L., & DeLozier, J. (1988). *Neurolinguistic programming: Volume I. The study of the structure of subjective experience.* Cupertino, CA: Meta Publications.

Donee, L. H. (1973, March). *Infant's development scanning patterns of face and non-face stimuli under various auditory conditions.* Paper presented at the meeting of the Society for Research in Child Development, Philadelphia, PA.

Dunn, J. (1982). Comment: Problems and promises in the study of affect and intention. In E. Tronick (Ed.), *Social interchange in infancy.* Baltimore, MD: University Park Press.

Dunn, J., & Kendrick, C. (1979). Interaction between young siblings in the context of family relationships. In M. Lewis & L. A. Rosenblum (Eds.), *The genesis of behavior: Vol. 2. The child and its family.* New York: Plenum.

Dunn, J., & Kendrick, C. (1982). *Siblings: Love, envy and understanding.* Cambridge, MA: Harvard University Press.

Emde, R. N., & Sorce, J. E. (1983). The rewards of infancy: Emotional availability and maternal referencing. In J. D. Call, E. Galenson, and R. Tyson (Eds.), *Frontiers of infant psychiatry* (Vol. 2). New York: Basic Books.

Emde, R. N., Gaensbauer, T. J., & Harmon, R. J. (1976). *Emotional expression in infancy.* New York: International Universities Press.

Ennis, R. H. (1971). Conditional logic and primary children. *Interchange, 2*, 126–132.

Fabricius, W. V., Sophian, C., & Wellman, H. M. (1987). Young children's sensitivity to logical necessity in their inferential search behavior. *Child Development, 58*, 409–423.

Fagan, J. F. (1973). Infants' delayed recognition memory and forgetting. *Journal of Experimental Child Psychology, 16*, 424–450.

Fagan, J. F. (1976). Infants' recognition of invariant features of faces. *Child Development, 47*, 627–638.

Fagan, J. F. (1977). Infant's recognition of invariant features of faces. *Child Development, 48*, 68–78.

Fagan, J. F., & Singer, L. T. (1979). The role of simple feature differences in infants' recognition of faces. *Infant Behavior and Development, 2*, 39–45.

Fairbairn, W. R. D. (1958). On the nature and aims of psychoanalytical treatment. *International Journal of Psychoanalysis, 39,* 374–385.

Fairbairn, W. R. D. (1963). Synopsis of an object-relations theory of the personality. *Journal of Psychoanalysis, 44,* 224–225.

Fairbairn, W. R. D. (1974). *Psychoanalytic studies of the personality.* New York: Routledge, Chapman & Hall. (Original work published 1952)

Field, T. M. (1978). The three R's of infant-adult interactions: Rhythms, repertoires and responsivity. *Journal of Pediatric Psychology, 3,* 131–136.

Field, T. M., Woodson, R. W., Greenberg, R., & Cohen, C. (1982). Discrimination and imitation of facial expressions by neonates. *Science, 218,* 179–181.

Fincham, F. D. (1981). Perception and moral evaluation in young children. *British Journal of Social Psychology, 20,* 265–270.

Fischer, K. W. (1980). A theory of cognitive development: The control and construction of hierarchies of skills. *Psychological Review, 87,* 477–531.

Flavell, J. H., Botkin, P. I., Fry, C. L., Wright, J. W., & Jarvis, P. E. (1975). *The development of role-taking and communications skills in children.* Melbourne, FL: Krieger. (Original work published 1968)

Flavell, J. H., Speer, J. R., Green, F. L., & August, D. L. (1981). The development of comprehension monitoring and knowledge about communication. *Monographs of the Society for Research in Child Development, 46* (5, Serial No. 192).

Fogel, A. (1977). Temporal organization in mother-infant face-to-face interaction. In H. R. Schaffer (Ed.), *Studies in mother-infant interaction.* New York: Academic Press.

Fogel, A. (1982). Affect dynamics in early infancy: Affective tolerance. In T. Field and A. Fogel (Eds.), *Emotions and early interactions.* Hillsdale, NJ: Erlbaum.

Fraisse, P. (1976). *The psychology of time* (J. Leith, Trans.). Westport, CT: Greenwood. (Original work published 1957)

Frances, A. J. (1986). *Diagnosis and treatment of DSM-III personality disorders.* (A Series of 4 audio tapes). New York: B.M.A. Audio, Division of Guilford Publishing Co.

Frank, J. P. (1982). Therapeutic components shared by all psychotherapies. In J. H. Harvey & M. M. Parks (Eds.), *Psychotherapy research and behavior change.* Washington, DC: American Psychological Association.

Freud, A. (1968). [Remarks in] Panel Discussion. *International Journal of Psycho-Analysis, 49,* 506–507.

Freud, S. (1911). Formulations on the true principles of mental functioning. In J. Strachey (Ed. and Trans.), *The standard edition of the complete psychological works of Sigmund Freud* (Vol. 12, 218–226). New York: Norton.

Freud, S. (1923). The ego and the id. In J. Strachey (Ed. and Trans.), *The standard edition of the complete psychological works of Sigmund Freud,* (Vol. 19, pp. 1–66). New York: Norton.

Friedman, E. R. (1977). Judgments of time intervals by young children. *Perceptual and Motor Skills, 45,* 715–720.

Friedman, M. (1985). Survivor guilt in the pathogenesis of anorexia nervosa. *Psychiatry, 48,* 25–39.

Gedo, J. E., & Goldberg, A. (1973). *Models of the mind: A psychoanalytic theory.* Chicago: University of Chicago Press.

Gelman, R., Spelke, E. S., & Meck, E. (1983). What preschoolers know about animate and inanimate objects. In D. Rogers & J. A. Sloboda (Eds.), *The acquisition of symbolic skills.* London: Plenum.

Geppert, U., & Küster, U. (1983). The emergence of "wanting to do it oneself:" A precursor of achievement motivation. *International Journal of Behavior Development, 6*, 355–369.

Gnepp, J., Klayman, J., & Trabasso, T. (1982). A hierarchy of information sources for inferring emotional reactions. *Journal of Experimental Child Psychology, 33*, 111–123.

Golden, M., Montare, A., & Bridger, W. (1977). Verbal control of delay behavior in two-year-old boys as a function of social class. *Child Development, 48*, 1107–1111.

Gopnik, A., & Aslington, J. (1988). Children's understanding of representational change and its relationship to the understanding of false belief and the appearance-reality distinction. *Child Development, 59*, 26–37.

Gopnik, A., & Meltzoff, A. N. (1984). Semantic and cognitive development in 15- to 21-month-old children. *Journal of Child Language, 2*, 495–513.

Gopnik, A., & Meltzoff, A. N. (1987). The development of categorization in the second year and its relationship to other cognitive and linguistic developments. *Child Development, 58*, 1523–1531.

Greenacre, P. (1959). Certain technical problems in the transference relationship. *Journal of the American Psychoanalytic Association, 7*, 484–502.

Greenberg, J. R., & Mitchell, S. A. (1983). *Object relations in psychoanalytic theory*. Cambridge, MA: Harvard University Press.

Gunther, M. (1961). Infant behavior at the breast. In B. M. Foss (Ed.), *Determinants of infant behavior* (Vol. 2). London: Methuen.

Gustafson, G. E., Green, J. A., & West, M. J. (1979). The infant's changing role in mother-infant games: The growth of social skills. *Infant Behavior and Development, 2*, 301–308.

Gustafson, J. P. (1986). *The complex secret of brief psychotherapy*. New York: Norton.

Haake, R. J., & Somerville, S. C. (1985). Development of logical search skills in infancy. *Developmental Psychology, 21*, 176–186.

Harter, S., & Buddin, B. J. (1987). Children's understanding of the simultaneity of 2 emotions: A 5-stage developmental acquisition sequence. *Developmental Psychology, 23*, 388–399.

Haviland, J. M., & Lelwica, M. (1987). The induced affect response: 10-week-old infants' response to 3 emotional expressions. *Developmental Psychology, 23*, 97–104.

Hetzer, H. (1931). *Kind und schaffen* [Child and creation]. Jena, Germany: Gustav Fischer.

Hogrefe, J., Wimmer, H., & Perner, J. (1986). Ignorance versus false belief: A developmental lag in attribution of epistemic states. *Child Development, 57*, 567–582.

Horner, A. (1979). *Object relations and the developing ego in therapy*. New York: Jason Aronson.

Horowitz, M. (1979). *States of mind*. New York: Plenum Press.

Horowitz, M. (1984). *Personality styles and brief psychotherapy*. New York: Basic Books.

Horowitz, M. (1986). *Stress response syndromes* (2nd ed.). Northvale, NJ: Jason Aronson.

Horowitz, M. (1987). *States of mind: Configurational analysis of individual personality* (2nd ed.). New York: Plenum.

Horowitz, M. J. (1989). *Introduction to psychodynamics: A new synthesis*. New York: Basic Books.

Horowitz, M., Marmar, C., Krupnick, J., Wilner, N., Kaltreider, N., & Wallerstein, R. (1984). *Personality styles and brief psychotherapy.* New York: Basic.

Izard, C. E., Hembree, E. A., Dougherty, L. M., & Spizzirri, C. L. (1983). Changes in facial expressions of 2- to 19-month-old infants following acute pain. *Developmental Psychology, 19,* 418–426.

Izard, C. E., Huebner, R. R., Risser, D., McGinnes, G., & Dougherty, L. M. (1980). The young infant's ability to produce discrete emotion expressions. *Developmental Psychology, 16,* 132–140.

Izard, C. E., & Malatesta, C. Z. (1985). *A developmental theory of emotions.* Unpublished manuscript, University of Delaware.

Johnson, S. M. (1985). *Characterological transformation: The hard work miracle.* New York: Norton.

Johnson, S. M. (1987). *Humanizing the narcissistic style.* New York: Norton.

Kagan, J. (1981). *The second year: The emergence of self-awareness.* Cambridge, MA: Harvard University Press.

Kaye, K. (1982). *The mental and social life of babies.* Chicago, IL: University of Chicago Press.

Kaye, K., & Fogel, A. (1980). The temporal structure of face-to-face communication between mothers and infants. *Developmental Psychology, 16*(5), 454–464.

Kegan, R. G. (1982). *The evolving self: Problem and process in human development.* Cambridge, MA: Harvard University Press.

Keller, H., & Scholmerich, A. (1987). Infant vocalizations & parental reactions during the first four months of life. *Developmental Psychology, 23,* 62–67.

Kernberg, O. (1975). *Borderline conditions and pathological narcissism.* New York: Jason Aronson.

Kernberg, O. (1976). *Object relations theory and clinical psychoanalysis.* New York: Jason Aronson.

Kernberg, O. F. (1984). *Severe personality disorders.* New Haven, CT: Yale University Press.

Kohut, H. (1971). *The analysis of the self: A systematic approach to the psychoanalytic treatment of narcissistic personality disorders.* (The Psychoanalytic Study of the Child Monograph No. 4). New York: International Universities Press.

Kohut, H. (1977). *The restoration of the self.* New York: International Universities Press.

Kohut, H. (1978). In P. Ornstein (Ed.), *The search for the self.* New York: International Universities Press.

Kohut, H. (1984). *How does analysis cure?* Chicago, IL: University of Chicago Press.

Kopp, C. B. (1982). Antecedents of self-regulation: A developmental perspective. *Developmental Psychology, 18,* 199–214.

Kuchuk, A., Vibbert, M., & Bornstein, M. H. (1986). The perception of smiling and its experiential correlates in three-month-old infants. *Child Development, 57,* 1054–1061.

Kuczynski, L., Zahn-Waxler, C., & Radke-Yarrow, M. (1987). Development and content of imitation in the second and third years of life: A socialization perspective. *Developmental Psychology, 23,* 363–369.

LaBarbera, J. D., Izard, E. E., Vietze, P., & Parisi, S. A. (1976). Four- and six-month-old infants' visual response to joy, anger, and neutral expressions. *Child Development, 47,* 535–562.

Langlois, J. H., Roggman, L. A., Casey, R. J., Ritter, J. M., Rieser-Danner, L. A.,

& Jenkins, V. Y. (1987). Infant preferences for attractive faces: Rudiments of a stereotype? *Developmental Psychology, 23*, 363–369.

Levy, A. W., & Bleecker, E. R. (1975). *Development of character structure*. Paper presented at the annual convention of the California State Psychological Association, Fresno, CA.

Lewcowicz, D. J., & Turkewitz, G. (1980). Cross-modal equivalence in early infancy: Audio-visual intensity matching. *Developmental Psychology, 16*, 597–607.

Lewis, M., Feiring, L., McGoffog, L., & Jaskin, J. (in press). Predicting psychopathology in six-year-olds from early social relations. *Child Development*.

Lichtenberg, J. D. (1983). *Psychoanalysis and infant research*. Hillsdale, NJ: Analytic Press.

Livesley, W. J., & Bromley, D. B. (1973). *Personality perception in childhood and adolescence*. London: Wiley.

Lowen, A. (1971). *The language of the body*. New York: Macmillan. (Original work published 1958)

Lowen, A. (1983). *Narcissism: Denial of the true self*. New York: Macmillan.

Lowenwald, H. W. (1979). The meaning of the Oedipus complex. *Journal of the American Psychoanalytic Association, 27*, 751–755.

MacFarlane, J. (1975). Olfaction in the development of social preferences in the human neonate. In M. Hofer (Ed.), *Parent-infant interaction*. Amsterdam: Elsevier.

MacKain, K., Stern, D. N., Goldfield, A., & Moeller, B. (1985). *The identification of correspondence between an infant's internal affective state and the facial display of that affect by an other*. Unpublished manuscript.

MacTurk, R. H., McCarthy, M. E., Vietze, P. M., & Yarrow, L. J. (1987). Sequential analysis of mastery behavior in 6- and 12-month-old infants. *Developmental Psychology, 23*, 199–203.

Mahler, M. S. (1968). *On human symbiosis and the vicissitudes of individuation*. New York: International Universities Press.

Mahler, M. S., Pine, R., & Bergman, A. (1975). *The psychological birth of the human infant*. New York: Basic.

Malan, D. H. (1979). *Individual psychotherapy and the science of psychodynamics*. London: Butterworth.

Mandler, J. M. (1983). Representation. In J. H. Flavell & E. M. Markman (Eds.), P. H. Mussen (Series Ed.), *Handbook of child psychology: Vol. 3. Cognitive development* (pp. 420–494). New York: Wiley.

Mant, C. M., & Perner, J. (1988). The child's understanding of commitment. *Developmental Psychology, 24*, 343–351.

Massey, C. M., & Gelman, R. (1988). Preschoolers' reasoning about movement. *Developmental Psychology, 24*(3), 307–317.

Masterson, J. (1976). *Psychotherapy of the borderline adult*. New York: Brunner/Mazel.

Masterson, J. (1981). *The narcissistic and borderline disorders*. New York: Brunner/Mazel.

Masterson, J. (1985). The real self: A developmental, self, and object relations approach. New York: Brunner/Mazel.

McArthur, D. S. (1988). *Birth of a self in adulthood*. Northvale, NJ: Jason Aronson.

Meissner, W. W. (1986). *Psychotherapy and the paranoid process*. Northvale, NJ: Jason Aronson.

Meissner, W. W. (1988). *Treatment of patients in the borderline spectrum*. Northvale, NJ: Jason Aronson.

Meltzoff, A. N. (1988). Infant imitation and memory: 9-month-olds in immediate
and deferred tests. *Child Development, 59*, 217–225.

Messer, S. B. (1986). Behavioral and psychoanalytic perspectives at therapeutic
choice points. *American Psychologist, 41*(11), 1261–1272.

Miller, A. (1984). *Thou shalt not be aware: Society's betrayal of the child*. New
York: Farrar, Straus & Giroux.

Minuchin, S., Rosman, B. L., & Baker, L. (1978). *Psychosomatic families: Anorexia nervosa in context*. Cambridge, MA: Harvard University Press.

Mitchell, S. A. (1988). *Relational concepts in psychoanalysis*. Cambridge, MA:
Harvard University Press.

Modell, A. (1965). On having the right to a life: An aspect of the superego's
development. *International Journal of Psycho-Analysis, 46*, 323–331.

Modell, A. (1971). The origin of certain forms of pre-oedipal grief and the implications for a psychoanalytic theory of affect. *International Journal of Psycho-
Analysis, 52*, 337–346.

Morrongiello, B., & Rocca, P. (1988). Infants' localization of sounds along the
horizontal axis: Estimates of minimum audible angle. *Developmental Psychology, 24*(1), 8–13.

Nachman, P. (1982). Memory for stimuli reacted to with positive and neutral
affect in seven-month-old infants. Unpublished doctoral dissertation, Columbia
University.

Nachman, P., & Stern, D. N. (1983). *Recall memory for emotional experience in
pre-linguistic infants*. Paper presented at the National Clinical Infancy Fellows
Conference, Yale University, New Haven, CT.

Niederland, W. G. (1961). The problem of the survivor. *Journal of Hillsdale Hospi-
tal, 10*, 233–247.

Nelson, C. A. (1987). The recognition of facial expressions in the first two years of
life: Mechanisms of development. *Child Development, 58*, 4. 889–909.

Nelson, C. A., & Dolgin, K. (1985). The generalized discrimination of facial expressions by 7-month-old infants. *Child Development, 56*, 58–61.

Nelson, C. A., & Ludemann, P. (1987). *The categorical representation of facial expressions by 4- and 7-month-old infants*. Manuscript submitted for publication.

O'Brien, T. C. (1972). Logical thinking in adolescence. *Educational Studies in
Mathematics, 4*, 401–405.

O'Connell, B., & Gerard, A. B. (1985). Scripts and scraps: The development of
sequential understanding. *Child Development, 56*, 671–681.

Paris, S. G., & Lindauer, B. K. (1976). The role of inference in children's comprehension and memory. *Cognitive Psychology, 8*, 217–227.

Piaget, J. (1936). *The origin of intelligence in children*. New York: International
Universities Press.

Piaget, J. (1986). *The construction of reality in the child*. New York: Ballantine.
(Original work published 1954)

Piaget, J., Grize, J-B., Szeminska, A., & Vinh Bang. (1977). *Epistemology and
psychology of functions*. (J. Castellanos and V. Anderson, Trans.). Norwell,
MA: Kluwer Academic. (Original work published 1968)

Pillow, B. (1988). Young children's understanding of attentional limits. *Child Development, 59*, 38–45.

Ratner, N., & Bruner, J. (1978). Games, social exchange and the acquisition of
language. *Journal of Child Language, 5*, 391–401.

Reich, W. (1949). *Character analysis* (3rd ed.). New York: Orgone Institute Press.

Richie, D. M., & Bickhard, M. H. (1988). The ability to perceive duration: Its relationship to the development of the logical concept of time. *Developmental Psychology, 24*(3), 318–323.

Robinson, E. J., & Whittaker, S. J. (1985). Children's responses to ambiguous messages and their understanding of ambiguity. *Developmental Psychology, 21*(3), 446–454.

Ross, H. S., & Kay, D. A. (1980). The origins of social games. In K. H. Rubin (Ed.), *Children's play* (pp. 17–31). San Francisco: Jossey-Bass.

Ross, H. S., & Lollis, S. P. (1987). Communication within infant social games. *Developmental Psychology, 23*, 241–248.

Rutter, D. R., & Durkin, K. (1987). Turn-taking in mother-infant interaction: An examination of vocalizations and gaze. *Developmental Psychology, 23*, 54–61.

Rycroft, C. (1973). *A critical dictionary of psychoanalysis.* New York: Basic.

Sachs, J., & Devin, J. (1976). Young children's use of age-appropriate speech styles in social interaction and role-playing. *Journal of Child Language, 3*, 81–98.

Sagi, A., & Hoffman, M. L. (1976). Empathic distress in newborns. *Developmental Psychology, 12*, 175–176.

Schafer, R. (1983). *The analytic attitude.* New York: Basic.

Schaffer, H. R. (1977). *Studies in mother-infant interaction.* London: Academic Press.

Schwartz, G. M., Izard, C. E., & Ansul, S. E. (1985). The 5-month-old's ability to discriminate facial expressions of emotion. *Infant Behavior and Development, 8*, 65–77.

Sedlak, A. (1979). Developmental differences in understanding plans and evaluating actors. *Child Development, 50*, 536–560.

Selvini-Palazzoli, M. (1978). *Self-starvation.* New York: Jason Aronson.

Shapiro, D. (1965). *Neurotic styles.* New York: Basic.

Shapiro, D. (1989). *Psychotherapy of neurotic character.* New York: Basic Books.

Sherrod, L. R. (1981). Issues in cognitive-perceptual development: The special case of social stimuli. In M. E. Lamb & L. R. Sherrod (Eds.), *Infant social cognition.* Hillsdale, NJ: Erlbaum.

Silverman, L. H., & Weinberger, J. (1985). Mommy and I are one: Implications for psychotherapy. *American Psychologist, 40*, 1296–1308.

Simner, M. L. (1971). The newborn's response to the cry of another infant. *Developmental Psychology, 5*, 136–150.

Sodian, B., & Wimmer H. (1987). Children's understanding of inference as a source of knowledge. *Child Development, 58*, 424–433.

Solomon, R. L., & Wynne, L. E. (1954). Traumatic avoidance learning: The principles of anxiety conservation and partial irreversibility. *Psychology Review, 61*, 353–385.

Somerville, S. C., Hadkinson, B. A., & Greenberg, C. (1979). Two levels of inferential behavior in young children. *Child Development, 50*, 119–131.

Sophian, C., & Wellman, H. (1980). Selective information use in the development of search behavior. *Developmental Psychology, 16*, 323–331.

Spangler, G., Bräutigam, I., & Stadler, R. (1984). Handlungsentwicklung in der frühen Kindheit und ihre Abhängigkeit von der kognitiven Entwicklung und der emotionalen Erregbarkeit des Kindes [Action development in early childhood and its relation to children's cognitive development and emotional excitability]. *Zeitschrift für Entwicklungspychologie und Pädagogische Psychologie, 16*, 181–193.

Spieker, S. J. (1982). *Infant recognition of invariant categories of faces: Person, identity and facial expression.* Unpublished doctoral dissertation, Cornell University.

Spitz, R. A., & Cobliner, W. G. (1965). *The first year of life.* New York: International Universities Press.

Spungen, L., & Goodman, J. (1983). Sequencing strategies in children 18–24 months: Limitations imposed by task complexity. *Journal of Applied Developmental Psychology, 4,* 109–124.

Stern, D. N. (1971). A micro-analysis of mother-infant interaction: Behaviors regulating social contact between a mother and her three-and-a-half-month-old twins. *Journal of American Academy of Child Psychiatry, 10,* 501–517.

Stern, D. N. (1974). The goal and structure of mother-infant play. *Journal of American Academy of Child Psychiatry, 13,* 402–421.

Stern, D. N. (1977). *The first relationship: Infant and mother.* Cambridge, MA: Harvard University Press.

Stern, D. N. (1980). *The early development of schemas of self, of other, and of various experiences of "self with other."* Paper presented at the symposium on Reflections on Self Psychology, Boston Psychoanalytic Society and Institute, Boston, MA.

Stern, D. N. (1985). *The interpersonal world of the infant: A view from psychoanalysis and developmental psychology.* New York: Basic.

Stern, D. N., Beebe, B., Jaffe, J., & Bennett, S. L. (1977). The infant's stimulus world during social interaction: A study of caregiver behaviors with particular reference to repetition and timing. In H. R. Schafer (Ed.), *Studies in mother-infant interaction.* London: Academic Press.

Stern, D. N., Hofer, L., Haft, W., & Dore, J. (1985). Affect attunement: The sharing of feeling states between mother and infant by means of inter-modal fluency. In T. Field & N. Fox (Eds.), *Social perception in infants.* Norwood, NJ: Ablex.

Sternberg, R. J. (1979). Developmental patterns in the encoding and combination of logical connectives. *Journal of Experimental Child Psychology, 28,* 469–498.

Strauss, M. S. (1979). Abstraction of prototypical information by adults and ten-month-old infants. *Journal of Experimental Psychology: Human Learning and Memory, 5,* 618–632.

Stroufe, L. S. (1987). Socioemotional development. In J. Osofsky (Ed.), *Handbook of infant development* (2nd ed., pp. 462–515). New York: Wiley.

Sugarman-Bell, S. (1978). Some organizational aspects of pre-verbal communication. In I. Markova (Ed.), *The social context of language* (pp. 49–66). Chichester, England: Wiley.

Taylor, M. (1985). *The development of children's ability to distinguish what they know from what they see.* Unpublished doctoral dissertation, Stanford University.

Tisak, M. S., & Turiel, E. (1988). Variation in seriousness of transgressions and children's moral and conventional concepts. *Developmental Psychology, 24*(3), 352–357.

Trevarthan, C., & Hubley, P. (1978). Secondary intersubjectivity: Confidence, confiders and acts of meaning in the first year. In A. Lock (Ed.), *Action, gesture and symbol.* New York: Academic Press.

Tronick, E., & Adamson, L. (1980). *Babies as people.* New York: Collier.

Tronick, E., Als, H., Adamson, L., Wise, S., & Brazelton, T. B. (1978). The infant's response to intrapment between contradictory messages in face-to-face interaction. *Journal of Child Psychiatry, 17,* 1–13.

Tronick, E., Als, H., & Brazelton, T. B. (1977). The infant's capacity to regulate mutuality in face-to-face interaction. *Journal of Communication, 27,* 74–80.

Tronick, E., Ricks, M., & Conn, J. F. (1982). Maternal and infant affective exchange. Patterns of adaptation. In T. Field and A. Fogel (Eds.), *Emotions and early interactions.* Hillsdale, NJ: Erlbaum.

Vaughan, B. E., Kopp, C. B., & Krakow, J. B. (1984). The emergence and consolidation of self-control from eighteen to thirty months of age: Normative trends and individual differences. *Child Development, 55,* 990–1004.

Walker-Andrews, A. S., & Lennon, E. M. (1984). *Auditory-visual perception of changing distance.* Paper presented at the International Conference of Infancy Studies, New York.

Watson, J. S. (1979). Perception of contingency as a determinant of social responsiveness. In E. Thomas (Ed.), *The origins of social responsiveness.* Hillsdale, NJ: Erlbaum.

Watson, J. S. (1980). *Bases of causal inference in infancy: Time, space and sensory relations.* Paper presented at the International Conference on Infant Studies, New Haven, CT.

Weiss, J., & Sampson, H. (1986). *The psychoanalytic process: Theory, clinical observation, and empirical research.* New York: Guilford.

Wellman, H. M., & Estes, D. (1986). Early understanding of mental entities: A reexamination of childhood realism. *Child Development, 57,* 910–923.

Wenar, C. (1982). On negativism. *Human Development, 25,* 1–23.

Wilkening, F. (1979). Combining of stimulus dimensions in children's and adult's judgments of area: An information integration analysis. *Developmental Psychology, 15,* 25–33.

Wilkening, F. (1981). Integrating velocity, time, and distance information: A developmental study. *Cognitive Psychology, 13,* 231–247.

Winnicott, D. W. (1951). Transitional objects and transitional phenomena. In D. W. Winnicott (1958). *Collected papers: Through pediatrics to psychoanalysis.* London: Tavistock.

Winnicott, D. W. (1958). *Collected papers.* London: Tavistock.

Winnicott, D. W. (1965). *The maturational processes and the facilitating environment.* New York: International Universities Press.

Winnicott, D. W. (1971). *Playing and reality.* New York: Basic Books.

Winnicott, D. W. (1989). *Holding and interpretation.* New York: Grove-Weidenfeld.

Young-Browne, G., Rosenfeld, H. M., & Horowitz, F. D. (1977). Infant discrimination of facial expression. *Child Development, 6,* 491–498.

Yuill, N. (1984). Young children's coordination of motive and outcomes in judgments of satisfaction and morality. *British Journal of Developmental Psychology, 2,* 73–81.

Yuill, N., & Perner, J. (1988). Intentionality and knowledge in children's judgments of actor's response and recipient's emotional reaction. *Developmental Psychology, 24,* 358–365.

abandonment:
  fear of, 96
  and hostility, 91
  resulting from self–expression, 191
abandonment depression, 90, 118
abstinence and neutrality, 2, 117
abuse, 152
Accidental Tourist, The (film), 31
accommodation, 85, 199
  of the "evoked companion", 89–90
Acredolo, C., 217, 218
Adamson, L., 29, 36, 210
adjustment, process of, 21–22
  to meet relational needs, 37
Adler, G., 201
affect:
  adopted, 100
  and the symbiotic character, 90–96
  tolerance for stimulation, 190
affective objectives:
  with the symbiotic character, 99–
    101
agency, defined, 199
aggression, 91–93, 149
  encouraging healthy, 151–52
  toward the libidinal self, 159
  natural, 45, 47
  and the oral character, 38–39
  in theoretical discussions, 120
alcoholism, parental, 35–36
Alice, case discussion, 153–70
Allen, case discussion, 172–74
Als, H., 29, 36, 209, 210
ambition, 50
ambivalence, defined, 199
American Psychiatric Association, 16
analytic attitude, 143

Anderson, N. H., 215
Andrulonis, P. A., 116
anorexia nervosa, 121–22, 125
Ansul, S. E., 211
antilibidinal object, 165, 182, 199
antilibidinal self, 110, 165, 199
  and the antilibidinal object, 152,
    168–69
  as a "demonic force", 159–60
  and the libidinal self, 182
  pathogenic beliefs of the, 129
anxiety, 51, 94
  triggered in therapy, 185
Ashmead, D., 212
Aslington, J., 215
assertiveness, healthy, 90
assimilation, defined, 199–200
attachment, 24, 199
  to a bad object, 108
  characterological issues of, 28–41
  exploitative and possessive, 135
attunement:
  in infancy, 29
  mirrored, 22
August, D. L., 216
autism, defined, 200
autonomy, 135
  and anorexia, 122
  choice between contact and, 158,
    178–79
  as a danger, 86
  and fear of abandonment, 98
  frustration of, 82
  issues for borderline patients, 116
  support for, 166
aversive stimulation, 30
avoidant personality disorder, 25

bad objects, 60, 106, 188, 189
    internalized, 21, 31, 160
        by the masochist, 56
    Siu, case discussion, 191
    splitting of, 107–8
Baillargeon, R., 210
Baker, L., 121
Bandler, L., 171
Bandler, R., 123, 171
Barrera, M. E., 210
Barrett, K. C., 212
Bateson, G., 188
Beebe, B., 209, 210
Beeghly, M., 213, 214
Beeghly–Smith, M., 213
behavioral channel, 147
    Robert, case discussion, 174
    Siu, case discussion, 188
behavioral objectives for the symbiotic
        character, 103–4
    list, 104
behavioral therapy, 1
    desensitization metaphor from, 10
behavior, symbiotic, 86–90
Bengtsson, H., 73, 216
Bennett, S. L., 209
Bergman, A., 17, 35, 200, 203, 204,
        205–6
Berne, E., 6, 37, 110, 111
Bertenthal, B. E., 214
Bickhard, M. H., 215
binding:
    hostility in response to, 90–91
    replication by the symbiotic, 88
bioenergetic exercise, 187
Blanck, G., 37
Blanck, R., 37
Bleecker, E. R., 20, 44
blocks, 20–21
    to meet relational needs, 37
Bloom, L., 212
body language, and deprivation, 35
body–related psychotherapy, 178
bonding, 19, 28–41, *see also* attach-
        ment
borderline personality, 115–21
    aggression in, 92
    and countertransference, 142–43
    symbiotic, 192–95
borderline triad, 186, 191–92
Bornstein, M. H., 210

Botkin, P. I., 216
bottomless pit of needs, 39–40
boundaries, 19
    in adult–adult relationships, 140–
        41
    defined, 200
    modulating, 100
    protective imaginary, 171
    and sexuality, 62
    and the symbiotic, 46, 86, 95–96
    in therapy, 190
    and vulnerability, 87
Bowlby, J., 19, 199
Brazelton, T. B., 29, 36, 209, 210
Bretherton, I., 213, 214
Breuer, 65
Bridger, W., 213
Bromley, D. B., 217
Brooks–Gunn, J., 214
Brown, A., 212
Brown, R., 212
Bruch, H., 121
Bruner, J. S., 211, 212
Bräutigam, I., 213
Buddin, B. J., 216, 217
Buie, D., 201
Burgner, M., 202

Call, J. D., 209
Campos, J. J., 212
caretakers, and the symbiotic, 85
caretaking:
    as an adjustment to deprivation,
        36
    primitive responses of, 37
Carol, case discussion, 170–72
Caron, A. J., 210, 211
Caron, R. F., 210, 211
Case, R., 216
Casey, R. J., 209
Chandler, M., 216
change:
    resistance to, 21, 112
    therapeutic, 161, 166
character:
    and environmental frustration, 17
    formation of, 11, 20–22
    reproduction in the family, 70
characterological–developmental
        theory, 5–6, 11, 15–27
    on infants' responses, 30

characterological issues:
  of attachment and bonding, 28–41
  combinations of, 162–63
  and existential issues, 16
  of self–development, 42–60
  and structural development, 24, 26
Characterological Transformation
  (Johnson), 41, 44
Chowdoff, P., 64
Cicchetti, D., 211
classical psychoanalytic theory, 2–3, 5
  a central conflict of, 17
  and the oedipal conflict, 61
Cobliner, W. G., 209
co–dependent behavior, 39
coercive borderline states, 192
cognition:
  experiential view of, 145
  reframing as direct learning, 9–10
  and the symbiotic, 96–99
cognitive map, 16, 17
cognitive objectives for the symbiotic
  character, 101–3
Cohen, C., 29, 208
coherence of self, 7
Cohn, J. F., 212
collaborative psychotherapy, 143–44
  Alice, case discussion, 169
collapsed self of the oral character, 38
communication, disordered, 125
competition, 61, 68
conflict:
  life–disrupting internal, 25
  and a negative therapeutic reaction,
    175
  origins of, 17
  over self–expression, 161–62
  in separation, 91–92
  symbiotic, 102
  in the symbiotic's affects, 94–95
confrontation, therapeutic, 118–19
consciousness, a child's, 6
continuum:
  of intervention, 193
  of psychopathology, 22–26
  of structural development, 27, 95–
    96, 120–21
control:
  and masochism, 54–55, 82
  mastery theory, 125, 126
conversion reactions, 65

core self, 111
corrective emotional experience, 7–9,
  34, 90, 127–28, 136–38, 144
  and negative therapeutic reaction,
    185–92
  see also psychotherapy; therapy
countertransference, 117, 180–81
  and the symbiotic character, 141–43
  in theoretical discussions, 120
criticism, responses to, 106
cross–generational alliances, 121–22
Crowder, A. M. H., 214
cultural perspective, 15
Cuneo, D. O., 215

Daehler, M., 212
danger situations, 162
Davidson, P. M., 216
death instinct, origin of Freud's hypothesis, 60
DeCasper, A. J., 28, 208
DeLoache, J., 212
DeLozier, J., 171
denial:
  confrontation of, 119
  in the family of the histrionic, 65
Dennis, S., 216
dependence, mature, 114
depletion guilt, 124–25
depression, 51
  abandonment, 90, 118, 177
  conceptualization of, 182
  and an infant's need gratification,
    35–36
  masochistic morass of, 58
  and the narcissistic character, 52
  in obsessive–compulsives, 71
  in the oral character, 38
deprivation, and masochistic expression, 59
desensitization:
  to the danger of self–expression,
    90
  as direct learning, 9–10
  with obsessive–compulsives, 74
  for a schizoid person, 32
Deutsch, F., 215
development:
  chronology of, 208–18
  flawed, obsessive–compulsive strate-
    gies for, 73

development (*continued*)
  limits to modeling, 18
  of separateness, research on, 44
developmental psychology, 5, 15
developmental psychotherapy, 5
developmental stages, 23
  and origins of narcissism, 49–50
  practicing period, 80
  rapprochement period, 81
Devin, J., 215
Diagnostic and Statistical Manual
  (DSM-III-R), 16, 25–26
difference, threatening, 136
differentiation, 200
  Carol, case discussion, 171–72
  and development of autonomy, 43
Diltz, R., 171
direct learning, 9–10
discipline, and individuation, 86
disclosure in therapy, 143
dissociation, 25
  and a harsh environment, 31–32
dissociative channel, 146, 170–71
Dolgin, K., 210, 211
Donee, L. H., 209
Dore, J., 212
Dougherty, L. M., 209
drive theory, 17
Dunn, J., 212
Durkin, K., 212, 213, 214

eclecticism, compared with integration,
  2
Edgecumbe, R., 202
educational channel, 147
ego functioning:
  dimensions of, 94
  dystonic thoughts, 71
  see also structural development;
    structural functioning
ego psychology, 5, 22–23
  and the oral issue, 37
Emde, R. N., 43, 80, 209, 211
empathy, 2
  of infants, 36–37
  mirroring, 79
  misdirected, 124–25
engulfment:
  fear of, 96
  and hostility, 91

enmeshment, 155–56, 164, 200
  of borderline patients, 192
  in infancy, 44
  rejection of, 184
  social, 102
  therapeutic separation from, 90
Ennis, R. H., 218
entitlement, defined, 200
environment, interaction with the developing child, 30, 82
envy, 175
Erickson, M. H., 10, 123
escape conditioning paradigm, 16
Estes, D., 73, 214
etiology:
  of masochism, 176
  of the symbiotic, 45, 79–86
evocative memory, defined, 200–201
evoked companion, 89–90
"exciting" object, 107, 116, 150, 184,
  201
existential issues, 5–6
  and character structure, 11, 16
  and "neurotic" psychopathology, 61
  personal profile on the dimensions of,
  26
  and structural integration, 23
expectations, parent's, and narcissistic
  injury, 48
experiential therapy, 144–52, 181
exploitation of a child's sexuality, 62
extinction, resistance to, 16–17

Fabricius, W. V., 215, 216, 217
Fagan, J. F., 210, 211
Fairbairn, W. R. D., 12, 17, 21, 30,
  31, 56, 60, 88, 105, 106–15, 116,
  118, 120, 123, 129, 137, 149,
  150, 158, 159–60, 168, 192–93,
  201, 202, 204–5
false self, 21–22, 49, 50, 70, 86, 111
  histrionic, 66
  and relationship with the other, 44
  of the oral character, 38
  symbiotic, 99
family of origin:
  of borderline patients, 192
  characterological reproduction in the,
  70
  separating from, 79, 102

family pain:
  carrier of responsibility for, 88–89
  intergenerational, 46
family therapy, 121–23
father–daughter relationship, and histri-
    onic behavior, 65
father figure, therapist as, 137–38
fear:
  activated by self–expression, 189
  based on deficit, 189–90
  and guilt, 182
  and obsessive–compulsive behavior,
    74
  of others and structural development,
    25
  of separation, 47
  in the symbiotic, 100
  triggered in therapy, 185
feeling channel, 147, 186–87
Field, T. M., 29, 208, 209
Fifer, W. P., 28, 208
Fincham, F. D., 216
Fischer, K. W., 213, 214
Flavell, J. H., 216
Fogel, A., 209, 212
Fraisse, P., 214
Frances, A. J., 68
Frank, J. P., 4
Freud, A., 202
Freud, S., 4, 5, 19, 60, 62, 65, 68,
    117–18, 126, 175, 189, 202
Friedman, E. R., 214
Friedman, M., 124, 125
Frit, J., 213
frustrations:
  and character development, 20–
    22
  narcissist's responses to, 49
  see also optimal frustration
Fry, C. L., 216
functional model, 26
fusion in the symbiotic:
  and cognitive errors, 96–97
  with a significant other, 102

Gaensbauer, T. J., 209, 211
Games People Play (Berne), 111
games that symbiotics play, 102
Gedo, J. E., 23
Gelman, R., 214, 215

generalization, the problem of, 144–52
genetic disorders, 26
Geppert, U., 214
Gerard, A. B., 212
gestalt therapy, 21, 105, 178
getting the story straight, 6–7, 10
  with obsessive–compulsive, 74
Gnepp, J., 215
Goldberg, A., 23
Goldberg, J., 216
Golden, M., 213
Goldfield, A., 36, 212
Goldsmith, H. H., 212
"good–enough" objects, 151, 184
"good–enough" relationship:
  external, 114
  with a mother, 135
  with a therapist, 136
Goodman, J., 212
Gopnik, A., 50, 72, 213, 215
grandiosity, 186
  in narcissistic individuals, 49
  and the oral character, 38
  and perfectionism, 72
gratification, isomorphism with feeding
    need, 35
Greco, C., 212
Green, F. L., 216
Green, J. A., 211
Greenacre, P., 173
Greenberg, C., 216
Greenberg, J. R., 17
Greenberg, R., 29, 208
grief:
  and personal growth, 100
  therapeutic experience of, 96
  for unmet needs of the past, 41
Grinder, J., 123, 171
Grize, J-B., 216
guilt, 94
  and fear, 182
  induced by parents, 181–82
  and a negative therapeutic reaction,
    175
  Siu, case discussion, 178–79
  triggered in therapy, 185
  unconscious, 123–26
Gunther, M., 36, 208
Gustafson, G. E., 211
Gustafson, J. P., 7, 188

Haake, R. J., 214
Hadkinson, B. A., 216
Haft, W., 212
Harmon, R. J., 209, 211
harshness, projection of, 31–32
Harter, S., 216, 217
Haviland, J. M., 36, 37, 209
healing, in a "strengthened context", 7–
    9
Helm, D., 216
helplessness, 56
Hembree, E. A., 209
hermeneutic intervention, 6–7, 8, 18
Hetzer, H., 214
histrionic behavior, 63–68
Hofer, L., 212
Hoffman, M. L., 29, 36, 209
Hogrefe, J., 215
Hohle, R. H., 214
holding, 34
    demands on the symbiotic, 88
    and maturation, 8
    in therapy, 190
holding back, as an obsessive–compul-
    sive symptom, 71
hopelessness, 56
Horner, A., 199
Horobin, K., 217, 218
Horowitz, F. D., 210
Horowitz, M., 4, 5, 64, 109, 110, 111,
    148, 205
Horowitz, M. J., 64, 124
hostility, 100, 164–65
    of the histrionic, 66
    to individuals of the opposite sex, 65,
        67
    natural, 45, 47
    of the oral character, 38–39
    in response to an impossible bind,
        90–91
Hubley, P., 211
humanistic psychoanalysis, 2–3
Humanizing the Narcissistic Style
    (Johnson), 50

idealization, 50, 151, 201
    narcissistic, 53
ideal self, formation of, 110–11
identification, 85, 201
    with the affective states of others,
        100

    and maturity, 84
    with a mother, 163–64
identity:
    externally imposed, 42
    formation in the symbiotic, 93
impressionistic cognitive style, 65
incorporative introjection, 84, 85
individuation, 19
    choosing between love and, 135
    guilt over, 97–98
    and natural aggression, 93
    need for, 17
    practicing subphase of, 43
    rapprochement period of, 44
    the role of aggression in, 91–92
    and the symbiotic character, 85
    a therapist's, 4–5
    in therapy, 95
infants:
    chronology of development, 208–14
    preprogrammed responses of, 28–
        29
insight channel, 147
instinctual needs:
    interaction with the interpersonal
        environment, 20
    object–seeking, 118
integration, compared with eclecticism,
    2
intellectualization, and structural devel-
    opment, 25
internalization, 83–84, 84–85, 107,
    201
    of bad objects, 21, 31, 56, 160
    of a good object, 110
internalization channel, 147–48, 187–
    88, 190
internal object relations:
    model of the borderline symbiotic,
        194
    symptoms as, 149, 153–74
internal saboteur, 150, 160, 201
interpersonal model:
    and drive theory, 17
    and instinctual needs, 20
interpretation, and maturation, 8
intervention:
    direct, 104
    exacerbation of symptoms in, 175
    hermeneutic, 6–7, 8, 18
    reasons for failure of, 145

structuring of, 106
with symbiotics, 80
therapeutic, 141
see also therapy
intimacy, 148–49
role–relationship model, 141
introjection, 83, 201–2
collusion between antilibidinal self
and object, 150
and the obsessive–compulsive's overseer, 69
unassimilated, 84
intrusion:
and masochism, 55
replicating in therapy, 187
in vivo desensitization, 9–10
irritability, 39
Izard, C. E., 208, 209, 211
Izard, E. E., 211

Jaffe, J., 209
Jarvis, P. E., 216
Johnson, L., 73, 216
Johnson, S. M., 5, 11, 16, 35, 41
Johnston, B., 145
joining, in therapy, 146

Kagan, J., 50, 213
Kay, D. A., 213
Kaye, K., 209, 212
Kegan, R. G., 18, 120
Keller, H., 208
Kendrick, C., 212
Kernberg, O. F., 5
Klayman, J., 215
Kohut, H., 2, 7, 19, 20, 50, 54, 84,
111, 114, 201, 202, 205, 207
Kopp, C. B., 213
Korzybski, A., 2, 3
Koslowski, B., 209
Krakow, J. B., 213
Küster, U., 214
Kuchuk, A., 210
Kuczynski, L., 44, 213

LaBarbera, J. D., 211
Lamb, M. E., 212
Langlois, J. H., 209
learning process, 8–9
age– and situation–appropriate,
19

development of rigid responses, 16–
17
direct, 9
and psychopathology, 10–11
Lelwica, M., 36, 37, 209
Lennon, E. M., 210
Levy, A. W., 20, 44
Lewcowicz, D. J., 29, 208
Lewis, M., 214
liberator, therapist as, 137–38
libidinal ego, defined, 202
libidinal object, 202
and the libidinal self, 150–51
libidinal self, 116, 158, 202
aggression toward the antilibidinal
self, 151, 183
and the libidinal object, 150–51
pathogenic beliefs of the, 129
libido, in Fairbairn's theory, 107
Lichtenberg, J. D., 29, 120
limit setting in therapy, 140
Lindauer, B. K., 214
Livesley, W. J., 217
Lollis, S. P., 211
loss of self, 158
and personal growth, 100
therapeutic strategies for, 170–74
love, 149
in oedipal issues, 61
Lowen, A., 5, 10, 19–20, 35, 44, 54,
55, 63, 70
low–functioning individuals, rigidity in,
70
loyalty, 149
Ludemann, P., 211

McArthur, D. S., 143, 156
McCarthy, M. E., 212
MacFarlane, J., 208
MacKain, K., 36, 212
McKeough, A., 216
McNew, S., 213
MacTurk, R. H., 212
magical thinking, defined, 202
Mahler, M. S., 17, 19, 29, 35, 43, 80,
83, 200, 203, 204, 205–6
Main, M., 209
Malan, D. H., 162, 186
Malatesta, C. Z., 208
Mandler, J. M., 212
Mant, C. M., 217

map:
  characterological–development
    theory, 15
  providing in therapy, 160
  for role–relationship models, 111
  see also PMAP
Marini, Z., 216
Marschak, M., 209
masochism, 54–60
  as adaptation, 154
  etiology of, 176
  and a negative therapeutic reaction,
    175
masochistic character, 24, 58–59
  and symbiosis, 179–80
Massey, C. M., 215
Masterson, J., 5, 12, 17, 23, 90, 94,
    115–21, 150, 175, 194
maturation, 6, 19
  in Fairbairn's theory, 113–14
  in Masterson's theory, 120
Maurer, E., 210
Meck, E., 214
Meissner, W. W., 69, 93
Meltzoff, A. N., 50, 72, 211, 213
Menninger, C., 186
mental bookkeeping, 98
mental migration, 30
merger, 202
  expressed as excessive responsibility,
    97
  narcissistic, 53
  of parents with the child, 79
  pressure for, 156
  sacrifice to obtain, 159
merger–object, idealized, 158–59
Messer, S. B., 1, 23
metaphor:
  desensitization, 10
  in therapy, 146
metaphor channel, 148
Miller, A., 62
Minuchin, S., 121
mirroring, 22, 81, 202
  demand in symbiotic's relationships,
    88
  empathic response, 79
  and formation of self, 83
  narcissistic, 53
Mitchell, S. A., 1, 17, 30, 120
Modell, A., 45, 97, 98, 124, 206
models as fictions, 120

Models of the Mind (Gedo and Gold-
    berg), 23
Moeller, B., 36, 212
Montare, A., 213
morass, masochistic, 56
Morrongiello, B., 211
mother–child interactions, 36
  in early infancy, 29
motivation, client's awareness of, 147
mourning, 189
  for antilibidinal objects, 183
  for the exciting object, 184
  for unmet needs of the past, 41
  see also grief; loss
multiple personality, 32
Myers, R. S., 210, 211
myth of self–righteous perfection, 143

Nachman, P., 211
narcissism:
  healthy, 54
  initial adjustment, 21–22
  and self–object relations, 113
  and the therapist's role, 140
narcissistic cathexis, defined, 202
narcissistic character, 24, 52–53
  and the libidinal self, 110
narcissistic issues, 48–54
  Allen, case discussion, 172
  injury, and oedipal issues, 63
  Robert, case discussion, 174
  transferences, 53
needs:
  for autonomy, 80
  gratification, isomorphic with feed-
    ing, 35
  organismic, 20, 108
  self–blocking of, 36
negative environmental response, 20
negative therapeutic reaction, 57, 58,
    60, 175–95, 185–92
negative transference, 129
Nelson, C. A., 210, 211
neurolinguistic programming, 123, 171
neutrality and abstinence, 2, 117
Niederland, W. G., 45, 124

object constancy, defined, 202
objectives:
  of active family therapies, 122
  behavioral, 103–4
  cognitive, 101–3

of therapy with the symbiotic, 99–104

of treatment, Fairbairn's model, 118–19

object permanence, defined, 203

object relations, 5, 105–6, 149
  analysis of symptoms, 157–70, 182–85
  developmental perspective on, 112–13
  fixed internal, 21
  internal, 109–10
  Object Relations Theory of the Personality, An, 107

object seeking, 107, 120
  and symptomatic behavior, 150, 188–89

object ties, need to preserve, 88

O'Brien, T. C., 218

observing ego, 194–95

obsessive–compulsive behavior, 68–76
  as an oedipal adaptation, 63

O'Connell, B., 212

oedipal character, 24, 66–68
  obsessive–compulsive, 75–76

oedipal issues, 61, 162
  Alice, case discussion, 157, 164
  and guilt, 162

omnipotence/worthlessness, defined, 203

omnipotent responsibility, 191, 203
  an interpretation of, 186

one–up/one–down relationships, 35, 76

on the way to object constancy, defined, 203

opposition, and assertion of autonomous identity, 81

optimal distance, defined, 203

optimal frustration, 83, 203

optimal indulgence, and formation of self, 83

oral character, 24, 40, 154
  and the libidinal self, 110
  self–object relations of, 113

oral issue, 34–41

Ordinary People (film), 31

organic disorders, 26

organismic needs, 108
  and reaction to frustration, 20

other, to the symbiotic character, 93–94, 98

overdetermined responses, 9

overeating, case discussion, 166–69

overseer, 69

owned child, 79–104

pacing, 146, 172

pain, masochistic tolerance of, 182–83
  see also family pain

parents:
  in an anorexic family, 121
  attachment of abused children to, 106
  and autonomy, 82–83
  dependence on children, 125
  expectations of, and narcissistic injury, 48
  guilt induced by, 181–82
  and a histrionic personality, 64–65
  individuation discouraged by, 97–98
  of obsessive–compulsives, 69
  and perfectionism, 73–74
  replicating self–destructive patterns of, 98
  respect for the client, 173
  symbiotic union with, 115–16

Paris, S. G., 214

Parisi, S. A., 211

part–object, defined, 203–4

passive:
  turning into active, 97, 128, 129–30, 139–40, 142, 152, 192

passive aggression, 58, 151, 183
  of the masochist, 56
  and resistance in the symbiotic, 89

pathogenic beliefs, 6, 127
  antilibidinal, 150
  challenging in therapy, 128–29
  and deprivation, 37
  masochistic, 181
  of the symbiotic, 98
  in the therapist–client relationship, 139

pathogenic relationship, preservation of, 88

pathology, interpersonal origins of, 125–26

perfectionism, 106
  myth of, 143
  narcissistic, 72
  in the obsessive–compulsive, 71–72
  and parents, 73–74

Perlmutter, M., 212

Perls, F., 4, 10
Perner, J., 73, 215, 216, 217
personality:
    correlation with symptoms, 31–32
    functioning level of disordered, 193
    histrionic, 67–68
    pre–oedipal origin of disordered, 61
phallic–narcissistic diagnosis, 63
physical illness:
    and the narcissistic character, 52
    and the oral character, 37–38
Piaget, J., 85, 199, 203, 210, 213, 216
Pillow, B., 215
Pine, R., 17, 35, 200, 203, 204, 205–6
plans, unconscious, 126–30
play–therapy, 126
pleasure principle, 117–18
PMAP (post-modern art psychother-
    apy), 2, 193
polarity, 3
    around aggression, 92
    in borderline patients, 117
    compensated-collapsed, 39
    in narcissistic individuals, 49
    and rage, 159
    in the symbiotic, 94
positive connotation, 122–23
positive transference, 108
post–modern art, 1
post–modern art psychotherapy, 2, 193
practicing, defined, 204
prescriptive family therapy, 122–23
preservation hypothesis, 123
primary identification, 84
problem solving, conscious and uncon-
    scious, 144
process, in psychotherapy, 6–12
projection, 110, 180
    as a cue in therapy, 142
    justified by choices, 137
    by the symbiotic character, 88, 93
psychic structure, Fairbairn's model of,
    109
psychoanalysis, 1
psychodynamic psychotherapy, 178
psychopathology:
    as accommodation to avoid pain, 22
    and attachment in infancy, 37
    and environmental frustration, 17
    functional model of, 26
    views of, 10

psychotherapy:
    abstinence and neutrality in, 117
    as an art form, 1–12
    see also corrective emotional experi-
        ence; therapy
punishment and self-expression, 191

racism, 176, 180
Radke–Yarrow, M., 44, 213
rage, 160–61
    natural, 41, 56
    retaliatory, 32
rapprochement, 81, 204
    crisis of, defined, 204
    and individuation, 44
rationalization, 65
Ratner, N., 211
reality, confrontation of, 119
reality principle, 118
real object, defined, 204
real self:
    avoiding fragmentation of, 88
    development of, 42
    and self–building in therapy, 48
reassessment by the symbiotic, 85
rebellion, 163–64, 177
    object of, 178
    passive–aggressive, 183
recognition memory, defined, 204
reframing, 18–19, 122–23
    of antilibidinal self-expressions, 185
Reich, W., 5, 10, 20, 55, 111, 115
rejecting object, 107, 150, 204–5
remembering, the purpose of, 7
reparenting process in therapy, 195
repertoire expansion, 9–12
repression, 108–10
    of bad objects, 107–8, *see also* bad
        objects
research:
    on a child's social sense, 43
    chronology of development based on,
        208–18
    contributions of, 22
    on developing separateness, 44
    developmental, 120
    on the development of self–concept,
        49–50
    on the need for social interaction,
        28–29
    on the need constellation, 35

on obsessive–compulsive development, 72–73
in parent–child relationships in
infancy, 79
on responses in infancy, 36–37
single–subject, 127
on understanding otherness, 81
resistance:
of the "evoked companion", 89–90
to extinction, 16–17
rewarding object relations unit
(RORU), 116, 118
Richie, D. M., 215
Ridgeway, D., 213
Rieser–Danner, L. A., 209
rigidity, in the symbiotic, 89
Ritter, J. M., 209
rivalry, experience of natural, 62
Robert, case discussion, 174
Robinson, E. J., 216
Rocca, P., 211
Rogers, C., 2
Roggman, L. A., 209
role–relationship model, 137, 141,
140, 205
reversal of self and object roles in,
152
Rosenfeld, H. M., 210
Rosman, B. L., 121
Ross, H. S., 211, 213
Rutter, D. R., 212, 213, 214
Rycroft, C., 175, 201–2, 203–4, 205,
206

Sachs, J., 215
sadness, case discussion, 183
safety:
parental signaling of, 80
in the social world, 29–30
Sagi, A., 29, 36, 209
Sampson, H., 6, 12, 206
Schafer, R., 143
Schaffer, H. R., 209
schizoid character, 23–25, 33, 107
schizoid issues, 28–34, 170–72
Scholmerich, A., 208
Schwartz, G. M., 211
script decision, 6, 98, 102, 127
and deprivation, 37
secondary identification, 84
security operation, 21–22, 81–82, 111

Sedlak, A., 217
self:
antilibidinal, 110
compared with "ego", 110
and incorporative introjection, 84
lack in the symbiotic, 83
and other, 24, 89
rejected, 108
symptomatic, 50
in system, 24
characterological issues, 61–76
self–affirmation, 20
self–building in therapy, 48
self–cohesion, and symbiosis, 93
self–concept, 99
child's development of, 50
and identification, 103
self–determined expression, 19–20
self–development, characterological
issues of, 42–60
self–directed activity, case discussion,
174
self–esteem, 48
child's development of, 50
false self as a source of, 49
self–expression, 161–62, 185
self–negation, 20–21, 22, 36, 55–56
hypothesis of, 30–31
selfobject, 19, 205
dual structures, 111
self–object relations, 113, 165
split, 108
symptoms modeled as internal, 148–
52
self–other relationship, 20
negative, 31
self psychology, 5
self–regulating:
as an obsessive–compulsive symptom, 71
by the other, defined, 205
self–respect, 174
loss of, 173
self–sacrifice, 177
self–soothing, defined, 205
Selvini–Palazzoli, M., 121, 124
separation:
Alice, case discussion, 154
anxiety about, defined, 205
from a cultural background, 184
fear of, 96

separation (*continued*)
  and natural aggression, 86
  support for, 139
  threatening, 136
separation guilt, 45, 46, 57, 97, 124–
  25, 179, 187, 188, 191, 205
separation–individuation, defined,
  205–6
sexuality and oedipal issues, 61
Shapiro, D., 5, 25, 65, 68–69
Sherrod, L. R., 29, 208
signal anxiety, defined, 206
significant others:
  phenomenology and motivation of, 9
  symbiotic's responses to, 87
Silverman, L. H., 92
Simner, M. L., 29, 36, 209
Singer, L. T., 211
Siu, case discussion, 176–95
Skinner, B. F., 4, 10
socialization:
  and autonomy, 82
  infant's responses to isolation, 30
  innate propensity for interactions,
    120
  obsessive–compulsive's, 71
sociopathic functioning, 26
Sodian, B., 216, 217
Solomon, R. L., 16
Somerville, S. C., 214, 216
Sophian, C., 214, 215, 216, 217
Sorce, J. E., 43, 80
Spangler, G., 213
Speer, J. R., 216
Spelke, E. S., 214
Spieker, S. J., 209
Spitz, R. A., 209
Spizzirri, C. L., 209
splitting, 21, 107–8
  in Masterson's theory, 117
  in the narcissistic character, 52
  in the symbiotic, 102
  see also bad objects
Spungen, L., 212
Stadler, R., 213
Stenberg, C., 212
Stern, D. N., 17, 20, 28, 29, 35, 36,
  37, 42, 43, 50, 79, 81, 89, 120,
  199, 200, 204, 205, 209, 210,
  211, 212, 213
Sternberg, R. J., 218

stimulus barrier, defined, 206
stranger anxiety/reactions, defined,
  206
Strauss, M. S., 212
Stroufe, L. A., 211
Stroufe, L. S., 212
structural development:
  in borderline patients, 116
  and characterological issues, 24
  continuum of, 27
  through "exercise of function", 173–
    74
  intersection with characterological is-
    sues, 26
structural functioning, 23
structural tripartite model, 189
success:
  as a danger, 165
  problems with, 156
  to the symbiotic, 98–99
  threat in, 136
suffering, need in the masochist, 56
Sugarman, S., 212
Sugarman-Bell, S., 211
suppression, as an obsessive–compulsive symptom, 71
survivor guilt, 45, 46, 57, 97, 124–25,
  179, 184, 191, 206
  Alice, case discussion, 154, 156
  Siu, case discussion, 187
Sybil (film), 31
symbiosis, defined, 92, 206
symbiotic character, 24, 46–47
  and masochistic parents, 57
  relationships of, 153
symbiotic issues, 42–48, 79
  Allen, case discussion, 172
  etiology of, 45, 79–86
  and resistance to change, 112
  Robert, case discussion, 174
symptoms:
  analysis of, 148
  as internal object relations, 148–52,
    149, 153–74
  object relations analysis, 182–85
systematic desensitization, 9–10
system, the self in, 61–76
Szeminska, A., 216

Taylor, M., 216
terror, and withdrawal, 31–32

tests:
  symbiotic, 138–41
  for the therapist, 127–29
theatrical art in therapy, 1–2
therapeutic alliance, 4, 7, 119, 143–44, 194–95
  strengthened context of, 189
therapeutic channels, 145–48
therapeutic reaction, negative, 175–95
therapeutic techniques, 2–3
  choice points in, 3
  reframing, 18–19
  spontaneity and intuition in, 4
therapist:
  artistic choice of forms by, 2
  interpretation of theory by, 11
  as liberator, 137–38
  needs of the, 141–42
  negative personal reactions of, 18
  reinjury by, case discussion, 178
  roles of, Fairbairn's model, 114–15
  and the symbiotic, 140–41
therapy, 12
  accounting for outcomes, 4
  collaborative approach to, 143–44
  desensitization experience in, 10
  with the histrionic personality, 65–66
  individuation in, 95
  with masochists, 57, 60
  with the narcissist, 51, 54
  objectives, with the symbiotic, 99–104
  with obsessive–compulsives, 74–75
  with the oral character, 39, 41
  with a schizoid person, 32, 34
  with the symbiotic character of, 47–48, 93, 99, 185–86
  see also corrective emotional experience of
timing of desensitization, 32, 34
Tisak, M. S., 73, 216
Trabasso, T., 215
trance utilization, 171
transactional analysis, 105
transference, 126–27, 145
  acting–out, 97, 192
  archaic, 19
  interpretation of, 136
  negative, 129
  positive, 108

symbiotic, 138–41
  twinship, 84
transference channel, 169
transference neurosis, 114
transference tests, 127, 182
transitional object, defined, 206–7
transmuting internalization, 85, 207
trauma:
  and character structure, 16
  mastery of, 126
treatment:
  analysis of symptoms as, 157–70
  objectives, Fairbairn's model, 118–19
  see also therapy
Trevarthan, C., 211
triangle of conflict, 186, 188, 191–92
Tronick, E., 29, 36, 209, 210, 212
true self, resurrection and development, 99
  for the narcissist, 51, 54
trust, and masochism, 56
Turiel, E., 73, 216
Turkewitz, G., 29, 208
twinship, 207
  narcissistic, 53
  transference, 84

unconscious guilt, 123–26
unconscious plans, 126–30
unified structure (core self), 111

Vaughan, B. E., 213
Vibbert, M., 210
Vietze, P., 211, 212
Vinh Bang, 216
volition, distorted, 68

Walker–Andrews, A. S., 210
Watson, J. S., 209
Weinberger, J., 92
Weiss, J., 6, 12, 30, 37, 45, 60, 97, 125, 126–29, 152, 205, 206
Wellman, H. M., 73, 214, 215, 216, 217
Wenar, C., 214
West, M. J., 211
Whittaker, S. J., 216
Wilkening, F., 215
will, masochistic show of, 180
Wimmer, H., 215, 216, 217

Winnicott, D. W., 8, 21, 30, 49, 91,
    111, 206–7
Wise, S., 29, 36, 210
withdrawal in response to harshness,
    31–32
  in an infant, 30
withdrawing object relations unit
    (WORU), 117, 118
Wolpe, J., 10
Woodson, R. W., 29, 208

worthlessness and narcissism, 49
Wright, J. W., 216
Wynne, L. E., 16

Yarrow, L. J., 212
Young–Browne, G., 210
youngest child, infantilized, 179
Yuill, N., 73, 215, 216, 217

Zahn-Waxler, C., 44, 213